AF689994

EU SECURITY AND JUSTICE LAW

The coming into force of the Lisbon Treaty has provided the EU with new powers in the fields of criminal law and security law while reinforcing existing powers in immigration and asylum law. The Stockholm Programme is the latest framework for EU action in the field of justice and home affairs. It includes a range of new legislation in the fields of immigration and asylum, substantive criminal law, criminal procedure and cooperation between national criminal justice systems. The combination of the new Treaty and Programme have made security and justice key areas of legislative growth in the EU. This volume brings together a range of leading scholars, as well as some of the most interesting new voices in the debate, to examine the state of EU security and justice law after the Lisbon Treaty and the Stockholm Programme. It provides a critical examination of EU law in the fields of immigration, asylum, counter-terrorism, citizenship, fundamental rights and external relations. The book also examines the evolving roles of the EU institutions and criminal justice agencies. It provides a critical account of EU law in this field under the developing constitutional and institutional settlement.

Volume 42 in the series Modern Studies in European Law

Modern Studies in European Law

Recent titles in this series:

Professional Services in the EU Internal Market: Quality Regulation and Self-Regulation
Tinne Heremans

Environmental Integration in the EU's External Relations: Beyond Multilateral Dimensions
Gracia Marín Durán and Elisa Morgera

The Constitutional Dimension of European Criminal Law
Ester Herlin-Karnell

EU Counter-Terrorism Law: Pre-Emption and the Rule of Law
Cian C Murphy

Children and the European Union: Rights, Welfare and Accountability
Helen Stalford

Federalism in the European Union
Edited by Elke Cloots, Geert De Baere and Stefan Sottiaux

Toward a Prosecutor for the European Union Volume 1: A Comparative Analysis
Edited by Katalin Ligeti

Empowerment and Disempowerment of the European Citizen
Edited by Michael Dougan, Niamh Nic Shuibhne and Eleanor Spaventa

Legal Reasoning and the European Court of Justice
Gunnar Beck

Lawyering Europe: European Law as a Transnational Social Field
Edited by Antoine Vauchez and Bruno de Witte

Services and the EU Citizen
Edited by Frank S Benyon

The Accession of the European Union to the European Convention on Human Rights
Paul Gragl

Normative Patterns and Legal Developments in the Social Dimension of the EU
Edited by Ann Numhauser-Henning and Mia Rönnmar

The European Neighbourhood Policy and the Democratic Values of the EU: A Legal Analysis
Nariné Ghazaryan

For the complete list of titles in this series, see 'Modern Studies in European Law' link at www.hartpub.co.uk/books/series.asp

EU Security and Justice Law

After Lisbon and Stockholm

Edited by
Diego Acosta Arcarazo
and
Cian C Murphy

•HART•
PUBLISHING
OXFORD AND PORTLAND, OREGON
2014

Published in the United Kingdom by Hart Publishing Ltd
16C Worcester Place, Oxford, OX1 2JW
Telephone: +44 (0)1865 517530
Fax: +44 (0)1865 510710
E-mail: mail@hartpub.co.uk
Website: http://www.hartpub.co.uk

Published in North America (US and Canada) by
Hart Publishing
c/o International Specialized Book Services
920 NE 58th Avenue, Suite 300
Portland, OR 97213-3786
USA
Tel: +1 503 287 3093 or toll-free: (1) 800 944 6190
Fax: +1 503 280 8832
E-mail: orders@isbs.com
Website: http://www.isbs.com

© The editors and contributors severally 2014

The editors and contributors have asserted their right under the Copyright, Designs and Patents Act 1988, to be identified as the authors of this work.

Hart Publishing is an imprint of Bloomsbury Publishing plc

All rights reserved. No part of this publication may be reproduced, stored in a retrieval system, or transmitted, in any form or by any means, without the prior permission of Hart Publishing, or as expressly permitted by law or under the terms agreed with the appropriate reprographic rights organisation. Enquiries concerning reproduction which may not be covered by the above should be addressed to Hart Publishing Ltd at the address above.

British Library Cataloguing in Publication Data
Data Available

ISBN: 978-1-84946-422-2

Typeset by Hope Services, Abingdon
Printed and bound in Great Britain by
TJ International Ltd, Padstow

to our teachers
and our students
for their inspiration
and to our families
for their support

Foreword

Immigration, asylum, policing and criminal justice are high on the political agenda and are of great public concern. Difficult and sensitive issues arise daily, requiring a delicate balance between the legitimate requirements of public order, national security and immigration control on the one hand, and the protection of human rights and civil liberties on the other. Increasingly, these issues now have a European dimension.

European Union law in these areas, especially since the entry into force of the Lisbon Treaty (closely modelled on the Constitutional Treaty) has been transformed: the previous, complex 'three-pillar structure' had preserved an essentially inter-governmental approach, requiring political consensus for the adoption of legal provisions, and largely excluding judicial interpretation and supervision. Today, after the demolition of the three-pillar structure, EU legislation in these areas is adopted (under a part of the Treaty which goes under the title 'Area of Freedom, Security and Justice') in the same way as other EU legislation: that is, by the European Parliament and with a qualified majority in the Council. Moreover, implementation in the 28 Member States of the EU is subject to the control of the European Court of Justice. And an ambitious programme of legislation is under way.

The present book thus examines issues of fundamental importance across a wide range of subjects: criminal law, counter-terrorism, migration, asylum, and others; it analyses the governmental structure, the concept of citizenship, the protection of fundamental rights. It discusses underlying constitutional principles, and also the external dimension.

One message which emerges clearly from the discussion is the importance of a bedrock principle, that of the rule of law. Now enshrined in Article 2 of the Treaty on European Union, there is a risk that the rule of law is taken for granted. Properly understood, it is a constant standard to be applied to all exercises of power, whether by legislature, executive or judiciary. Legislation, if it is to be a successful guide to citizens and officials, needs to be properly thought out; not the product of political compromise but of careful crafting with expert scrutiny. The executive has to act within its competences, and – need it be said? – to act within the law: sadly, there is increasing evidence in Europe today of defiance even of court judgments in the interest of political expediency. And as for the courts themselves, the ultimate guardians of the rule of law, there seems a risk of increasing incoherence and unforeseeability in the case-law. This may partly result from inadequate and complex legislation, but also, as chapters in this book demonstrate, from the handling of such central concepts as European citizenship and fundamental rights. The resulting unpredictability and uncertainty of some areas of the case law may even suggest that, paradoxically, the emergence of new systems to uphold the rule of law may endanger the values which they are designed to protect.

In any event, this book will certainly enlighten discussion and stimulate debate in several crucial areas of public life, and on that account is to be warmly welcomed.

Francis G Jacobs

Acknowledgements

This book has its genesis in our shared interest in the development of the European Union as an 'area of freedom security and justice'. It was brought into being thanks to the ongoing support of the Centre of European Law at King's College London as we brought together various groups of scholars and practitioners over the past three years to discuss the implications of the coming into force of the Lisbon Treaty and the launch of the Stockholm Programme. Three events were held, a conference: Explaining the Stockholm Programme in January 2010, with the support of the European Commission in the United Kingdom, a roundtable: Freedom, Security and Justice in June 2011, and a book workshop: EU Security and Justice Law in November 2012. None of these events could have taken place without the Centre's support and we are grateful to its Director, Andrea Biondi, his predecessor, Piet Eeckhout, and the Centre staff of Christine Copping, Andrea Cordwell-James and Renee Olivel for their organisational support. The Centre's luminaries, in particular the brilliant and generous Francis Jacobs, offer us constant support and an example we can but hope to follow. We are also thankful to the various participants on each of those days – a list of scholars and practitioners that includes, but is not limited, to the authors of this book, and especially to Elspeth Guild whose ideas and support were essential for the organisation of the first conference, and Christian Krappitz of the European Commission Representation in the UK for financial assistance for that conference.

The law in this field is ever-changing and so we must caution our readers that we endeavour to state the law as it was on 1 June 2013. There have been some subsequent developments, such as the judgment in *Kadi II*, of which note has been taken. We are delighted to have the book in the Hart Publishing Modern Studies in European Law series. Richard Hart's support for this project was steadfast from the start and his team, in particular Rachel Turner, Mel Hamill, Tom Adams and Emma Swinden, have been efficient in bringing the manuscript through production and forgiving of our own tardiness in responding to various questions and queries. A large portion of the editorial work was done in Washington DC and New York City thanks to the generosity of the Fulbright Commission. Cian Murphy is grateful to the Fulbright Commission for funding and to David Cole (Georgetown) and Joseph Weiler (NYU) for hosting his visit in the US. Adrienne Yong provided excellent assistance as we brought the editing to a close. The task of editors of a collection of essays can sometimes be an arduous one. We are very grateful to our authors that this was not the case for the book you hold in your hands. Indeed, the experience has been so painless that our collective response is less 'never again' and more 'what's next'? It will come as a relief to our friends and families, for whose patience we are most grateful of all, that we have no answer to that question yet!

DA and CM
Madrid and New York
31 May 2013

Table of Contents

List of Contributors

Diego Acosta Arcarazo is Lecturer in Law at the University of Bristol.

Stephen Coutts is a Researcher at the European University Institute.

Christina Eckes is Associate Professor in EU Law at the University of Amsterdam.

Ester Herlin-Karnell is Assistant Professor of EU Law at VU University of Amsterdam.

Sir Francis Jacobs QC is former Advocate General at the Court of Justice of the European Union and Jean Monnet Professor of European Law at King's College London.

Theodore Konstadinides is Lecturer in Law at the University of Surrey.

Dora Kostakopoulou is Professor of Law at Warwick University.

Valsamis Mitsilegas is Head of the Department of Law and Professor of European Criminal Law at Queen Mary University of London.

Violeta Moreno-Lax is Lecturer in Law at Queen Mary University London.

Tine Munk is a PhD student and Part-time Research Associate at the University of Manchester.

Cian C Murphy is Lecturer in Law at King's College London.

Noreen O'Meara is Lecturer in Law at the University of Surrey.

Steve Peers in Professor of Law at the University of Essex.

Jorrit Rijpma is Assistant Professor at the University of Leiden.

Table of Cases

Court of Justice of the European Union and General Court

European Court of Human Rights

National Courts

Austria

Germany

United States

Table of Legislation

EU Treaties and Conventions

EU Secondary Legislation

Decisions

Regulations

International Conventions

1

Rethinking Europe's Freedom, Security and Justice

CIAN C MURPHY AND DIEGO ACOSTA ARCARAZO*

> There is a precipice between two steep mountains: the city is over the void, bound to the two crests with ropes and chains and catwalks . . . suspended over the abyss . . . the net will last only so long.**

I. INTRODUCTION: CONSTITUTIONAL MOMENTS AND THE TEMPTATION OF THE NEW

THERE IS A tendency in EU law scholarship to over-emphasise novelty and to pronounce a new dawn with each new treaty. For EU law scholars it is always tempting to view the most recent European constitutional moment as the most significant. Yet it may well be more appropriate to accept the inevitable impermanence of any EU constitutional settlement. In counterpoint to the United States' claims of its striving for a 'more perfect Union', even as it perpetuates the fossilisation of its constitution, the EU engages in ongoing constitutional reinvention, while promising its people(s) that everything remains the same. It may be that Europe's constitutional progress may only take place when it denies it is taking place – slinking forward while convincing its citizens that there is nothing to see. Witness the demise of the Constitutional Treaty, agreed in Dublin but signed, in a self-conscious act of constitutional grandeur, in Rome. The Lisbon Treaty that later proved to be acceptable to the European people is very similar in its content and effects as the Constitutional Treaty. It is more different in appearance than it is in reality.

The European Union has seen four major revisions to its constitutional text in two decades (and several minor ones, and a further aborted attempt).[1] It has also

* We are grateful to Stephen Coutts and Christina Eckes for comments on an earlier draft. Any errors and all flights of imagination are our own.

** Italo Calvinho, *Invisible Cities* (London, Vintage Classics New Ed edn, 1997).

[1] Following the Maastricht Treaty (1992) are the Amsterdam Treaty (1997), the Nice Treaty (2001), and the Lisbon Treaty (2007). The failure of the Constitutional Treaty (2004) prompted the reversion

seen the adoption of three programmes to develop its 'area of freedom, security and justice' in the past 15 years. These treaties and agreements are known by the cities in which they were adopted: Maastricht, Amsterdam, Nice, and Lisbon for the treaties, Tampere, The Hague, and Stockholm for the programmes. As scholars we refer to 'before Lisbon' and 'after Stockholm' when in our discussions of legal and policy developments. The naming practice seems to emphasise both the geographic dispersion of Europe's constitutional process and also the tendency to conceive of European constitutional history as progressing in a series of 'moments' at various European towns and cities. It is understandable, in seeking to better understand the nascent EU, for us to glance across the Atlantic at the United States (US). Yet Europe does not have a single moment of birth, such as the signing of the US Constitution in Philadelphia, but a succession of moments of lurching growth and development.

The Schumann Declaration, as foundational to Europe as Jefferson's Declaration of Independence is across the Atlantic, states that the purpose of this enterprise was no less than world peace.[2] This peace, the Schumann Declaration claims, 'cannot be safeguarded without the making of creative efforts proportionate to the dangers which threaten it'.[3] Despite the rhetorical grandeur the aims of the Declaration were much more modest, focusing on control of the means of production and the fusion of European markets. Although peace was the aim its achievement was to be through economic rather than political or security integration. Therefore for almost half a century the European institutions did not have formal roles in relation to security and any such measures adopted were public international law rather than what would come to be known as supranational law.[4] The entry into force of the Maastricht Treaty in 1993 marked the beginning of the EU's formal involvement in security matters – both internal and external. The role of the EU in external security was through the common foreign and security policy, the Union's 'second pillar', while internal security, known as justice and home affairs, was the 'third pillar' of the new Union.[5]

Over the following decade, through a series of revisions of the treaties, this role was increased as more policy fields were made subject to supranational law-making and adjudication.[6] For instance, in 1999 the Amsterdam Treaty saw immigration and asylum law move from the third pillar to the first pillar and therefore to the

to amending treaties with the Lisbon Treaty. Minor amendments have been brought about by accession treaties, such as the Treaty concerning the Accession of the Republic of Croatia (2011) and the Irish Protocol on the Lisbon Treaty (2012). See in general P Craig, *The Lisbon Treaty: Law, Politics and Treaty Reform* (Oxford, Oxford University Press, 2010). The simplified revision procedure to the treaties was put into use for the first time in 2011 to allow for the European Stability Mechanism (amending Art 136 TFEU). See Council Decision 2011/199/EU of 25 March 2011, 2011 OJ L91/1.

[2] Robert Schuman Declaration of 9 May 1950.

[3] ibid.

[4] See, for an overview of the justice and home affairs area since its inception, S Peers, *EU Justice and Home Affairs Law*, 3rd edn (Oxford, Oxford University Press, 2011) ch 2.

[5] For the classic account, see E Denza, *The Intergovernmental Pillars of the European Union* (Oxford, Oxford University Press, 2002).

[6] K Hailbronner, 'European Immigration and Asylum Law under the Amsterdam Treaty' (1998) 35 *CML Rev* 1047.

supranational legal sphere. Although this led to an increase in the EU's role in these fields, constraints on that role did remain.[7] Thus, there was the sharing of the right of legislative initiative between the Commission and the Member States, reliance on unanimity amongst the Member States in the Council, the limitation of the European Parliament to a consultative role, and significant limitations on the jurisdiction of the Court of Justice of the European Union (ECJ).[8] The Nice Treaty did little to develop this constitutional and institutional settlement. Now, the Lisbon Treaty has brought the pillar structure to an end. The remaining fields of justice and home affairs have been made subject to supranationalism. However, with each increase in integration comes a new reservation of power by the Member States, leading to greater complexity and, perhaps, the fragmentation of the Union's legal supranationalism.[9]

In the Union legislature, most fields are now, after Lisbon, subject to the ordinary legislative procedure, with proposals requiring the support of a qualified majority in the Council and with equal legislative powers for the European Parliament alongside the Council.[10] This supranationalisation of the legislative process through the Parliament's involvement, alongside the shift from unanimity to qualified majority voting in the Council,[11] may not necessarily result in a more open political process or, indeed, in better legislation.[12] Whether such improvements have been, or will be, brought about is a question that recurs throughout this book. Elsewhere scholars have identified 'a difficult relationship' between supranationalism and intergovernmental processes in relation to justice and home affairs.[13] Alongside the change in legislative process come some new powers to legislate. The Lisbon Treaty develops the Union's legislative power in the fields of criminal law and security law and consolidates its existing powers in immigration and asylum law.

There remain idiosyncratic arrangements for these precious policy fields in justice and home affairs that have so close an association with sovereign power. This is perhaps most notable in respect of criminal law and justice. Therefore, although the Commission now has principal responsibility for the initiation of legislation, a group of Member States (at least a quarter) may still propose criminal justice

[7] See, for a discussion on immigration and asylum after the Amsterdam Treaty, E Guild and C Harlow, *Implementing Amsterdam: Immigration and Asylum Rights in EC Law* (Oxford, Hart Publishing, 2001).

[8] J Monar, 'Justice and Home Affairs in the Treaty of Amsterdam: Reform at the Price of Fragmentation' (1998) 23 *EL Rev* 320.

[9] S Peers, 'Mission Accomplished? EU Justice and Home Affairs Law after the Treaty of Lisbon' (2011) 48 *CML Rev* 661, 661–62.

[10] In certain areas a more restrictive legislative process persists. See Peers, ibid, 665.

[11] According to Lewis, the Council rarely votes but always tries to find a consensus even if qualified majority applies. J Lewis, 'Informal Integration and the Supranational Construction of the Council' (2003) 10 *Journal of European Public Policy* 996.

[12] D Acosta, 'The Good, the Bad and the Ugly in EU Migration Law: Is the European Parliament Becoming Bad and Ugly? (The Adoption of Directive 2008/115: The Returns Directive)' (2009) 11 *European Journal of Migration and Law* 19.

[13] E Guild, S Carrera and T Balzacq, 'The Changing Dynamics of Security in an Enlarged European Union' in D Bigo, S Carrera, E Guild and RBJ Walker (eds), *Europe's 21st Century Challenge. Delivering Liberty* (Aldershot, Ashgate, 2010) 36.

legislation.[14] The ECJ has ordinary jurisdiction over all justice and home affairs but limitations remain on the exercise of that jurisdiction and operational matters are still exempt.[15] The extension of the Court's jurisdiction does further the development of the rule of law. The Court provides for effective remedies, ensures the right to a fair trial, and upholds the principle that any exercise of power should be subject to review.[16] The Court's ordinary jurisdiction now permits individuals to access the ECJ through references by all national courts and not merely courts of last instance (as was the case before Lisbon).[17] This better guarantees judicial protection and has already had an impact in the number of cases before the Court. This is essential for the correct interpretation of new legislative instruments and for the protection of rights in such a sensitive area.[18] A further consideration, of relevance to the work of the Parliament and especially the Court of Justice, is the coming into full force of the Charter of Fundamental Rights. For so long dependent on the Council of Europe's European Convention on Human Rights (ECHR), the Union now has its own Bill of Rights, a timely development for a Union that must 'offer its citizens' an 'area of freedom, security and justice'.

II. POLITICS FROM TAMPERE TO STOCKHOLM VIA THE HAGUE (AND NEW YORK)

Article 3(2) TEU now states that the Union

> shall offer its citizens an area of freedom, security and justice without internal frontiers, in which the free movement of persons is ensured in conjunction with appropriate measures with respect to external border controls, asylum, immigration and the prevention and combating of crime.

This is an objective of the EU, second only to the promotion of 'peace, its values and the well-being of its peoples' and is 'loaded with social contract connotations'.[19] The most recent articulation of this objective is not its first mention in a European treaty. Rather it was the Amsterdam Treaty that first sought to create an area of freedom, security and justice. However, since that first citation of the idea, the 'plurality of values in the headline' has led to much discussion as to their relative weight and the extent to which EU action to achieve this objective would require a balance between the three.[20]

[14] Art 76 TFEU.

[15] Peers (n 4) 666.

[16] FG Jacobs, *The Sovereignty of Law: The European Way* (Cambridge, Cambridge University Press, 2007) 62.

[17] The Court's jurisdiction over preliminary references on third pillar measures before the Lisbon Treaty was subject to a national declaration in accordance with the EU Treaty. See Art 35 TEU(L).

[18] D Acosta Arcarazo and A Geddes, 'The Development, Application and Implications of an EU Rule of Law in the Area of Migration Policy' (2013) 51 *Journal of Common Market Studies* 179.

[19] See Eckes, ch 11.

[20] N Walker, 'In Search of the Area of Freedom, Security and Justice: A Constitutional Odyssey' in N Walker (ed), *Europe's Area of Freedom, Security and Justice* (Oxford, Oxford University Press, 2004) 5.

If the process of legal integration leading to the area of freedom, security and justice through treaty developments is notable for its cautious approach to the transfer of power to EU institutions, the use of multi-annual programmes has proven to be much more ambitious. The first five-year programme for this field, the Tampere Programme of 1999, saw the main challenge of the Amsterdam Treaty as being to ensure that freedom, including the right to free movement, was enjoyed 'in conditions of security and justice accessible to all'.[21] In order to achieve this, the Tampere Programme identified four priorities to address. The first was the establishment of a Common European Asylum and Migration Policy, which would permit third-country nationals to enjoy certain freedoms, alongside measures to control external borders to prevent irregular migration and to combat related international crime.[22] The second priority was the creation of a genuine European area of justice allowing for the mutual recognition and enforcement of judgments and decisions throughout the Union.[23] The third priority sought to develop Union-wide efforts to coordinate action 'to prevent and fight crime and criminal organisations through the Union'.[24] The fourth priority made reference to the Union's need to develop a stronger external role so as to be recognised as an important partner in the international arena.[25] These priorities would prove to be too ambitious for the rudimentary post-Amsterdam legislative instruments, and too sensitive for Member State governments, for much to be done before the attacks in New York and Washington DC on September 11 2001.

The attacks by Al-Qaeda in New York, Washington DC, and Pennsylvania do not constitute a 'constitutional moment' in the sense of Amsterdam, Nice or Lisbon. However, they did have a profound effect on EU law and policy – an effect that was made greater by subsequent attacks in Europe.[26] Therefore it may be possible to speak of the area of freedom, security and justice 'after New York'. Alongside its Action Plan on Combating Terrorism, the European Council sought through the Hague Programme of 2004 to take with urgency stronger action on a series of cross-border challenges including terrorism and organised crime.[27] Therefore the Hague Programme addresses the same priorities as the Tampere Programme, such as migration and free movement of EU citizens, the strengthening of criminal justice and security cooperation and the development of a coherent external dimension of the Union policy in this area. Nevertheless, the later Programme is notable for its

[21] European Council (1999) Presidency Conclusions of the Tampere European Council, 15 and 16 October 1999, para 2.

[22] ibid, para 3.

[23] ibid, para 5.

[24] ibid, para 6.

[25] ibid, para 8.

[26] See, in general, CC Murphy, *EU Counter-terrorism Law: Pre-emption and the Rule of Law* (Oxford, Hart Publishing, 2012). See further Murphy's chapter in this volume.

[27] Brussels European Council 4/5 November, Presidency conclusions, the Hague Programme, Brussels 8 December 2004, 14292/1/04 REV 1, 25.

stronger emphasis on security.[28] The Hague Programme fits with government action across the world in the 'war on terror' and the field of EU counter-terrorism law is just as problematic as US policy.[29] In the academy, works were written on the dangers of 'balancing' freedom with security,[30] on achieving justice when both freedom and security are at stake,[31] and on the position of the individual – both in terms of EU citizens and third-country nationals.[32] However, illiberalism has been in evidence in EU security law and policy since long before the September 11 attacks and the events of that day, and their effects, must be understood in broader historical context.[33]

If the Hague Programme was in part a product of the 'war on terror' then the Stockholm Programme belongs in the post-'war on terror' world. It gives prevalence to fundamental rights and the role of the EU citizen and largely discards the security rhetoric of its predecessor.[34] The principal challenge for the coming years, according to the Programme, 'will be to ensure respect for fundamental freedoms and integrity while guaranteeing security in Europe'. Hence, it is important to ensure that 'law enforcement measures and measures to safeguard individual rights, the rule of law, [and] international protection rules go hand in hand in the same direction and are mutually reinforced'.[35] In order to achieve its objectives, the Stockholm Programme benefits from the new constitutional and institutional framework after Lisbon, with the enhancement of the roles of the European Commission, European Parliament and the ECJ, as well as the new binding effect of the Charter of Fundamental Rights.

The Stockholm Programme represents a form of maturation in some respects. The Tampere Programme was too ambitious and the Hague Programme was reactionary. The Stockholm Programme promises, at least, a more considerate approach. One of the Hague Programme's failures, for example, was the inability of the Council to agree legislation to protect the rights of suspects. This led to criticism of criminal justice cooperation which was, the argument goes, taking place without

[28] T Balzacq and S Carrera, 'The Hague Programme: The Long Road to Freedom, Security and Justice' in T Balzacq and S Carrera (eds), *Security versus Freedom?: A Challenge for Europe's Future* (Aldershot, Ashgate, 2006).

[29] See, in general, Murphy (n 26).

[30] Bigo, Carrera, Guild and Walker (n 13).

[31] M Anderson and J Apap (eds), *Striking a Balance between Freedom, Security and Justice in an Enlarged European Union* (Brussels, Centre for European Policy Studies, 2002); T Balzacq and S Carrera (eds), *Security versus Freedom?: A Challenge for Europe's Future* (Aldershot, Ashgate, 2006).

[32] A Baldaccini, E Guild and H Toner (eds), *Whose Freedom, Security and Justice? EU Immigration and Asylum Law and Policy* (Oxford, Hart Publishing, 2007); C Kaunert, 'Liberty versus Security? EU Asylum Policy and the European Commission' (2009) 5 *Journal of Contemporary European Research* 148.

[33] For a classic critique, see T Bunyan, 'Towards an Authoritarian European State' (1991) 32 *Race & Class* 19.

[34] E Guild and S Carrera, 'The European Union's Area of Freedom, Security and Justice Ten Years On' in E Guild, S Carrera and A Eggenschwiler (eds), *The Area of Freedom, Security and Justice Ten Years On. Successes and Future Challenges under the Stockholm Programme* (Brussels, Centre for European Policy Studies, 2010).

[35] Council of the European Union, The Stockholm Programme – An Open and Secure Europe Serving and Protecting the Citizens, 17024/09, Brussels, 2 December 2009, 3.

appropriate safeguards. Today the Stockholm Roadmap for Suspects' Rights, adopted at the same time as the Programme, calls for six legislative proposals to address six different aspects of the criminal justice process. Instead of an all-or-nothing approach to the legislation, the Council has thus taken an 'incrementalist' approach, which may yield better results.[36] This 'incrementalist' approach is not new and is similar to the one the Commission has taken when proposing legislation on regular migration.[37] Furthermore, the centrality of the citizen in the Stockholm Programme may, as the authors in this book discuss, play a legitimising function for the area of freedom, security and justice.[38] If the Hague Programme's overt obsession with security was the source of criticism then taking citizenship as the focus for the Stockholm Programme provides the Council and Commission with a degree of political capital in dealing with both Member States and the European Parliament. After all, it is difficult to be against action done in the name of the citizen.

Of course some Member States remain deeply sceptical about Schuman's European project. The position of the United Kingdom presents a particular political complication. The exercise of the opt-out in Protocol 36 to the Treaty of Lisbon will pose a critical, perhaps even a fatal, challenge to cooperation in this field.[39] It will, to borrow a metaphor, be akin to taking a mallet to the still-drying frieze of Europe's criminal justice mosaic. A picture will still emerge but its fragmentation will be even greater. The UK has also, as Peers notes in this volume, sought to increase the use of justice and home affairs legal bases so as to broaden the scope of its opt-out from EU law. Furthermore, at the time of writing the UK Government is debating holding a referendum on UK membership of the EU. Nevertheless, even if British opposition appears to be at a new height, it is merely the predictable consequence of the return to government of the Conservative Party. Margaret Thatcher was antipathetic, noting that she had not 'rolled back the frontiers of the state in Britain, only to see them re-imposed at a European level, with a European super-state exercising a new dominance from Brussels'.[40] John Major's cabinet was torn asunder over European Monetary Union. The posturing by David Cameron appears to marry traditional Conservative Party anti-European ideology with a greater tendency towards populist grandstanding. This is in part because of the national political landscape. The strong showing of the UK Independence Party in the 2013 local elections heightens the pressure on the Prime Minister from his Eurosceptic supporters. However, he openly courts that support and so the rise of Euroscepticism is in part the product of his own actions (such as his refusal to sign the Fiscal Treaty in 2012). It would be hostage to fortune to guess as to how all of this will resolve itself but perhaps, today more so

[36] See ch 3 by Konstadinides and O'Meara in this volume.

[37] See ch 8 by Kostakopoulou, Acosta Arcarazo and Munk in this volume.

[38] See ch 6 by Coutts in this volume.

[39] For the leading discussion of the opt-out and its implications, see A Hinarejos, JR Spencer and S Peers, 'Opting out of EU Criminal Law: What is Actually Involved?' (2012) CELS Working Paper, New Series, No 1, Cambridge University, September 2012.

[40] M Thatcher, Speech to the College of Europe – 'The Bruges Speech' (Bruges, 20 September 1988).

than at any time in the past, there appears a risk that populism will outweigh the pragmatic advantages of EU membership for British political leaders.

The decade between the agreement of the Nice Treaty in 2001 and the eventual coming into force of the Lisbon Treaty in 2010 therefore gives lie to the view that the European Union is marching towards an inevitable federal unity. In some respects the outcome of the past decade has not been a Union that moves 'ever closer' but rather one that has become deeper and more intricate. Much of what follows from the Lisbon and Stockholm constitutional moments has not been new integration but rather the fulfilment of the promises of earlier integration (such as in respect of the rights of suspects). The developments that this book explores reflect the need to come to terms with the swing towards securitisation in the aftermath of the September 11 2001 attacks. The deepening of integration in relation to intra-European rendition, whether of suspects or refugees, has become essential because of the failure of national systems of justice to ensure adequate protection for those subject to that rendition. However, it has not, in most cases, been national political actors that have sought to force such change, but rather European and national judiciaries who have done so. The history of the EU is one of periodic progress by political institutions with the legal institutions – courts – needing to keep the engine ticking over between treaty revisions. It is therefore necessary not just to rethink the politics of freedom, security and justice, but also to rethink its law.

III. THE LAW OF FREEDOM, SECURITY AND JUSTICE

The history of the EU is one of political and legal action and reaction. The relationship between the treaty reform process and the jurisprudence of the Court of Justice is a reflexive one. The internal market was brought about as the Court sought to build on the broad foundations in the treaties. The decisions in cases such as *Dassonville*, *Cassis de Dijon*, and *Keck* are now part of the grammar of EU law and legal scholarship.[41] In recent years a similar dynamic is emerging in respect of the area of freedom, security and justice. Thus, the early foundational case of *Pupino* (criminal justice) sits alongside *Kadi I* (counter-terrorism) and *NS* (asylum) as touchstones of the Court's work on freedom, security and justice.[42] These cases may, over time, assume the same significance as *Van Gend en Loos* and *Costa v ENEL* have in relation to the European constitution.[43] They have certainly prompted political reaction. The decision in *Kadi I* saw a revision not just

[41] Case 8/74 *Dassonville* [1974] ECR 837; Case 120/78 *Rewe-Zentral AG v Bundesmonopolverwaltung für Branntwein* (*Cassis de Dijon*) [1979] ECR 649; Joined Cases C-267/91 and C-268/91 *Keck and Mithouard* [1993] ECR I-6097.

[42] Case C-105/03 *Criminal proceedings against Maria Pupino* [2005] ECR I-5285; Joined Cases C-402/05 P and C-415/05 P *Kadi and Al Barakaat International Foundation v Council and Commission* [2008] ECR I-6351 (*Kadi I*); C-411/10 *NS v Secretary of State for the Home Department* [2011] ECR I-0000 (*NS*).

[43] Case 26/62 *Van Gend en Loos* [1963] ECR 1; Case 6/64 *Costa v ENEL* [1964] ECR 585.

of EU law, but also of the administrative practices of the UN Security Council.[44] Of course, the sanctions system at the core of the case blurs the line between internal and external security, a trait of recent action in this field. The European Commission was already taking action in the field of asylum policy even before the *NS* judgment as it sought to respond to the already crucial judgment in *MSS v Belgium and Greece* from the European Court of Human Rights (ECtHR).[45] There is therefore as salient a relationship between litigation before the European courts (national, supranational and international) and the political process at the EU level as there is in national constitutional systems.[46]

This relationship between law and politics was the subject of explicit acknowledgement in the Opinion of Advocate General Sharpston in the citizenship case of *Ruiz Zambrano*.[47] The Advocate General proposes in her Opinion a revolution in the law on EU citizenship and fundamental rights. However, she is mindful of the appropriate means to bring about such a change and notes that a revolution 'requires both an evolution in the case-law and an unequivocal political statement from the constituent powers of the EU (its Member States), pointing at a new role for fundamental rights in the EU'.[48] There is a reflexive dynamic at work here that envisages progress in the development of the EU constitution emerging from cooperation between the Court and the Council.

Before we leave the reader believing that there is a healthy and happy relationship between the law and politics of European integration it is necessary to consider some caveats. There are at least two reasons to believe that the work of the Court of Justice will be more difficult in relation to freedom, security and justice than it was in respect of the internal market. First, when the Court of Justice sought to establish a new legal order and to build the internal market it was drawing on a blank slate. The treaties were less complex and the institutional arrangement subject to less contortion than they are now. Thus, whereas the Court was able to devise the doctrine of direct effect of directives using the *telos* of integration, it was told in plain terms that framework decisions under the Amsterdam Treaty 'shall not entail direct effect'.[49] The Member States, which had never before made reference to the doctrine in a treaty, sought to ensure that the Court did not engage in the same creative exercise that it had in relation to directives.

The absence of a blank slate is in part a consequence of the second reason to anticipate difficulties: the differences in ideology in Member States' attitudes to freedom, security and justice. The internal market was the common expression of a commitment to liberal economic principles (albeit subject to some tempering for welfarist reasons). The *telos* that the Court of Justice sought to pursue took

[44] See Murphy (n 26) ch 5.

[45] *MSS v Belgium and Greece* Judgment of the European Court of Human Rights Grand Chamber, 21 January 2011.

[46] For an early exploration of these ideas, see JHH Weiler, 'The Transformation of Europe' *The Yale Law Journal*, vol 100, no 8, Symposium International Law, 2403.

[47] Case C-34/09 *Gerardo Ruiz Zambrano v Office National de l'Emploi* [2011] ECR I-1177.

[48] ibid, para 173.

[49] Art 34 TEU(L).

this economic liberalism as its central tenet and built a common European market for labour, goods and services on this basis. The Member States were willing to acquiesce in this enterprise due to the peace, and perhaps more pertinently the prosperity that it brought. Since 2001 that peace has been subject to rupture – not by the actions of state actors but because of non-state networks and individuals.[50] However, even after September 11, there is not a common ideology on security amongst the Member States.

Taken together, the constraints of more complex treaties, and the political hesitancy of the Member States to cede control in a field where they have deep ideological differences, leave the dialogue between law and politics much more fractious than it was in the past. The decisions of the ECJ in cases such as *Kadi I*, *NS* and *Ruiz Zambrano*, are filling in the gaps of a system of integration after the political actors could only agree to sketch an outline. As with *Dassonville*, *Cassis de Dijon* and *Keck*, the three more recent judgments seek to empower people. However, unlike the earlier judgments, the more recent ones empower natural people, within and outside the EU, in social and political ways. They do not merely empower legal persons in economic ways. Is it for this reason that the political actors shudder in response? All three judgments are the subject of critique for the challenges they pose to the existing constitutional order. And yet, these challenges have their genesis not in judicial activism by the ECJ, but in the political activism by the Member States, which sought to enable political cooperation in fields that affect security. The Member States therefore find themselves facing the consequences of wish fulfilment.

Where does all of this leave law in the area of freedom, security and justice? In Europe, further integration and simplification often leads to complexity, dissonance and fragmentation.[51] Thus, the integration of the Schengen Agreement into EU law has led to more complex arrangements amongst the Schengen states and between those states and the non-Schengen members of the EU. As the legal reality becomes ever more complex, the tale of an 'ever-closer union' becomes even more of a fairy tale. The search for coherence is a common theme in relation to the area of freedom, security and justice. At a conceptual level the search entails grappling with the three ideas in the area's title. As Walker notes in his seminal

[50] Since 2007 the prosperity has also come to an end, with the embodiment of EU prosperity, Ireland, one of five PIIGS states in dire economic condition (Portugal, Ireland, Italy, Greece, Spain). The economic problems of Europe have begun to highlight dormant disagreements over fiscal policy that may, in time, demonstrate that the ideology of market economics was itself more hegemony than consensus. See, for example, the speech of the Irish President, Michael D Higgins, to the European Parliament on 17 April 2013 wherein he notes that European citizens feel 'the economic narrative of recent years has been driven by dry technical concerns; for example, by calculations that are abstract and not drawn from real problems, geared primarily by a consideration of the impact of such measures on speculative markets, rather than driven by sufficient compassion and empathy with the predicament of European citizens who are members of a union, and for whom all of the resources of Europe's capacity, political, social, economic and intellectual might have been drawn on, driven by the binding moral spirit of a union'.

[51] It is little surprise then that one of our authors, Steve Peers, is currently writing a monograph on *The Unravelling of EU Law* (Oxford, Hart Publishing, forthcoming 2014).

work, these three ideas tend to militate against coherence. Although his examination sought to consider various forms of coherence here the focus is on jurisprudential coherence: to what extent is the Court of Justice forging coherence in the law of the area of freedom, security and justice?[52]

The challenge of coherence applies both within and across fields of law. Thus, the ECJ is clearly struggling with the law on EU citizens. Its recent judgments in cases such as *Ruiz Zambrano*, *McCarthy* and *Dereci* stretch to breaking point principles such as the 'purely internal situation' rule.[53] The Court's difficulties in this field have led to a claim that it is suffering a constitutional crisis.[54] Because of recent ECJ case law, and because of the emphasis of the Stockholm Programme on the citizen, it is this concept more so than any other that may pose the greatest challenge in future years. There are difficulties of incoherence in law and policy apparent throughout this book – in citizenship but also in relation to constitutional principles in general and fundamental rights in particular.[55]

Some areas of Court jurisprudence may exhibit greater coherence. In respect of due process in the imposition and maintenance of restrictive measures, previously known as 'sanctions', the ECJ and ECtHR are developing complementary jurisprudence. There remains a struggle to articulate with precision rules on the right to be heard, the standard of proof that maintenance of restrictive measures requires, and the extent to which evidence must be subject to disclosure. However, following its judgment in *Kadi II*, it appears that the Court of Justice is holding firm.[56] The coherence of the law is subject to reinforcement from the ECtHR, which, in its *Nada v Switzerland* judgment, offered its approval of *Kadi I*, though its judgment is not as bold as that of its EU counterpart.

There has also been convergence of reasoning on asylum rights. The judgment of the Court of Justice in *NS* complements the judgment of the ECtHR in *MSS v Belgium and Greece* and offers protection for those seeking refuge. However, the achievement of coherence in some policy fields poses questions for the coherence of the law across policy fields. Thus, the path-breaking judgment in *NS* may herald difficulties for other fields of freedom, security and justice. If it is unacceptable to transfer an asylum seeker to a Member State with chronic problems with its reception conditions and application processing systems then is it also unacceptable to transfer a suspect or convict to a Member State with such problems in its criminal justice system? The *NS* judgment undermines the idea that EU law requires Members States to presume the existence of conditions for mutual trust

[52] N Walker (ed), *Europe's Area of Freedom, Security and Justice* (Oxford, Oxford University Press, 2004).

[53] N Nic Shuibhne, 'Seven Questions for Seven Paragraphs' (2011) 36 *EL Rev* 161; *Ruiz Zambrano*, n 47; Case C-434/09 *McCarthy* [2011] ECR I-0000; Case C-256/11 *Dereci* [2011] ECR I-0000.

[54] P Eeckhout, 'EU Human Rights Law in 2012' 9 March 2012, available www.europeanideas.eu/pages/ human-rights/human-rights/eu-human-rights-law-in-2012.php, last accessed 16 May 2013.

[55] See ch 3 by Herlin-Karnell, ch 5 by Konstadinides and O'Meara, and ch 6 by Coutts, respectively.

[56] Joined Cases C-584/10 P, C-593/10 P and C-595/10 P *Kadi II* [2013] ECR I-0000. The Court's judgment of 18 July 2013 largely upheld its decision in *Kadi I* even though the Opinion of AG Bot of 19 March 2013 gives reason to believe that the wisdom of the *Kadi I* line of reasoning is subject to debate in at least some corridors of the Court of Justice. See also *Nada v Switzerland* (2013) 56 EHRR 18.

and thus casts doubt on the operation of mutual recognition in police and judicial cooperation in criminal matters.[57] If the ECJ seeks jurisprudential coherence then it may in the process cause further fragmentation of EU law. It may be for this reason that in *Radu* the Court declined the opportunity to transfer its *NS* reasoning to the operation of the European Arrest Warrant.[58]

Even at its best, there is cause for concern about the satisfactory operation of the European courts in respect of the area of freedom, security and justice. The judicial architecture of the EU is not necessarily suitable for litigation on these matters. First, cases tend to require speedy resolution as personal liberty, rather than financial interests, are often at stake. The design of the EU courts for an economic union has not been subject to significant revision in light of this new role. Although procedures for the speedy resolution of matters before the Court of Justice have been put in place these are extraordinary mechanisms whose operation is still not wholly satisfactory. Problems of delay may not be manifest to date but there is a serious risk that the Court will struggle in terms of its caseload. Second, the court faces a new role in the interpretation and application of fields of law that did not, in the past, feature on its docket. The more it moves beyond the market the more it engages substantive fields of law in which there is no classic EU law to apply and where the common constitutional traditions of the Member State offer differences both stark and subtle.[59] These differences are between common law and civil law systems, between accusatorial and investigatory criminal justice, and between different philosophies of crime and punishment. The emerging EU criminal justice system has the potential to either exacerbate or ameliorate the Member States' worst excesses and the ECJ will play a key role in shaping that system.[60]

The Court of Justice therefore has a rather difficult task ahead of it. Of course, the ECtHR has also had a pan-European jurisdiction this past half-century – even in relation to criminal justice and security matters. Yet the ECtHR operates as a last resort. For example, in relation to a criminal trial, the Court determines whether the proceedings as a whole comply with European human rights law.[61] This allows it to tailor rather broad principles to the specifics of each case and therefore to accommodate the idiosyncrasies of each criminal justice system. The ECJ is the constitutional court for the EU as a whole and may, through preliminary references, be a court of first instance in terms of the interpretation and application of the law under the emerging EU criminal justice system. This means

[57] See the discussion by Herlin-Karnell (ch 3) in this book, and see also V Mitsilegas, 'The Limits of Mutual Trust in Europe's Area of Freedom, Security and Justice: From Automatic Interstate Cooperation to the Slow Emergence of the Individual' (2012) 31 *Yearbook of European Law* 319.

[58] Case C-396/11 *Radu* [2013] ECR I-000. See further the discussion by Herlin-Karnell in ch 3 in this book.

[59] On the difficulties of applying classic principles of EU constitutional law to the area of freedom, security and justice, see ch 3 by Herlin-Karnell in this volume.

[60] See ch 7 by Mitsilegas in this volume.

[61] For a discussion, see SJ Summers, *Fair Trials: The European Criminal Procedural Tradition and the European Court of Human Rights* (Oxford, Hart Publishing, 2007).

that it does not have the comfort of taking as broad an approach as the ECtHR. Its interpretation of EU law will, with some exceptions, be binding on all Member States. It is therefore in the difficult position of striving for coherence in an increasingly complex union of legal systems.

IV. THE PEOPLES OF EUROPE AND THEIR AREA

Our survey thus far has taken in the constitutional moments of the past two decades, political power struggles, and the jurisgenerative role of the courts. It is now necessary to consider for whom all this has been done. This question points to a philosophical challenge at the heart of the European project: in seeking a union of states and peoples that goes beyond the Westphalian settlement the EU is a challenge for political theory. To borrow from the title of another collection: *whose area of freedom, security and justice* is it?[62] The answer to that question, at least as far as the Lisbon Treaty and the Stockholm Programme make clear, is the citizens of the EU. The Union offers the area to its citizens who are, in turn, the centerpiece of the Stockholm Programme.

If the citizens are indeed the referent object for the area of freedom, security and justice then that would explain the persistence of heavy regulation of both regular and irregular migration. The idea of 'fortress Europe' may be trite and yet the barriers for those seeking entry continue to mount. The regulation of migration in Europe, both regular and irregular, has long been 'in the borderlands of law, politics and ideology'.[63] In the field of regular migration Kostakopoulou, Acosta Arcarazo and Munk argue that the EU is moving towards a comprehensive migration code that may constitute a liberalization of policy. Moreno-Lax unveils the structural causes of Europe's illiberalism in respect of irregular migration. Therefore, in contrast to the citizen, who is emerging as a participatory subject of EU law, asylum seekers remain mere objects of EU control.[64] Is this distinction the future of the Union–Westphalia writ large with the EU seeking to 'replicate injustices of misframing on a broader scale'?[65]

There may be reasons to hope for better. First, the crisis in, and incoherence of, EU citizenship law is a direct result of the Court's efforts to do justice in the face of an EU law that creates injustice (the purely internal situation rule). Therefore the judgment in *Ruiz Zambrano*, which may appeal more to the heart than to the head, stretches to the limits our existing understanding of what it means to be a European citizen.[66] Furthermore, the judgment was to the benefit of Mr Ruiz

[62] A Baldaccini, E Guild and H Toner, *Whose Freedom, Security and Justice?: EU Immigration and Asylum Law and Policy* (Oxford, Hart Publishing, 2007).

[63] See ch 8 by Kostakopolou, Acosta Arcarazo and Munk in this book.

[64] See ch 9 by Moreno-Lax and ch 6 by Coutts in this book.

[65] N Fraser, *Scales of Justice* (New York, Columbia University Press, 2009) 114.

[66] *Ruiz Zambrano* (n 47) above. See on this, D Kochenov and R Plender, 'EU Citizenship: From an Incipient Form to an Incipient Substance? The Discovery of the Treaty Text' (2012) 37 *EL Rev* 369.

Zambrano, who himself is a third-country national. Perhaps the greatest recent judgment in the field of European human rights law, *Kadi I*, did not concern EU citizens at all, but rather a third-country national who does not even reside in the EU. Although dealing with an external matter the Court's sleight of hand had its basis in the need, *within* the Union, to uphold constitutional principles.[67] There has long been something of a symbiotic relationship between the development of citizenship law and human rights in the EU. Yet citizenship, which seeks to draw boundaries on political community, and fundamental rights, which transcend boundaries in favour of common humanity, are in tension as much as they are in harmony. Thus, although the citizen is the focus of the Stockholm Programme it may well be that it is fundamental rights that seize the moment.

In this volume two authors note that the Treaty of Lisbon creates a 'surfeit of rights protection'.[68] Others refer to a 'consolidation effect' that a single code on migration rights might bring about.[69] It is also worth noting the reliance on the Charter of Fundamental Rights in the *NS* judgment on asylum law. Indeed, in discussions of EU litigation in London it is now common to hear barristers debate whether there is a 'Charter argument' applicable in the case. The overall standard of fundamental rights protection in Europe may not alter significantly as a result of the Charter, but in the hands of Europe's lawyers it may facilitate creative new arguments to be made. If this occurs it may not be our common citizenry, but our common humanity, that is most important.

Can fundamental rights help the Union forge a transnational 'imagined community'?[70] The challenge is not just to imagine a transnational political community for citizens, but also for those whose migration into and across Europe is subject to control by the Union.[71] The separation of citizenship, fundamental rights, and the area of freedom, security and justice was an exercise in power limitation by the Member States. Now, the coming together of those fields may present possibilities for a new dynamic of political belonging. Perhaps the idea that any of this is possible in a time of austerity is unrealistic. The Union may have gone beyond the 'neo-Hobbesian'[72] approach of the Hague Programme but it still struggles to articulate with any coherence its vision of freedom, security and justice. Such a vision remains essential if the area is not to continue a utopia beyond the reach of citizens and non-citizens alike.

[67] Yassin Abdullah Kadi is an Egyptian national who resides in Saudi Arabia.

[68] See ch 5 by Konstadinides and O'Meara.

[69] See ch 8 by Kostakopolou, Acosta Arcarazo and Munk.

[70] For a discussion of the creation of a political community in Europe, see ch 6 by Coutts and ch 11 by Eckes that concludes this volume. The term 'imagined community' is of course from the classic work by Benedict Anderson. See B Anderson, *Imagined Communities: Reflections on the Origins and Spread of Nationalism*, Rev Ed edn (London, Verso Books, 2006).

[71] This owes a debt to Fraser's idea of the all-subjected principle. See Fraser (n 65) 96.

[72] Coutts, ch 6.

V. SCHOLARSHIP, CASTLES AND INVISIBLE CITIES

All of this begs the question of the task for scholarship? In public international law scholarship can be a persuasive source of authority. This creative role of scholarship has been part of public international law since Grotius' *De Jure Belli ac Pacis.* In European law many scholars have sought to offer accounts of EU law that blur the line between descriptive and prescriptive accounts and thus that seek not just to observe but also to shape history. In this volume our authors do not seek to rewrite the laws of war and peace but rather to complete two modest tasks in the hope of improving our understanding of security and justice law today. The balance between these two tasks varies from author to author but both aspects are present in all of the accounts that follow.

The first task is simply to catalogue: to take note of the myriad legal developments and present them for consideration and debate. If the academy is to grapple with ongoing developments in law and policy then it is necessary to chronicle those developments and to describe them in as plain a language as possible. In a field such as justice and home affairs this requires Trojan work. Any reader familiar with the law will be aware of the work of Steve Peers to present his classic legal empirical research and render the area of freedom, security and justice accessible to all. Peers does the same in this book with his survey and critique of the law after the Lisbon Treaty and Stockholm Programme. But this work is too arduous for one scholar and all of our authors contribute to map the landscape.

The second task is to critique: to point to the achievements, and more often the shortcomings, in European law and policy. In doing so the authors offer different ways of imagining the future of the area of freedom, security and justice. In this volume we gather the thoughts of 15 scholars of European law. They range from leaders of the debate such as Kostakopolou, Mitsilegas and Peers, to new voices including Coutts, Herlin-Karnell, and Moreno-Lax. The authors have all had the opportunity to discuss and comment on each other's work and the conversation that follows ranges far and wide in its discussion.

The title of this book merits some explanation. Our work encompasses the law, politics and policy of the area of freedom, security and justice. The volume does not aim to be entirely comprehensive and nor is it coextensive with the field of justice and home affairs law (which is, in any event, already the subject of a canonical text of that title). Our choice of 'security and justice law' is therefore in part a pragmatic one. We have chosen to omit 'freedom' from our title. There are at least two elements of the 'law of freedom' missing from this volume. First, there are the classic fundamental freedoms of the internal market. These free movements are the subject of a rich literature and are distinct from our focus in this work.[73] Second, there is civil law cooperation, which might be seen as central to

[73] See, eg C Barnard, *The Substantive Law of the EU: The Fundamental Freedoms*, 3rd edn (Oxford, Oxford University Press, 2010).

both freedom and justice under the Stockholm Programme. This omission is difficult to defend in some respects. Civil law cooperation does feature in the Stockholm Programme and is part of the area of freedom, security and justice. However, it remains distinct in thematic terms. Such cooperation, unlike criminal justice and migration control, does not trigger the same concerns as security.[74] Perhaps similar dynamics are nonetheless at play, but if so, their examination is work for another day. In this book our focus is the rise of security as a field of EU law and the struggle to maintain a narrative of justice in that field. Peers' question is one with which all of our other authors engage: does the EU now offer a more liberal area of freedom, security and justice than it did before Lisbon and Stockholm? We would be wise not to rush to judgment. In this field political tensions are greater than ever, the law is increasingly complex, and in any event, the present constitutional moment too will pass.

It remains striking that the metaphors of choice for European lawyers are often architectural – we are still struggling for a blueprint. An earlier exploration of the area of freedom, security and justice carries on its cover a fortress in the sky.[75] The image resonates: fortress Europe is not built on solid foundations but is a lawyer's trick of conjuring something seemingly solid out of thin air. The challenges this poses have become all too clear in the decade since that volume. There has been change but much also remains the same. Then, as now, a debate was raging as to the coherence of this novel field of EU law. Then, as now, the very existence of an area of freedom, security and justice was open to debate. The fact that these concerns endure over 10 years after that text is salient. Perhaps it is simply a function of Europe's perpetual constitutional reinvention. It may also be that the area's existence becomes more precarious as it becomes more manifest. The constitutional history that has arisen from a series of moments in European cities might itself have given rise to one of Italo Calvinho's 'invisible cities'.[76] Perhaps the area of freedom, security and justice is strung across various precipices, hung between integration and fragmentation, between politics and law, between a philosophy of inclusion and exclusions born of fear. It persists despite, but also because of, the dynamic tension between the various peaks. It may be gone tomorrow – but today, for all of its existential doubt, it endures.

[74] Note though that Peers' overview of legislative proposals in ch 2 does capture the proposals in civil law and other chapters refer, in passing, to some matters of civil law cooperation.

[75] See Walker (n 52).

[76] The resonance is also visual – an early edition of Calvino's classic bore the same image on its cover.

2

*Justice and Home Affairs Law since the Treaty of Lisbon: A Fairy-Tale Ending?**

STEVE PEERS

I. INTRODUCTION

DOES EVERY STORY have a happy ending? For many years, the area of EU justice and home affairs (JHA) law has been the 'wicked stepmother' of the EU system, dismaying many supporters of judicial control, democratic accountability, the rule of law and human rights protection with its limited role for parliaments and courts and an array of legislation unbalanced towards migration control and criminal prosecution, with insufficient regard for substantive individual protection or procedural justice.

But the end of 2009 was the chance for a new beginning for EU JHA law. First of all, the entry into force of the Treaty of Lisbon, on 1 December 2009, significantly reformed the institutional framework for the adoption of JHA measures, largely bringing it into line with the rules that generally applied to the rest of EU law. Secondly, a few days later, the adoption of the Stockholm Programme by the European Council gave a new impetus to the development of JHA policies.[1] Over three years after these key developments,[2] it is possible to suggest provisional answers to two key questions: (a) is the institutional framework for JHA law now essentially supranational, rather than intergovernmental? (b) is substantive JHA law now essentially liberal, rather than conservative?

* This paper is an updated and extended version of S Peers, 'Mission Accomplished? EU Justice and Home Affairs Law after the Treaty of Lisbon' (2011) 48 *CML Rev* 661.

[1] OJ 2010 C115.

[2] This paper is updated to 25 Feb 2013. For more detailed analysis of the institutional framework and the substance of all JHA measures up until Sep 2010, see S Peers, *EU Justice and Home Affairs Law*, 3rd edn (Oxford, Oxford University Press, 2011) – hereinafter '*JHA Law*'. As regards the Lisbon Treaty and specific issues, see V Mitsilegas, *EU Criminal Law* (Oxford, Hart Publishing, 2009) 36–57 and C Ladenburger, 'Police and Criminal Law in the Treaty of Lisbon: A New Dimension for the Community Method' (2008) 4 *European Constitutional Law Review* 20.

II. THE INSTITUTIONAL FRAMEWORK

A. Background

Following the entrenchment of a 'formal intergovernmental' structure in the form of the so-called 'third pillar' system by the Maastricht Treaty, the significant amendments made by the Treaty of Amsterdam and the modest amendments made by the Treaty of Nice had resulted in a mixture of intergovernmental and supranational elements as regards JHA law.[3] After the end of a transitional period on 1 May 2004,[4] many immigration, asylum and civil law issues were already subject to the usual first pillar rules:[5] a Commission monopoly over making proposals, qualified majority voting (QMV) in Council and co-decision for the European Parliament (EP) over legislation.[6] However, even after this point, the jurisdiction of the Court of Justice over these issues was restricted (references for a preliminary ruling from final courts only);[7] there were also opt-outs for the UK, Ireland and Denmark, which had been the quid pro quo for applying the 'Community method' to these issues; and several areas remained subject to unanimity in Council with consultation of the EP (family law, legal migration), or to QMV in Council and consultation of the EP (visa lists and visa formats).[8]

As for the issues of policing and criminal law, they had remained in a reformed third pillar.[9] This entailed the use of different legal instruments as compared to EC law, in particular framework decisions, which resembled directives, except for an express lack of direct effect.[10] The Commission had to share power with

[3] For a detailed analysis of the historical evolution of the institutional system and models of integration in JHA matters, see S Peers, 'Justice and Home Affairs Law: Non-civil' in P Craig and G de Búrca (eds), *The Evolution of EU Law*, 2nd edn (Oxford, Oxford University Press, 2011).

[4] From 1999–2004, there was shared competence to introduce legal proposals as between the Commission and Member States, a limited role for the European Parliament (consultation), and mostly unanimous voting in the Council. See Art 67 EC.

[5] Arts 61–69 EC, known as 'Title IV' of Pt 3 of the EC Treaty.

[6] In part, this was due to a Council decision extending QMV and co-decision to certain areas, which took effect slightly later (1 Jan 2005): OJ 2004 L396/45. For discussion, see S Peers, 'Transforming Decision-Making on EC Immigration and Asylum Law' (2005) 30 *EL Rev* 283. As regards most asylum issues, Art 67(5) EC required the prior adoption of initial basic legislation before QMV and co-decision applied. For interpretation of Art 67(5), see Case C-133/06 *EP v Council* [2008] ECR I-3189.

[7] Art 68(1) EC. See also the further special rules in Art 68(2) and (3) EC. The Commission's proposal to extend the Court's jurisdiction (COM(2006) 346, 28 June 2006) was not adopted by the Council.

[8] On the latter point, see Art 67(3) EC.

[9] Title VI of the TEU (Arts 29–42).

[10] See Case C-105/03 *Pupino* [2005] ECR I-5285 and the discussion in E Spaventa, 'Opening Pandora's Box: Some Reflections on the Constitutional Effects of the Ruling in Pupino' (2007) 3 *European Constitutional Law Review* 5. The question of whether other EC law principles, such as primacy and damages liability, apply to the third pillar has not yet been decided by the Court: see the discussion in K Lenaerts and T Corthaut, 'Of Birds and Hedges: The Role of Primacy in Invoking Norms of EU Law' (2006) 31 *EL Rev* 287, 289–91; A Hinarejos, *Judicial Control in the European Union: Reforming Jurisdiction in the Intergovernmental Pillars* (Oxford, Oxford University Press, 2009) 29–49; and S Peers, 'Salvation outside the Church: Judicial Protection in the Third Pillar after the *Pupino* and *SEGI* Judgments' (2007) 44 *CML Rev* 883. Note that the Opinion of 2 Oct 2012 in Case C-399/11 *Melloni*, pending, assumes the primacy of third pillar law over national law in the same terms as EC law.

Member States as regards proposing measures, and the EP was only consulted on most measures. The Court of Justice had jurisdiction over references from national courts, except that Member States had the power to opt-out entirely from that jurisdiction.[11]

B. Treaty of Lisbon

Following the entry into force of the Treaty of Lisbon, the various issues falling within the scope of JHA law are now set out in Title V of Part Three of the renamed EC Treaty, the Treaty on the Functioning of the European Union, or 'TFEU'. The institutional framework for JHA law-making is now much more closely aligned with the general rules. First of all, most of the issues that were still subject to unanimous voting in the Council and consultation of the EP before the Treaty of Lisbon entered into force are now subject to QMV in Council and the 'ordinary legislative procedure' (previously known as 'co-decision'), in particular legal migration and most aspects of criminal law and police cooperation.[12] The ordinary legislative procedure also applies to the issues of visa lists and visa formats,[13] whereas previously QMV in Council with only consultation of the European Parliament had applied. QMV with consultation of the European Parliament, instead of unanimity in Council, applies to the adoption of measures on administrative cooperation in the fields of policing and criminal law.[14]

However, the Council must still vote unanimously as regards issues relating to passports, family law, the creation of a European Public Prosecutor and operational police cooperation (including cross-border operations).[15] Unanimity would also apply if the Council wants to change aspects of the JHA institutional framework, either to shift to the ordinary legislative procedure as regards family law, extend EU competence in relation to criminal law or extend the subject matter which the European Public Prosecutor would be competent to deal with.[16] Also, in certain areas of criminal law, the move to QMV is qualified by the power for any Member State to pull a so-called 'emergency brake', which would block discussions if that Member State considers that a draft measure 'would affect fundamental aspects of its criminal justice system'.[17] If such a brake is pulled, there is the possibility of a move to 'fast-track' enhanced cooperation (ie the legislation would only apply to

[11] See further Hinarejos (ibid), 55–94. In practice, 19 Member States opted in to the Court's jurisdiction: all except the UK, Denmark, Ireland, Estonia, Poland, Slovakia, Bulgaria and Malta (see OJ 2010 L56/14).

[12] See Arts 79, 82–85, 87 and 88 TFEU.

[13] Art 77 TFEU.

[14] Art 74 TFEU, which has widened the scope of the prior Art 66 EC.

[15] Arts 77(3), 81(3), 86(1), 87(3) and 89 TFEU, which all constitute 'special legislative procedures'. In each case the EP is consulted, except for Art 86(1) (concerning the European Public Prosecutor), where it has the power of consent.

[16] Arts 81(3), 82(2)(d), 83(1) and 86(4) TFEU.

[17] Arts 82(3) and 83(3) TFEU. For discussion of this procedure, see S Peers, 'EU Criminal Law and the Treaty of Lisbon' (2008) 33 *EL Rev* 507, 522–29.

those Member States willing to participate in it, as long as there are at least nine of them). Conversely, a Member State's veto as regards the creation of the European Public Prosecutor or operational police cooperation is softened by an equivalent possibility of a fast-track authorisation of enhanced cooperation.[18]

In conjunction with the shift to QMV in Council, the EU's competence over most JHA matters has been clarified, for instance by limiting EU competence specifically to certain categories of crime and types of criminal procedure with a cross-border element, and also ruling out EU competence as regards the volumes of admission of third-country nationals coming from third countries.[19]

Secondly, the role of the Commission has been strengthened in that it no longer shares power with each individual Member State as regards proposals for police and criminal law measures. Instead, the Treaty requires at least one-quarter of the Member States to make a proposal.[20] So, while the Commission's role is still weaker than it is in the rest of EU law, it is stronger than it was before as regards policing and criminal law.

Thirdly, the move toward the 'Community' method is unqualified as regards the use of the usual legal instruments of directives and regulations, in place of the previous third pillar instruments of conventions, framework decisions and so on. This change automatically entails application of the usual rules on the legal effect of such measures to the fields of policing and criminal law. However, it should be noted that the EU is obliged to use directives as regards the harmonisation of national criminal law.[21]

Fourthly, the Court of Justice gained its normal jurisdiction as regards immigration, asylum and civil law as well as policing and criminal law, subject to a residual limitation on the Court's jurisdiction as regards policing and criminal law: it cannot

> review the validity or proportionality of operations carried out by the police or other law-enforcement services of a Member State or the exercise of the responsibilities incumbent upon Member States with regard to the maintenance of law and order and the safeguarding of internal security.[22]

Fifthly, the three Member States with the greatest misgivings about the changes to the JHA institutional framework – the UK, Ireland and Denmark – were again 'bought off' by the extension of scope of their existing opt-out Protocols from Title IV matters to cover the whole of the JHA field. There were also a number of amendments to these Protocols.

[18] Arts 86(1) and 87(3) TFEU. For discussion of this procedure, see *JHA Law* (n 2 above), 70–71.

[19] Arts 83(1), 82(2) and 79(5) TFEU respectively. On the interpretation of these provisions, see ibid and S Peers, 'EU Immigration and Asylum Competence and Decision-Making in the Treaty of Lisbon' (2008) 10 *European Journal of Migration and Law* 219, 241–46.

[20] Art 76 TFEU.

[21] Arts 82 and 83 TFEU; this does not apply to the adoption of measures concerning mutual recognition (Art 82(1)). On the other hand, the EU must use regulations to adopt rules concerning Europol, Eurojust or the European Public Prosecutor (Arts 88, 85 and 86 TFEU).

[22] Art 276 TFEU.

Next, the rules on external relations in JHA matters were, as regards policing and criminal law, aligned with the general rules on these matters in the treaties.[23] Similarly, the general rules on enhanced cooperation now also apply to this area, subject to the possibility of fast-track authorisation of enhanced cooperation in several areas of criminal law.

Finally, there are transitional rules for policing and criminal law measures adopted before the Treaty of Lisbon, set out in a transitional protocol.[24] These rules limit the Court of Justice's jurisdiction over such measures for a five-year period up to 1 December 2014; during that period, the pre-Lisbon rules on the Court's jurisdiction continue to apply. Also, the legal effect of such measures continues indefinitely, until those measures are amended or repealed. Furthermore, the UK is entitled to decide to opt-out en masse of all such measures as of 1 December 2014, although it can apply to opt-in to some of those acts.

III. THE REVISED INSTITUTIONAL FRAMEWORK IN PRACTICE

A. Legislative Decision-making

As regards legislative decision-making, in the field of criminal law the EU has adopted three directives on criminal procedure issues,[25] two directives on substantive criminal law,[26] and one directive on mutual recognition.[27] Legislation has been proposed as regards: a European investigation order;[28] attacks on information systems;[29] access to a lawyer and communication rights;[30] criminal sanctions against market abuse;[31] the freezing and confiscation of criminal proceeds;[32] and counterfeiting currency.[33] Also, a proposal on the protection of EU's financial interests by means of criminal law,[34] while based on Article 325 TFEU, is closely related to JHA law, and may ultimately be adopted pursuant to a JHA legal base.[35] In 2013, the

[23] Art 218 TFEU (ex-Art 300 EC, as amended). See further, S Peers *JHA Law* (n 2 above), 127–35.

[24] Arts 9 and 10, Protocol 36.

[25] Directives: 2010/64 on the right to interpretation and translation for criminal suspects (OJ 2010 L280/1); 2012/13 on information about rights and accusations (OJ 2012 L142/1); and 2012/29 on the role of crime victims in criminal procedure (OJ 2012 L315/57).

[26] Directives 2011/36 on trafficking in persons (OJ 2011 L101/1) and 2011/92 on sexual offences against children (OJ 2011 L335/1).

[27] Directive 2011/99 on the European Protection Order (OJ 2011 L338/2).

[28] OJ 2010 C165/22. The Council has agreed its position on this proposal: Council docs 18918/11, 21 Dec 2011 and 9445/12, 29 May 2012. EP/Council negotiations are underway.

[29] COM(2010) 517, 30 Sep 2010. The Council and the EP have agreed a deal on this measure: Council doc 11399/12, 15 June 2012.

[30] COM(2011) 326, 8 June 2011. The Council has agreed its position on this proposal: Council doc 10467/12, 31 May 2012. EP/Council negotiations are underway.

[31] COM(2011) 654, 20 Oct 2011; revised: COM(2012) 420, 25 July 2012. The Council has agreed its position on this proposal: Council doc 17642/12, 12 Dec 2012. EP/Council negotiations are underway.

[32] COM(2012) 85, 12 March 2012. The Council has agreed its position on this proposal: Council doc 17287/12, 11 Dec 2012. EP/Council negotiations are underway.

[33] COM(2013) 42, 5 Feb 2013.

[34] COM(2012) 363, 11 July 2012.

[35] See Council doc 17359/12, 11 Dec 2012.

Commission's aim was to propose legislation on Eurojust, the European Public Prosecutor, legal aid for criminal suspects, the presumption of innocence, designer drugs, drug trafficking and the criminal records of third-country nationals.[36]

As regards policing matters, the EU has adopted a directive on the exchange of information on traffic offences,[37] as well as regulations on the development of the second-generation Schengen Information System (SIS II) as regards policing and criminal law.[38] Other adopted or proposed legislation has a 'dual' legal base relating to both criminal law and immigration matters.[39] The Commission has also proposed a directive on passenger name records.[40] In 2013, the Commission sought to propose legislation on Europol, the European Police College and domestic terrorist asset freezing.[41]

Next, in the area of civil law, the EU has adopted regulations on: the choice of law and jurisdiction as regards inheritance;[42] the choice of law in divorce (known as the 'Rome III' Regulation), pursuant to the rules on enhanced cooperation;[43] and civil jurisdiction and mutual recognition, replacing the previous Brussels I Regulation.[44] The Commission has also proposed five new regulations in this area: two new regulations concerning jurisdiction and choice of law as regards divorce and dissolution of non-marital partnerships;[45] a regulation on civil law enforcement of protection orders;[46] a regulation on European account preservation orders;[47] and a proposal to amend the existing regulation on insolvency proceedings.[48] In 2013, the Commission sought to propose legislation on service of documents, civil jurisdiction (as regards the planned Unified Patent Court), the recognition of civil status documents and simplification of legalisation of documents.[49]

On the issue of asylum, the EU has adopted legislation concerning the creation of a European Asylum Support Office,[50] revising the directive on the qualification of persons for refugee or subsidiary protection status,[51] and amending EU funding

[36] See the Commission's forward programming for 2013, last accessed 25 Feb 2013: ec.europa.eu/atwork/pdf/forward_programming_2013.pdf.

[37] Dir 2011/82 (OJ 2011 L288/1). On the 'legal base' dispute concerning this measure, see s F below.

[38] Regs 542/2010 (OJ 2010 L155/23) and 1272/2012 (OJ 2012 L359/12).

[39] See the discussion below as regards the regulation establishing the agency managing JHA databases and the proposal for police access to Eurodac.

[40] COM(2011) 32, 2 Feb 2011. The Council has agreed its position on this proposal: Council doc 8916/12, 23 April 2012.

[41] n 36 above.

[42] Reg 650/2012 (OJ 2012 L201/107).

[43] Reg 1259/2010 (OJ 2010 L343/10). For the decision authorising enhanced cooperation, see OJ 2010 L189/12. Fourteen Member States initially participated in the Regulation, and Lithuania joined them later (OJ 2012 L323/18). For further discussion, see S Peers, 'Divorce, European Style: The First Authorisation of Enhanced Cooperation' (2010) 6 *European Constitutional Law Review* 339.

[44] Reg 1215/2012 (OJ 2012 L351/1).

[45] COM(2011) 126 and 127, 16 March 2011.

[46] COM(2011) 276, 18 May 2011. The EP and Council agreed a deal on this proposal in Feb 2013: see Commission press release MEMO/13/119, 19 Feb 2013.

[47] COM(2011) 445, 25 July 2011.

[48] COM(2012) 744, 12 Dec 2012.

[49] n 36 above.

[50] Reg 439/2010 (OJ 2010 L132/11) and an amendment to the refugee fund Decision (OJ 2010 L129/1).

[51] Dir 2011/95 (OJ 2011 L337/9).

rules to provide more support for resettlement,[52] and for EU Member States in financial difficulties.[53] It has not yet, however, been able to adopt key legislation establishing the second phase of the Common European Asylum System as regards: asylum responsibility; Eurodac (the EU-wide database of asylum-seekers' fingerprints); reception conditions; and procedures for applications for international protection.[54] Having said that, the European Parliament and Council have in principle agreed on the legislation concerning responsibility and reception conditions,[55] and are negotiating the legislation on asylum procedures and Eurodac. There are no plans for further proposals for legislation for now.

In the area of visas and border controls, the EU has adopted legislation: amending its visa list;[56] amending the Regulation establishing Frontex (the EU's border control agency);[57] establishing rules regarding the issue of travel documents;[58] creating an agency to manage the Visa Information System (VIS), SIS II and Eurodac;[59] concerning the project management of the development of SIS II;[60] amending the legislation on local border traffic; changing the transit visa rules in the EU's visa code;[61] and developing the rules concerning the issue of long-stay visas.[62] At the time of writing, there are also proposals concerning: general amendments to the Schengen Borders Code;[63] specific amendments to the Code to make it easier for Member States to re-introduce internal border checks;[64] closely connected amendments to the Schengen evaluation process;[65] a codification of the EU's visa list;[66] further amendments to the visa list;[67] amendments to the EU funding legislation;[68] and establishing Eurosur, an EU-wide border surveillance system.[69] In 2013, the

[52] OJ 2012 L92/1.

[53] For the text of this legislation ready for adoption, see Council doc 71/12, 14 Feb 2013.

[54] See respectively: COM(2008) 820, 3 Dec 2008; COM(2008) 825, 3 Dec 2008 (revised in: COM(2009) 342, 10 Sep 2009; COM(2010) 555, 11 Oct 2010; and COM(2012) 254, 30 May 2012); COM(2008) 815, 3 Dec 2009 (revised in COM(2011) 320, 1 June 2011); and COM(2009) 554, 21 Oct 2009 (revised in COM(2011) 319, 1 June 2011).

[55] For the agreed text of these measures, see respectively Council docs 15605/12, 14 Dec 2012 and 14654/12, 14 Dec 2012.

[56] Regs 1091/2010 and 1211/2010 (OJ 2010 L329/1 and L339/6).

[57] Reg 1168/2011 (OJ 2011 L304/1).

[58] OJ 2011 L287/9.

[59] Reg 1077/2011 (OJ 2011 L286/1).

[60] Regs 541/2010 (OJ 2010 L155/19) and 1273/2012 (OJ 2012 L359/32). The parallel Regs 542/2010 and 1272/2012 (n 38 above) concern the policing and criminal law aspects of SIS II.

[61] Reg 154/2012 (OJ 2012 L58/3).

[62] Reg 265/2010 (OJ 2010 L85/1).

[63] COM(2011) 118, 10 March 2011. The EP and Council have agreed on the text of this measure: see Council doc 18006/12, 19 Dec 2012.

[64] COM(2011) 560, 16 Sep 2011. For the Council's agreed text, see: Council doc 6161/4/12, 4 June 2012. EP/Council negotiations are underway.

[65] COM(2010) 624, 16 Nov 2010; amended proposal: COM(2011) 559, 16 Sep 2011. See previously COM(2009) 102, 4 March 2009. For the Council's agreed text, see: Council doc 11846/1/12, 29 June 2012. EP/Council negotiations are underway.

[66] COM(2008) 761, 28 Nov 2008. Discussion of this proposal has ceased.

[67] For general amendments, see COM(2011) 290, 24 May 2011; EP/Council negotiations are underway. For amendments to the lists, see COM(2012) 650, 7 Nov 2012.

[68] COM(2012) 527, 20 Sep 2012. The EP and Council have agreed on the text of this measure: see Council doc 72/12, 14 Feb 2013.

[69] COM(2011) 873, 12 Dec 2011. EP/Council negotiations are underway.

Commission planned legislation to establish an entry–exit system and registered traveller programme, as well as a review of the visa code, rules on the surveillance of maritime borders and a codification of the borders code.[70]

As for irregular immigration, the EU has only adopted one measure: an amendment of the prior regulation on immigration liaison officers.[71] The Commission intended to propose legislation on the issue of advance passenger information in 2013.[72] In the area of regular migration, the EU has adopted legislation revising the rules on social security for third-country nationals who move within the EU,[73] as well as a directive which extends the prior long-term residence directive to refugees and beneficiaries of subsidiary protection,[74] and a directive which sets out a single permit procedure and common rights for third-country nationals who work within the EU.[75] Proposals on seasonal workers and intra-corporate transferees are under discussion.[76] In 2013, the Commission planned to propose amendments to the prior legislation on admission of students and researchers.[77]

As regards JHA funding, the Commission has proposed a number of measures that will regulate EU funding regarding JHA for the period 2014–20.[78] These measures will likely be adopted shortly after the basic rules on the EU's multi-annual financial framework have been agreed between the EP and the Council.

Finally, as for non-legislative acts, there has been no proposal to use the provisions concerning changes to decision-making rules or extension of competence,[79] but the Court of Justice has delivered an important judgment limiting the use of implementing powers (and presumably also delegated acts) to regulate coercive measures or issues raising human rights concerns.[80]

B. Role of Commission

One obvious indicator of the Commission's increased role in JHA matters since the entry into force of the Treaty of Lisbon was the appointment of two Commissioners with two Directorate-Generals to cover JHA matters, rather than (as before) one Commissioner and one Directorate-General. As for the Commission's role initiating proposals for legislation, there were three initiatives by Member States for criminal

[70] n 36 above.

[71] Reg 493/2011 (OJ 2011 L141/13).

[72] n 36 above.

[73] Reg 1231/2010 (OJ 2010 L344/1).

[74] Dir 2011/51 (OJ 2011 L132/1).

[75] Dir 2011/98 (OJ 2011 L343/1).

[76] COM(2010) 378 and 379, 13 July 2010. For the Council's position on these measures, see Council docs 10618/12, 6 June 2012 and 17100/12, 3 Dec 2012.

[77] See n 36 above.

[78] See COM(2011) 750–53 and 759, 15 Nov 2011.

[79] A pre-Lisbon proposal to change the decision-making rules on the issue of maintenance is no longer under consideration (COM(2005) 648, 15 Dec 2005). The Council has also adopted a non-legislative decision establishing the Standing Committee on Operational Cooperation on Internal Security (see Art 71 TFEU) pursuant to Art 240(3) TFEU (OJ 2010 L52/50).

[80] Case C-355/10 *EP v Council*, judgment of 5 Sep 2012 (not yet reported).

law legislation shortly after the entry into force of the Treaty of Lisbon.[81] However, there have been no further such initiatives since the spring of 2010, and there do not seem to be any further Member States' initiatives planned at the time of writing.

C. Court of Justice

The Treaty of Lisbon brought about a significant extension of the Court's jurisdiction over JHA issues,[82] and it was generally assumed that the Treaty would lead to a large increase in the number of JHA cases referred to the Court by national courts, thereby enhancing the Court's role as an actor in JHA law.

In practice, dividing JHA cases into three categories,[83] first of all, leaving aside the cases referred to the Court regarding the prior Brussels Conventions and Rome Conventions, which have been repealed by regulations,[84] the first admissible reference to the Court on civil law matters came in 2003. The number of references rose gradually afterward, with five references in 2004, three references in 2005, six references in 2006, 10 references in 2007, 15 references in 2008, and 11 admissible references in 2009.[85] In 2010, after the entry into force of the Treaty of Lisbon, there were 23 references from national courts concerning EU civil law legislation.[86] There were then 18 references in 2011,[87] and 23 references in 2012.[88]

[81] These were the proposals for directives on suspects' rights to translation and interpretation (*OJ 2010 C69/1*), the European Protection Order (*OJ 2010 C69/5*) and the European Investigation Order (n 28 above).

[82] See further, Hinarejos, *Judicial Control in the European Union* (n 10 above), 100–21.

[83] Inadmissible cases are not counted, and joined cases referred in the same year are counted as one case.

[84] Regs 44/2001 (OJ 2001 L12/1) and 593/2008 (OJ 2008 L177/6).

[85] For details of the cases, see S Peers, *JHA Law* (n 2 above), 602. Case C-509/09 *eDate Advertising* (judgment of 25 Oct 2011) was received in December 2009, ie after the entry into force of the Treaty of Lisbon, but referred beforehand.

[86] Cases: C-87/10 *Electrosteel* (judgment of 9 June 2011); C-112/10 *Zaza Retail* (judgment of 17 Nov 2011); C-139/10 *Prism Investments* (judgment of 13 Oct 2011); C-144/10 *Berliner Verkehrsbetriebe* (judgment of 12 May 2011); C-145/10 *Painer* (judgment of 1 Dec 2011); C-161/10 *Martinez* (judgment of 25 Oct 2011); C-191/10 *Rastelli Davide and C* (judgment of 15 Dec 2011); C-213/10 *F-Tex* (judgment of 19 April 2012); C-211/10 PPU *Povse* [2010] ECR I-6669; C-292/10 *G* (judgment of 15 March 2012); C-296/10 *Purrucker II* [2010] ECR I-11163; C-315/10 *Companhia Siderúrgica Nacional* (withdrawn); C-327/10 *Lindner* (judgment of 17 Nov 2011); C-400/10 PPU *McB* [2010] ECR I-8965; C-412/10 *Homawoo* (judgment of 17 Nov 2011); C-491/10 PPU *Aguirre Zarraga* [2010] ECR I-14247; C-494/10 *Bahr* (withdrawn); C-497/10 PPU *Mercredi* [2010] ECR I-14309; C-514/10 *Wolf Naturprodukte* (judgment of 21 June 2012); C-523/10 *Wintersteiger* (judgment of 19 April 2011); C-527/10 *Erste Bank* (judgment of 5 July 2012); C-543/10 *Refcomp* (judgment of 7 Feb 2013); C-616/10 *Solvay* (judgment of 12 July 2012); and C-619/10 *Trade Agency* (judgment of 6 Sep 2012) (all judgments not yet reported, except where noted otherwise).

[87] Cases: C-54/11 *JP Morgan Chase Bank* (withdrawn); C-116/11 *Handlowy* (judgment of 22 Nov 2012); C-133/11 *Folien Fischer* (judgment of 25 Oct 2012); C-154/11 *Mahamdia* (judgment of 19 July 2012); C-170/11 *Lippens* (judgment of 6 Sep 2012); C-190/11 *Muhlleitner* (judgment of 6 Sep 2012); C-215/11 *Syrocka* (judgment of 13 Dec 2012); C-228/11 *Melzer* (pending); C-325/11 *Alder and Alder* (judgment of 19 Dec 2012); C-332/11 *ProRail* (judgment of 21 Feb 2013); C-419/11 *Ceská Sporite a* (pending); C-456/11 *Gothaer Allgemeine Versicherung* (judgment of 15 Nov 2012); C-464/11 *Galioto* (order of 8 Feb 2013); C-490/11 *Ibis* (withdrawn); C-492/11 *Di Donna* (pending); C-552/11 *Thone* (withdrawn); C-634/11 *Anglo-Irish Bank* (pending); and C-645/11 *Sapir* (pending) (no judgments yet reported).

[88] C-9/12 *Corman-Collins* (pending); C-49/12 *Sunico* (pending); C-92/12 PPU *Health and Safety Executive* (judgment of 26 April 2012, not yet reported); C-98/12 *Slot* (withdrawn); C-144/12 *Goldbet*

Next, as regards immigration and asylum cases, the first admissible reference to the Court of Justice came in 2005.[89] There were then no references in 2006, one reference in 2007,[90] five references in 2008,[91] and four references in 2009.[92] Following the entry into force of the Treaty of Lisbon, there were 10 references from national courts in 2010,[93] 18 distinct references in 2011,[94] and 17 references in 2012.[95]

Finally, as for policing and criminal law cases, the first reference was in 2001,[96] followed by three references in 2003,[97] two in 2004,[98] five in 2005,[99] three in

Sportwetten (pending); C-147/12 *OFAB* (pending); C-156/12 *GREP* (order of the Court, 13 June 2012); C-157/12 *Salzgitter Mannesmann Handel* (pending); C-170/12 *Pinckney* (pending); C-218/12 *Emrek* (pending); C-251/12 *Van Buggenhout* (pending); C-324/12 *Novontech-Zala* (pending); C-328/12 *Schmidt* (pending); C-360/12 *Coty Prestige Lancaster Group* (pending); C-386/12 *Schneider* (pending); C-387/12 *Hi Hotel HCF* (pending); C-438/12 *Weber* (pending); C-452/12 *NIPPONKOA Insurance* (pending); C-469/12 *Krejci Lager & Umschlagbetriebs* (pending); C-478/12 *Maletic and Maletic* (pending); C-508/12 *Vapenic* (pending); C-519/12 *OTP Bank* (pending); and C-548/12 *Brogsitter* (pending). There are already two references in 2013: Cases C-1/13 *Cartier Parfums-Lunettes* and C-45/13 *Kainz*, both pending.

89 Case C-241/05 *Bot* [2006] ECR I-9627.

90 Case *C-465/07 Elgafaji and Elgafaji [2009] ECR I-921.*

91 Cases: C-19/08 *Petrosian* [2009] ECR I-495; C-139/08 *Kqiku* [2009] ECR I-2887; Cases C-175/08–C-179/08 *Abdulla and others* [2010] ECR I-1493; C-261/08 and C-348/08 *Zurita Garcia* and *Choque Cabrera* [2009] ECR I-10143; and C-578/08 *Chakroun* [2010] ECR I-1493.

92 Cases: C-57/09 and C-101/09 *B and D* [2010] ECR I-10979; C-31/09 *Bolbol* [2010] ECR I-5539; C-247/09 *Xhymshiti* [2010] ECR I-11845; and C-357/09 PPU *Kadzoev* [2009] ECR I-11189.

93 Cases: C-69/10 *Samba Diouf* (judgment of 28 July 2011); C-105/10 PPU *Gataev and Gataeva* (withdrawn); C-188/10 and C-189/10 *Melki and Abdeli* [2010] ECR I-5667; C-411/10 and C-493/10 *NS* (judgment of 21 Dec 2011); C-430/10 *Gaydarov* (judgment of 17 Nov 2011); C-502/10 *Singh* (judgment of 18 Oct 2012); C-563/10 *Khavand* (withdrawn); C-571/10 *Kamberaj* (judgment of 24 April 2012); C-606/10 *Association Nationale d'Assistance aux Frontières pour les Etrangers* (judgment of 14 June 2012); and C-620/10 *Kastrati* (judgment of 3 May 2012) (all judgments not yet reported, except *Melki and Abdeli*).

94 Cases: C-4/11 *Puid* (pending); C-15/11 *Sommer* (judgment of 21 June 2012); C-61/11 PPU *El Dridl Hassan* [2011] ECR I-3015; C-71/11 and C-99/11 *Y and Z* (judgment of 5 Sep 2012); C-155/11 *Imran* (order of 10 June 2011); C-175/11 *HID* (judgment of 31 Jan 2013); C-179/11 *CIMADE and GISTI* (judgment of 27 Sep 2012); C-245/11 *K* (judgment of 6 Nov 2012); C-254/11 *Shomodi* (pending); C-277/11 *MM* (judgment of 22 Nov 2012); C-329/11 *Achughbabian* (judgment of 6 Dec 2011); C-364/11 *El Kott* (judgment of 19 Dec 2012); C-430/11 *Sagor* (judgment of 6 Dec 2012); Case C-522/11 *Mbaye* (pending); C-528/11 *Halaf* (pending); C-534/11 *Arslan* (pending); C-648/11 *MA* (pending); and C-666/11 *M and others* (withdrawn) (all judgments not yet reported, except *Hassan*). This tally leaves aside 11 repetitive cases which were withdrawn: Cases C-50/11 *Emegor*; C-60/11 *Mrad*; C-63/11 *Austine*; C-94/11 *Godwin*; C-113/11 *Cherni*; C-120/11 *Kwadwo*; C-140/11 *Ngagne*; C-43/11 *Samb*; C-156/11 *Music*; C-169/11 *Conteh*; and C-187/11 *Vermisheva*.

95 Cases: C-23/12 *Zakaria* (judgment of 17 Jan 2013); C-39/12 *Dang* (withdrawn); C-51/12–54/12 *Zhu and others* (withdrawn); C-73/12–75/12 *Ettaghi and others* (withdrawn); C-83/12 PPU *Vo* (judgment of 10 April 2012); C-84/12 *Koushkaki* (pending); C-88/12 *Jaoo* (withdrawn); C-199/12–201/12 *X, Y and Z* (pending); C-278/12 PPU *Adil* (judgment of 19 July 2012); C-285/12 *Diakite* (pending); C-291/12 *Schwarz* (pending); C-297/12 *Filev and Osmani* (pending); C-394/12 *Abdullahi* (pending); C-446/12–C-449/12 *Willems and others* (pending); C-513/12 *Ayalti* (pending); C-575/12 *Air Baltic* (pending); and C-604/12 *HN* (pending). There is one case referred in 2013 already: C-79/13 *Saciri*, pending.

96 Cases C-187/01 and C-385/01 *Gozutok and Brugge* [2003] ECR I-1345.

97 *Pupino* (n 10 above) and Cases C-469/03 *Miraglia* [2005] ECR I-2009 and C-491/03 *Hiebeler* (withdrawn).

98 Cases C-436/04 *Van Esbroek* [2006] ECR I-2333 and C-467/04 *Gasparini* [2006] ECR I-9199.

99 Cases C-150/05 *Van Straaten* [2006] ECR I-9327; C-272/05 *Bowens* (withdrawn); C-288/05 *Kretzinger* [2007] ECR I-6441; C-303/05 *Advocaten voor de Wereld* [2007] ECR I-3633; C-367/05 *Kraaijenbrink* [2007] ECR I-6619; and C-467/05 *Dell'Orto* [2007] ECR I-5557.

2007,[100] four in 2008,[101] and four in 2009.[102] There were no references in 2002 or 2006. Following the entry into force of the Treaty of Lisbon, there were four references in 2010,[103] five in 2011,[104] and three in 2012.[105]

As for the urgent procedure for JHA issues, which was created already in 2008,[106] to date, the Court has had to decide on a modest number of references in this area on the basis of this procedure: three such procedures in 2008,[107] two in 2009,[108] four in 2010,[109] one in 2011,[110] and four in 2012.[111] The Court also decided two cases via an accelerated procedure as regards persons in detention, pursuant to the relevant provision in Article 267 TFEU inserted by the Treaty of Lisbon.[112]

More broadly, taking all three areas of JHA law together, there was one reference to the Court in 2001, followed by three references in 2003, seven in 2004, nine in 2005, six in 2006, 14 in 2007, 24 in 2008, 19 in 2009, 37 in 2010, and 43 in each of 2011 and 2012.

D. Opt-Outs[113]

The existence of specific opt-outs for JHA matters is the sole remaining fundamental distinction between the JHA Title and the rest of EU law.[114] In a nutshell, the Treaty of Lisbon extended the previous opt-out rules (which covered the

[100] Cases C-297/07 *Bourquain* [2008] ECR I-9425; C-404/07 *Katz* [2008] ECR I-7607; and C-491/07 *Turansky* [2008] ECR I-11039.

[101] Cases C-66/08 *Koslowski* [2008] ECR I-6041; C-296/08 PPU *Santesteban Goicoechea* [2008] ECR I-6307; C-388/08 PPU *Leymann and Pustovarov* [2008] ECR I-8993; and C-123/08 *Wolzenburg* [2009] ECR I-9621.

[102] Cases C-205/09 *Eredics* [2010] ECR I-10231; C-261/09 *Mantello* [2010] ECR I-11477; C-306/09 *IB* [2010] ECR I-10341; and C-403/09 *Gueye*, judgment of 15 Sep 2011, not yet reported.

[103] Cases: C-1/10 *Salmeron Sanchez* (judgment of 15 Sep 2011, not yet reported); *C-105/10 PPU Gataev and Gataeva (withdrawn);* C-264/10 *Kita* (withdrawn); and C-507/10 *X* (judgment of 21 Dec 2011, not yet reported).

[104] Cases: C-27/11 *Vinkov* (judgment of 7 June 2012); C-42/11 *Lopes da Silva Jorge* (judgment of 5 Sep 2012); C-79/11 *Giovanardi* (judgment of 12 July 2012); C-396/11 *Radu* (judgment of 29 Jan 2013); and C-399/11 *Melloni* (judgment due 26 Feb 2013) (no judgments reported yet).

[105] Cases: C-60/12 *Balasz*, pending; C-192/12 PPU *West* (judgment of 28 June 2012, not yet reported); and Case C-398/12 *M*, pending.

[106] Amendments to the Court's Statute and Rules of Procedure, and related statement: OJ 2008 L24/42, 39 and 44. On this procedure in practice, see C Barnard, 'The PPU: Is it Worth the Candle? An Early Assessment' (2009) 34 *EL Rev* 281.

[107] Cases C-195/08 PPU *Rinau* [2008] ECR I-5271; C-296/08 PPU *Santesteban Goicoechea* [2008] ECR I-6307; and C-388/08 PPU *Leymann and Pustovarov* [2008] ECR I-8993.

[108] Case C-357/09 PPU *Kadzoev* (n 92 above); and C-403/09 PPU *Deti ek* [2009] ECR I-12193.

[109] *Povse, McB, Mercredi* and *Aguirre Zarraga* (n 86 above). Also, the case of *Gataev and Gataeva* (n 93 above) was withdrawn after the Court had decided to apply the PPU procedure.

[110] *El Dridl Hassan* (n 94 above).

[111] *West* (n 105 above); *HSE* (n 88 above); *Vo* (n 95 above); and *Adil* (idem).

[112] *Melki and Abdeli* (n 93 above); and Case C-550/09 *E and F* [2010] ECR I-6213.

[113] For details, see S Peers, 'In a World of Their Own? Justice and Home Affairs Opt-outs and the Treaty of Lisbon' (2008–09) 10 *Cambridge Yearbook of European Legal Studies* 383.

[114] On the relevance of 'legal base' disputes to the opt-outs, see s F below. For pre-Lisbon disputes concerning the opt-outs, see Cases C-77/05 *UK v Council* [2007] ECR I-11459; C-137/05 *UK v Council* [2007] ECR I-11593; and C-482/08 *UK v Council* [2010] ECR I-10413.

issues of immigration, asylum and civil law) to the areas of policing and criminal law as well, allowing the UK and Ireland to opt-in or out of individual proposals and excluding Denmark from participating in all JHA measures (except those building upon the Schengen *acquis*). As regards the UK and Ireland, the rules were also amended to provide for a special procedure in the event that the UK or Ireland refuse to participate in measures amending JHA acts which they are already bound by, although in practice this procedure has not been used.

In practice, the UK and Ireland initially opted into most post-Lisbon criminal law and policing measures, although the UK has subsequently become more reluctant to opt-in to proposals.[115] Prior to the entry into force of the Treaty of Lisbon, both Member States opted out of the proposals to amend the directives on asylum procedures, refugee definition and reception conditions, which already bind them. The UK also opted out of the social security regulation regarding third-country nationals, which was adopted after the Treaty of Lisbon. As regards civil law, these Member States opted into the amendment to the Brussels Regulation and the protection orders legislation, but out of the proposals concerning succession, matrimonial property and civil partnerships. The UK opted out of the proposal concerning account preservation orders.

More fundamentally, in autumn 2012 the UK indicated its intention to invoke the 'block opt-out' as regards pre-Lisbon policing and criminal law measures, so that none of those prior measures would apply to the UK unless they had been amended in the meantime.[116] However, the UK indicated that it would seek to opt back in to some of the measures concerned.[117]

There is a possible argument that where a JHA act in which these Member States do not participate *repeals* a prior JHA act in which they do participate, the Member States concerned are relieved from their prior obligations under that act. However, the relevant agreed or adopted post-Lisbon legislation (the regulation on social security, the directive on crime victims' rights and most legislation on asylum and substantive criminal law) consistently specifies that the prior legislation is replaced as regards the participating Member States only; implicitly the prior legislation still applies to the non-participating Member States.

[115] In particular, both Member States opted out of Dir 2011/82 on road traffic offences and the proposed directive on access to a lawyer. The UK initially opted out of Dir 2011/36 on trafficking in persons, but opted in later (see the Commission decision on the UK's opt-in: OJ 2011 L271/49), and it opted out of the proposals on market abuse and freezing orders. For its part, Ireland opted out of the initiative for the Investigation Order and from Dir 2011/99 establishing the Protection Order.

[116] On the issue of amendments of pre-Lisbon policing and criminal law measures, see s E below.

[117] *Hansard*, 15 Oct 2012, col 34. For discussion of the legal issues of the block opt-out, see A Hinarejos, J R Spencer and S Peers, 'Opting out of EU Criminal Law: What is Actually Involved?' online at: www.cels.law.cam.ac.uk/Media/working_papers/Optout%20text%20final.pdf.

E. Transitional Rules[118]

Although a declaration attached to the Treaty of Lisbon and the Stockholm Programme both invited the EU institutions to amend pre-Lisbon third pillar measures before the end of the transitional period,[119] in practice there have been few such amendments.[120] More specifically, one pre-existing third pillar measure has been amended,[121] and three pre-existing third pillar measures have been replaced.[122] Furthermore, there have been six proposals to repeal or amend pre-existing third pillar acts.[123]

Of the 34 framework decisions adopted during the Amsterdam era, 29 are still in force,[124] and only seven more would be amended by the currently proposed legislation. So far there has been no attempt to amend the flagship framework decision establishing the European Arrest Warrant (EAW) or many other mutual recognition measures (as regards in absentia trials, the mutual recognition of custodial sentences, probation and parole and pre-trial decisions, and of the consequences of prior convictions),[125] most of the framework decisions on substantive

[118] For detailed discussion of these provisions, see S Peers, 'Finally "Fit for Purpose?" The Treaty of Lisbon and the End of the Third Pillar Legal Order' (2008) 27 *Yearbook of European Law* 47.

[119] For a list of these pre-existing measures, see S Peers, *JHA Law* (n 2 above), App II. For the Stockholm Programme, see OJ 2010 C115, point 1.2.10.

[120] The impact of the transitional period on the Court might be slightly reduced since arguably, by analogy with the case law concerning the Court's extra jurisdiction over civil law, national courts can send questions to the Court even before the end of the transitional period: see Case C-283/09 *Werynski* [2011] ECR I-601.

[121] Reg 542/2010 (n 38 above) amended a third-pillar decision of 2008 concerning the development of the SIS II system (Dec 2008/839, OJ 2008 L299/43).

[122] Dirs 2011/36, 2011/92 and 2012/29 (nn 26 and 25 above) replaced the Framework Decisions on (respectively) trafficking in persons, sexual offences against children and crime victims' rights (OJ 2002 L203/1; OJ 2004 L13/44; and OJ 2001 L82/1).

[123] The proposed directive on attacks on information systems (n 29 above) would replace the Framework Decision on this subject (OJ 2005 L69/67), while the proposed directive establishing a European Investigation Order (n 28 above) would repeal the Framework Decision establishing the European Evidence Warrant (OJ 2008 L350/72), and part of the Framework Decision on freezing orders (OJ 2003 L196/45), as regards freezing evidence (but not as regards freezing the proceeds of crime). The latter proposal would also 'replace' the 'corresponding' provisions of the Schengen Convention and the EU's mutual assistance Convention and its Protocol (OJ 2000 C197/1 and OJ 2001 C326/1) as between Member States, which would leave such provisions in force to the extent that they do not concern requests falling within the scope of the Directive (Art 29 of the proposal). The proposed directives on data protection as regards policing and criminal law and counterfeiting currency (respectively COM(2012) 10, 25 Jan 2012 and n 33 above) would replace the existing Framework Decisions on these issues (respectively OJ 2008 L350/60 and OJ 2000 L140/1), while the proposed directive on protection of EU financial interests (n 34 above) would replace the Convention on this issue and its three Protocols (OJ 1995 C316/48, along with OJ 1996 C313/1, OJ 1997 C151/1 and OJ 1997 C221/12). Finally, the proposed directive on criminal assets (n 32 above) would repeal the Joint Action on money laundering (OJ 1998 L333/1) as well as parts of the Framework Decisions on confiscation of assets (OJ 2005 L68/49) and money laundering (OJ 2001 L182/1).

[124] In addition to the three that were replaced by directive (n 122 above), two were annulled by the Court of Justice: Cases C-176/03 *Commission v Council* [2005] ECR I-7879; and C-440/05 *Commission v Council* [2007] ECR I-9097.

[125] See OJ 2002 L190/1 (EAW); OJ 2009 L81/24 (in absentia trials); OJ 2008 L327/27 (custodial sentences); OJ 2008 L337/102 (probation and parole); OJ 2009 L294/20 (pre-trial decisions); and OJ 2008 L220/32 (prior convictions). See also OJ 2001 L329/3 (counterfeiting currency, prior convictions).

criminal law (as regards counterfeiting non-cash instruments, terrorism, drug trafficking, organised crime, corruption and racism and xenophobia),[126] or the sundry framework decisions (concerning conflict of jurisdiction, the exchange of police information, the accreditation of forensic labs, criminal records and joint investigation teams).[127]

As for third-pillar decisions, 57 formal third pillar decisions were adopted during the Amsterdam era, of which 43 were still applicable when the Treaty of Lisbon entered into force.[128] Only one of these decisions has been amended since.[129] Thus, 42 decisions are still in force, dealing with issues such as exchange of information, EU agencies, law enforcement networks and EU funding. Implicitly the two third-pillar funding decisions will expire anyway at the end of 2013.[130]

As for conventions, there are no plans to replace the Conventions on corruption, on driving disqualifications or on customs cooperation ('Naples II'),[131] and no proposals yet to replace the Common Positions on 'domestic' terrorists or the exchange of information with Interpol.[132] Some third pillar joint actions or joint positions are also still in force.[133] Finally, as for the Schengen *acquis*, portions of the Schengen Convention and a number of measures implementing it are still in force, although some apply as between Member States on the one hand and Schengen associates only.[134] There are proposals to amend, replace or repeal some of these provisions,[135] and some would cease to apply as soon as the legislation establishing SIS II is applicable.[136]

F. Legal Base Issues

It is clear that despite the general application of the 'Community method' to JHA issues pursuant to the Treaty of Lisbon, there are still 'legal base' disputes about

[126] OJ 2001 L149/1 (non-cash instruments); OJ 2002 L164/3; and OJ 2008 L 330/21 (terrorism); OJ 2004 L335/8 (drug trafficking); OJ 2008 L300/42 (organised crime); OJ 2003 L192/54 (corruption); and OJ 2008 L328/55 (racism and xenophobia).

[127] OJ 2009 L328/42 (conflict of jurisdiction); OJ 2006 L386/89 (police information); OJ 2009 L322/14 (forensic labs); OJ 2009 L 93/23 (criminal records); and OJ 2002 L162/1 (joint investigation teams).

[128] For a list, see S Peers, *JHA Law* (n 2 above), App II.

[129] See, n 122 above.

[130] See Art 1(2) of the Decision on crime prevention (OJ 2007 L58/7) and the Decision on criminal justice (OJ 2007 L58/13).

[131] See respectively OJ 1997 C195/1; OJ 1998 C216/1; and OJ 1998 C24/1.

[132] See respectively OJ 2009 L346/58 and OJ 2005 L27/61.

[133] See again S Peers, *JHA Law* (n 2 above), App II.

[134] eg the Schengen Convention provisions on extradition, which were replaced as regards Member States by the Framework Decision establishing the EAW (n 125 above), which does not build upon the Schengen *acquis*.

[135] eg see the proposals concerning the EIO and Schengen evaluation and the travel documents Decision (nn 28, 65 and 58 above).

[136] See Art 52 of Reg 1987/2006 (OJ 2006 L381/4). At the time of writing, it is intended that SIS II will be operational in spring 2013.

the boundary between the JHA Title and the other provisions of the EU Treaties.[137] Furthermore, there are also still disputes about the boundaries *within* the JHA Title, given that the Commission still shares powers with Member States to make proposals as regards criminal law and policing, but not as regards other JHA issues.

For its part, the EP has argued for an *increased* scope of the JHA provisions of the treaties, in order to increase its powers over certain EU measures which the Council believes are covered by the Treaty rules relating to foreign policy.[138] This trend clearly indicates that the decision-making framework for JHA policy has been 'communautarised' as compared to the foreign policy provisions of the treaties.

Conversely, the Commission has sought to *reduce* the use of the JHA provisions of the treaties in order to defend its prerogatives,[139] by means of both threatened and actual litigation. It has brought proceedings to challenge the legal base of three EU measures: the legislation on exchange of information regarding traffic offences, on the grounds that the transport provisions of the Treaty apply instead; a treaty on conditional access devices, on the grounds that it falls within the scope of the EU's common commercial policy; and a partnership agreement with the Philippines, inter alia, on the grounds that the legal base concerning readmission treaties should not have applied.[140] The Commission had also threatened litigation as regards the proposed criminal law directive on the European Protection Order, arguing that it could not apply to civil proceedings. After a number of Member States backed the Commission and blocked the adoption of the directive,[141] its scope was narrowed,[142] and the Commission proposed a parallel measure that will apply to civil proceedings.[143]

Next, the UK has sought to *increase* the use of the JHA provisions, in order to widen the scope of its opt-out, in particular as regards social security rules

[137] For the relevant 'legal base' disputes before the entry into force of the Treaty of Lisbon, see Case C-170/96 *Commission v Council* [1998] ECR I- 2763; C-176/03 *Commission v Council* (n 124 above); C-317/04 and C-318/04 *EP v Council and Commission* [2006] ECR I-4721; C-440/05 *Commission v Council* (n 124 above); C-127/08 *Metock* [2008] ECR I-6241 (implicitly); C-301/06 *Ireland v Council and EP* [2009] ECR I-593; and C-482/08 *UK v Council* (n 114 above).

[138] Cases C-130/10 *EP v Council*, judgment of 19 July 2012, not yet reported, and C-658/11 *EP v Council*, pending. In the former case, the Court of Justice rejected the EP's argument that Art 75 TFEU (involving the ordinary legislative procedure), rather than Art 215 TFEU (which entails no role for the EP), applies to the adoption of general rules on anti-terrorist sanctions. In the latter case, the EP argues that a treaty relating to the treatment of pirates captured in the Indian Ocean was not purely a foreign policy treaty, but also concerns development and criminal law issues – giving it the power of consent over that treaty, instead of exclusion from the decision-making process. The choice of legal base in both cases also affects the position of the UK and Denmark (the position of Ireland is also affected by the latter case), but in Case C-130/10 this issue was not discussed.

[139] In Case C-130/10 (ibid), however, the Commission backed the Council's position.

[140] Cases C-43/12 *Commission v EP and Council*, regarding Dir 2011/82 (n 37 above); C-137/12 *Commission v Council* (note that the Council excluded the criminal law provisions of the relevant treaty from the EU's signature); and C-377/12 *Commission v Council*, all pending. Again, all of these cases would affect the position of the UK, Ireland and Denmark.

[141] See s IV below.

[142] Dir 2011/99 (n 27 above). On this issue, there is no effect on the position of the UK, Ireland and Denmark.

[143] n 46 above.

applicable pursuant to association agreements.[144] Finally, the institutions dispute whether the rules on Schengen evaluation can be amended pursuant to Article 74 TFEU (which provides for a non-legislative procedure, on which the EP is only consulted) or Article 77 (which provides for the ordinary legislative procedure).[145]

As regards these disputes, first of all, the European Parliament has a good case that the treaty which regulates in some detail the criminal law aspects of the status of any pirates who are apprehended by the EU ought to have been concluded in part pursuant to the EU's criminal law powers. Secondly, as regards the exchange of information on drivers and protection orders, the better view is that the EU's criminal and policing law competences do not extend to civil or administrative law proceedings.[146] Thirdly, if provisions on criminal liability are purely ancillary to a treaty mainly concerning trade in services, only the EU's common commercial policy should apply. Fourthly, the Commission's argument that readmitting its own citizens (and a fortiori the citizens of other states) will assist the development of the Philippines is simply preposterous. Fifthly, it is implicit in the case law of the Court of Justice that association agreements aim to extend, inter alia, the EU's internal market to third states[147] – so the correct legal bases to this end are the EU's internal market powers, not its immigration law powers, to the extent to which the former powers apply.[148] Finally, the Treaty rules on adoption of measures concerning the evaluation of JHA policies are clearly a *lex specialis* which takes precedence over the rules on the adoption of measures concerning the substance of those policies – although there is no reason why the measures concerning Schengen evaluation and the amendment of the EU's border code cannot be adopted in a single legal act, pursuant to a joint legal base. Of course, it remains to be seen what view the Court of Justice takes of these matters.

IV. ASSESSING THE IMPACT OF THE TREATY OF LISBON

First of all, as regards the legislative process, the very large majority of measures proposed and adopted have been subject to QMV and the ordinary legislative procedure.[149] The only exceptions concern family law, where the Rome III Regulation and the more recent proposals on property relating to marriage or registered partnerships concern family law, so are subject to a 'special legislative

[144] Cases C-431/11 and C-656/11 *UK v Council*, pending.

[145] nn 28 and 31 above.

[146] For elaboration, see S Peers, *JHA Law* (n 2 above), 673. See also the analysis of the Commission legal service (Council doc 10005/10, 19 May 2010).

[147] See particularly Case 12/86 *Demirel* [1987] ECR 3719.

[148] This means that Art 48 TFEU is the correct legal base for extending EU social security rules for migrant workers or self-employed persons to third-country nationals pursuant to association agreements. But since Art 48 does not apply to other categories of persons, it is not the correct legal base for the extension of EU social security rules to such persons.

[149] For more detail, see S Peers, 'Mission Accomplished? EU Justice and Home Affairs Law after the Treaty of Lisbon' (2011) 48 *CML Rev* 661, 674.

procedure'. Here it is striking that the enhanced cooperation process was used to circumvent the lack of unanimity on the Rome III Regulation.

As compared to the position prior to the Treaty of Lisbon, the proposals concerning legal migration, criminal law and policing would all have been (or were in fact) subject to unanimous voting in the Council and mere consultation of the European Parliament, while visa list measures were subject to QMV and European Parliament consultation. It is clear that the impact of the Treaty of Lisbon was decisive as regards the legal migration measures, which had previously been blocked, although probably the impact was less radical as regards some criminal law measures that had already been agreed in principle.[150] In the criminal law area, it is striking that Member States have consistently sought to reach a consensus. The exception that proves the rule is the European Protection Order, where the Spanish Council presidency attempted in 2010 to push ahead despite the opposition of a number of Member States, overcoming a blocking minority by removing the UK's participation in the measure.[151] Subsequent presidencies instead sought a solution (the severability of the civil law aspects of the proposal) that all Member States could support. Perhaps this striving for consensus explains why no Member State has (publicly, at least) threatened to pull the 'emergency brake' as regards criminal law proposals.[152]

In a large majority of cases, the Council has agreed on EU measures within 6–12 months of each proposal. There have been certain exceptions for politically difficult issues, where the Council has needed more time to agree a deal even with the use of QMV,[153] but that is equally true of other areas of EU law. The more difficult part of the legislative process is clearly the European Parliament/Council relationship, with the number of protracted disputes between the co-legislators on JHA matters escalating in 2012.[154] In particular, it appears that Council presidencies (particularly the Danish and Cypriot presidencies of 2012) have been highly competent at brokering agreement within the Council, but correspondingly ineffective at bridging differences between the Council and the European Parliament – perhaps an echo of the intergovernmentalist legacy of this policy area. Time will tell whether the post-Lisbon JHA regime will recover fully from this childhood illness.

Conversely, as regards non-legislative acts, it is striking that the Court of Justice's judgment in this area strengthens the EU legislative institutions as compared to the

[150] For more detail, see Peers (ibid), 675–76.

[151] For more detail, see Peers (ibid), 676.

[152] It should be noted that the proposal for a European Protection Order was not subject to the 'emergency brake'.

[153] Most notably, the European Investigation Order, succession rules, the economic migration proposals and some asylum proposals (reception conditions, procedures and the Dublin rules).

[154] In particular: the dispute over the legal base and content of the Schengen evaluation proposal has led to the EP blocking the proposals on attacks on information systems, passenger name records, the European Investigation Order and the borders code; the outstanding asylum legislation is being treated by the Council as a package deal; and the proposals on visa lists and access to a lawyer have been individually difficult to negotiate.

EU executive *in particular* as regards JHA matters – the exact opposite of the Court's position a decade earlier.[155]

As for the Commission's monopoly of initiative, after a short transition, it looks as if the power of Member States to make proposals in the area of policing and criminal law has indeed become a 'dead letter', as some had predicted.[156]

Moving on to the role of the Court of Justice, the statistics set out above make clear that before the Treaty of Lisbon, national courts were far more willing to refer civil law cases to the Court of Justice than other types of JHA cases. The entry into force of the Treaty of Lisbon led to a jump in references of civil law cases by about 50 per cent in 2010 compared to 2009; the numbers then dipped in 2011 but returned to the 2010 level in 2012. In the area of immigration and asylum, the small number of pre-Lisbon cases more than doubled in 2010 and then nearly doubled again in 2011 (leaving aside a batch of repetitive cases), matching the number of civil law cases; the number of cases then held steady in 2012. However, in the area of criminal law, the number of cases reaching the Court of Justice has not increased compared to the pre-Lisbon position, presumably due to the transitional restrictions on the Court's jurisdiction. The number of criminal law cases is likely to increase once the post-Lisbon criminal law measures (which are not subject to such transitional restrictions) become due for transposition, starting in 2013,[157] and once the transitional rules expire near the end of 2014.

As regards the emergency procedure, so far, the number of cases concerned appears to be manageable and the Court has been able to give rulings in these important cases in time periods of between one month and three months. Time will tell if this is sustainable in the longer term.[158]

In total, the average number of JHA cases per year in 2010–12 (41) was about double the average number per year for 2008–09 (21.5). The impact of the Treaty of Lisbon has been greatest as regards immigration and asylum cases (a four-fold increase), although the total number of such cases is still modest. Overall, the expansion of the Court's jurisdiction over JHA matters has had a limited impact on the Court's overall workload (rising from about 4 per cent to about 7 per cent of the total number of cases). But conversely, it is arguable that this expanded jurisdiction *has* had a major impact on the implementation of JHA legislation – an issue considered further below.

[155] See Case C-257/01 *Commission v Council* [2005] ECR I-345.

[156] See Ladenburger (n 2 above), 31.

[157] As regards suspects' rights (presumably a likely topic for references), Dir 2010/64 must be applied by 27 Oct 2013 (Art 9(1)) and Dir 2012/13 must be applied by 2 June 2014 (Art 11(1)) (both n 25 above). As for substantive criminal law and exchanges of police information (less likely topics for references), Directive 2011/36 must be applied by 6 April 2013 (Art 22(1), n 26 above); Directive 2011/82 must be applied by 7 Nov 2013 (Art 12(1), n 37 above); and Directive 2011/92 must be applied by 18 Dec 2013 (Art 27(1), n 26 above). Directive 2011/99 on the European Protection Order does not have to be transposed until 11 Jan 2015 (Art 21(1), n 27 above), and Dir 2012/29 on crime victims' rights (replacing a Framework Decision which has already attracted a significant number of references) does not have to be transposed until 16 Nov 2015 (Art 27(1), n 25 above).

[158] See also the Court's discussion paper on the procedure: Council doc 6140/12, 6 Feb 2012.

As for the opt-out issues, they have not complicated the adoption of JHA measures, but if anything speeded it up, since those Member States who are most reluctant to see the adoption of EU measures in this area can simply remove themselves from the decision-making process. The complex scenarios created by the opt-outs have been manageable to date, but there will be a further layer of complexity in the near future when the UK exercises its block opt-out (and its partial opt back in) as regards pre-Lisbon third pillar measures, and the UK and Ireland remain subject to first-phase asylum legislation while the other Member States become subject to second-phase measures in this area.

Finally, the move to the usual EU procedures as regards JHA law has been hindered by the very limited moves to replace pre-Lisbon third pillar measures with post-Lisbon acts. However, as regards the Court of Justice the transitional period has less than two years to run at the time of writing, and as regards the legal effect of the pre-Lisbon measures, the application of the principle of indirect effect and (possibly) also the principle of primacy to those measures limits the impact of the transitional protocol.[159]

V. SUBSTANTIVE CHANGES

Has the Treaty of Lisbon resulted in a move towards a more liberal regulation of JHA issues? This question will be answered as regard legislation and case law in turn.

A. Legislation

The key question as regards legislation is the impact of the expanded role of the European Parliament, coupled with the extension of qualified majority voting. Even before the entry into force of the Treaty of Lisbon, in cases where co-decision applied the European Parliament clearly had a significant impact on the content of JHA legislation, for example as regards procedural rights and data protection provisions in the borders code, the visa code and the legislation establishing SIS II and the VIS, as well as some of the protections for irregular migrants in the Returns Directive and some of the social provisions of the directive on employment of irregular migrants.[160] After the entry into force of the Treaty of Lisbon, the European Parliament's extended legislative powers over JHA matters have had

[159] See respectively *Pupino* and the opinion in *Melloni* (both n 10 above).

[160] See the analyses of the relevant negotiations in (2006) 8 *European Journal of Migration and Law* 321 (borders code); (2008) 10 *European Journal of Migration and Law* 77 (SIS II); (2009) 11 *European Journal of Migration and Law* 69 (VIS); (2009) 11 *European Journal of Migration and Law* 387, 411–26 (employer sanctions); (2010) 12 *European Journal of Migration and Law* 105 (visa code); and, as regards the Returns Directive, D Acosta, 'The Good, the Bad, and the Ugly in EU Migration Law' (2009) 11 *European Journal of Migration and Law* 19 and the Statewatch analysis of June 2008: www.statewatch.org/news/2008/jun/eu-analysis-returns-directive-june-2008-final.pdf.

a modest but real impact to date, for example as regards: limiting the waiting period for refugees and persons with subsidiary protection to gain long-term residence status;[161] sundry amendments to the Anti-trafficking Directive (inter alia, improving the rights of victims, particularly children);[162] raising the standards in the Qualification Directive;[163] and improvements in the procedural rights of persons needing a European Protection Order[164] and in the interpretation and translation rights of suspects generally. On the latter measure, the European Parliament ensured the addition of provisions regarding the quality of interpretation and translation (including challenges to the quality of interpretation and translation), the strengthening of suspects' rights as regards the possible waiver of their translation rights, registers of translators and interpreters, training of and confidentiality obligations for translators and interpreters and record-keeping concerning the application of the directive.[165] Moreover, the European Parliament's enhanced powers as regards the conclusion of international agreements in the JHA field entailed the rejection of one agreement due to insufficient data protection provisions,[166] resulting in the negotiation of a revised treaty that the European Parliament then approved.[167] As for the use of qualified majority voting, it resulted in a more liberal policy as regards legal migration issues,[168] and more generally unblocked negotiations as regards suspects' rights.[169]

B. Case law

As regards case law, the increased volume of judgments of the Court of Justice has by now established clear patterns, in particular as regards immigration and asylum. A very large majority of judgments have condemned the relevant Member States' application of the EU legislation in question, leading to a rise in standards relating to third-country nationals. More specifically, while the Court has been deferential as regards Member States' application of the Asylum Procedures Directive,[170] it has consistently improved standards as regards implementation of the Qualification Directive,[171] and has addressed the human rights abuses arising

[161] See the Statewatch analysis of this agreement: www.statewatch.org/analyses/no-114-ltr.pdf.

[162] See the Statewatch analysis of this agreement: www.statewatch.org/analyses/no-113-trafficking.pdf.

[163] See generally, S Peers, 'The Recast Qualification Directive' (2012) 12 *European Journal of Migration and Law* 199.

[164] Compare the final Dir 2011/99 (n 27 above) to the Member States' proposal (n 81 above).

[165] Compare the final Dir 2010/64 (n 25 above) to the Member States' proposal (n 81 above).

[166] OJ 2010 L8/9.

[167] OJ 2010 L195/1.

[168] See Peers, 'Mission Accomplished?' (n 149 above), 675–76.

[169] The Commission's proposed Framework Decision on this subject (COM(2004) 328, 28 April 2004) had been previously blocked by Member States' vetoes.

[170] See *Diouf* and *HID* (nn 93 and 94 above).

[171] See, in particular, *Elgafaji*, *X and Y* and *El Kott* (nn 90 and 94 above).

from the EU's Dublin system.[172] As regards legal migration, it has applied exceptions narrowly, insisted often on uniform interpretation of the legislation, and interpreted the rules in light of human rights concerns.[173] For irregular migrants, it has curtailed Member States' tendencies towards criminalisation and detention – although admittedly with the end of expediting their removal from the territory.[174]

VI. CONCLUSION

In terms of decision-making, both in theory and in practice, there is now no significant difference between JHA law and other areas of EU law other than the opt-outs for certain Member States – which are becoming more common in other areas of EU law in any event – and the greater incidence of difficult negotiations between the European Parliament and the Council, which is not unknown in other areas (for instance, economic governance and banking regulation) either.

As regards the substance of EU law, the EU's JHA rules cannot yet be described as a liberal regime, at least in part because of the legacy of the measures adopted before the various moves (cemented by the Treaty of Lisbon) towards the application of the usual 'Community method' in this field. But there are signs of a clear move in that direction following the Treaty of Lisbon – aided both by the decision-making changes and by the increasing jurisprudence of the Court of Justice. Of course, there is still some way to go to this end, and liberalism in one area (such as the qualification of refugees) may well be undercut by a conservative policy in other respects (border controls, and the likely more limited improvements as regards asylum procedures). On the whole, then, while EU justice and home affairs law has gone to the ball, a fairy-tale ending is not yet certain.

[172] See *NS*, and also the other judgments favouring asylum-seekers' positions (*K* and *Kastrati*) as well as the *MA* Opinion (nn 93 and 94 above).

[173] See particularly, *Chakroun*, *Singh*, *Kamberaj*, *Sommer* and *Commission v Netherlands* (nn 91 and 93 above).

[174] See particularly, *Kadzoev*, *Hassan* and *Achughbabian* (nn 92 and 94 above).

3

*Constitutional Principles in the Area of Freedom, Security and Justice**

ESTER HERLIN-KARNELL

I. INTRODUCTION

THIS CHAPTER BEGINS with the premise that EU constitutional principles play an important role in shaping the European space of the area of freedom, security and justice (AFSJ). But what are the constitutional principles in the AFSJ? Are these principles different from the constitutional principles of EU law in general and to what extent do they represent the same values as set out in the Charter of Fundamental Rights? The ambition of this chapter is not to answer these questions in full but to highlight the importance of a debate on what principles should underpin the AFSJ. In addition, the chapter calls for recognition of how critical justice and home affairs is becoming as a part of the core of EU constitutional law.

The abolition of the complex pillar system and the extended jurisdiction of the Court of Justice of the European Union (ECJ) to cover this area have been of great importance for the development, robustness and legitimacy of the AFSJ project. The EU promises to deliver an area of freedom and security built on (and reconcilable with) the concept of justice indicating the demand for a balance to be struck between these sometimes-conflicting values. Yet there is a need to identify the adequate legal framework for reference when searching for an appropriate theoretical foundation in this area. Such identification involves pinning down the extent to which we can translate supranational EU principles developed on the basis of the former EC Treaty to the AFSJ.

The AFSJ is a very broadly defined field of law dealing with a wide EU policy area that ranges from security and criminal law to border control and civil law cooperation. While asylum, immigration and civil law cooperation were subject to communitarisation with the entry into force of the Treaty of Amsterdam in

* I would like to thank the editors for their very useful comments on this chapter. Thanks also to my discussant Dr Theodore Konstadinides as well as to all the participants and organisers of the workshop at King's College London in November 2012 for helpful suggestions. The usual disclaimer applies.

1999, criminal law cooperation and security were subject to less integration under the third pillar.[1] The Lisbon Treaty has now recast this whole framework by incorporating the AFSJ *acquis* into the Treaty on the Functioning of the European Union (TFEU). Therefore, although the AFSJ is identified as one policy area, it is quite obvious that the task of identifying the underlying principles in this divergent area and how these principles drive the development of an AFSJ is of paramount importance. The Stockholm Programme[2] represents an important step in the direction of an AFSJ policy field and should be viewed in the context of the entry into force of the Lisbon Treaty. The Programme sets out a very ambitious agenda for the EU to be achieved by 2014, with its successor already under negotiation. A proposal for a regulation establishing a justice programme that aims to establish guidelines for the funding of this area and thereby facilitate the implementation of the various AFSJ policies at national level is under discussion.[3]

This chapter focuses on the constitutional principles that are currently shaping the AFSJ. It will investigate the extent to which there is a common constitution theme uniting this sphere of EU law and policy. In doing so, it will ask whether the existing EU *acquis* is readily transferable to the AFSJ. Moreover, it seems as if the EU's promotion of values is closely connected to the greater ambition of ensuring justice in the EU as a whole and in this respect the AFSJ is becoming an important testing ground for the development of these values.[4] The chapter argues that the constitutional principles in the AFSJ are intimately connected to the values that the EU seeks to protect and therefore there is a relationship between the EU's objectives and normative values pertaining to the AFSJ.

II. CONSTITUTIONAL PRINCIPLES AS UNIFYING VALUES

When discussing the constitutional basis of the AFSJ, it is appropriate to recall the legal framework as set out in the Lisbon Treaty. The AFSJ as an *objective* of the EU is defined in Article 3(2) TEU. This provision lays down the EU's mission in this area by promising that the EU shall offer its citizens an AFSJ in which the free movement of persons is ensured in conjunction with appropriate measures with respect to external border controls, asylum, immigration and the prevention and combating of crime. Article 4 TFEU confirms this mission by explicitly

[1] See S Peers, *EU Justice and Home Affairs* (Oxford, Oxford University Press, 2011) for an extensive overview of the history of the third pillar, ch 1.

[2] The Stockholm Programme – An Open and Secure Europe Serving and Protecting the Citizen (Council of the European Union Brussels, 2 December 2009) available at: register.consilium.europa.eu/pdf/en/09/st17/st17024.en09.pdf.

[3] Proposal for a regulation establishing for the period 2014–20 the Justice Programme, COM(2011) 759 final.

[4] For an elaboration around this argument, see E Herlin-Karnell, 'EU Values and the Shaping of the International Context' in Amtenbrink and Kochenov (eds), *The European Union's Shaping of the International Legal Order* (Cambridge, Cambridge University Press, 2013); S Douglas-Scott, 'The Problem of Justice in the European Union' in P Eleftheriadis and J Dickson (eds), *Philosophical Foundations of EU law* (Oxford, Oxford University Press, 2012) ch 16.

acknowledging the EU's competence within the AFSJ and making clear that in achieving such a constitutional space the EU shares its competences with the Member States. Article 67 TFEU adds to this by setting out the AFSJ objectives in further detail. These objectives are phrased as values and stipulate that:

> The Union shall endeavour to ensure a high level of security through measures to prevent and combat crime, racism and xenophobia, and through measures for coordination and cooperation between police and judicial authorities and other competent authorities, as well as through the mutual recognition of judgments in criminal matters and, if necessary, through the approximation of criminal laws.

What then are the constitutional principles that underpin the development of this area and how do they operate?

A. The Anchor: Rule of Law, Legality or Conferral of Powers

The starting point for any discussion of the constitutional principles of the EU is the rule of law and by extension the principle of legality as well as the principle of conferral of powers. The rule of law is a constitutional principle of the EU as recognised in Article 2 TEU and is listed as one of the principles that inspired the EU's creation. In addition, Article 21 TEU makes it clear that not only is the EU founded on the rule of law but that foundational value guides the international action of the Union.[5] Central to the rule of law is the idea of bounded government restrained by law from acting outside its powers.[6] Therefore, given the public law nature of the AFSJ, the rule of law is of crucial importance to control coercive power and ensure respect for human rights.

In *Les Verts*[7] the ECJ assessed the compatibility of the EU system with the rule of law. The Court held that there is compliance with the rule of law in the EU legal order in as much as neither the Member States nor its institutions can avoid review of the question whether the measures adopted by them are in conformity with the basic constitutional charter of the Treaty. In the *Kadi* case, the ECJ went further and referred to the 'constitutional principles of the EU'.[8] The Court did not issue a birth certificate for the EU legal order but rather pointed to *Costa v ENEL* and *Van Gend en Loos* in which the new legal order in the EU was established.[9] The new Article 19 TEU is also an expression of the rule of law by

[5] G De Baere, 'European Integration and the Rule of Law in Foreign Policy' in Dickson and Eleftheradis (n 4) ch 14.

[6] Among many commentators, see M Kumm, 'Constitutionalism and the Moral Point of Constitutional Pluralism' in Dickson and Eleftheriadis, ibid, ch 9. See also T Bingham, *The Rule of Law* (Allen Lane, 2010) cited in F Jacobs, 'The Lisbon Treaty and the Court of Justice' in A Biondi, P Eeckhout and S Ripley (eds), *EU Law after Lisbon* (Oxford, Oxford University Press, 2012) ch 9.

[7] Case C-294/83 *Les Verts* [1986] ECR 1339.

[8] Case C-415/05 P *Kadi* [2008] ECR I-6351.

[9] Case C-6/64 *Costa v ENEL* [1964] ECR 585; Case 26/62 *Van Gend en Loos* [1963] ECR 1, eg L Pech, 'The Rule of Law as a Constitutional Principle of the European Union' (2009) Jean Monnet Working Paper 04/09.

specifically stating that the ECJ shall ensure the interpretation of Union law in accordance with the treaties.

In addition, the rule of law is deeply connected to the constitutional question in the EU regarding the objectives the EU should safeguard and the limits set by the Treaty. Therefore, the rule of law is closely related to the principle of conferral of powers too.[10] Yet the rule of law is wider than conferral of powers in that it also presupposes a democratic and just system indicating a certain quality of the law.[11] The rule of law and the principle of legality are a *sine qua non* for any discussion of the AFSJ.[12] Obviously, the principle of legality is central to whether the EU can legislate at all (Articles 4 TEU, 5 TEU and 7 TFEU), insofar as it encapsulates the principle of conferred powers. The challenge in the AFSJ is then to adequately balance the different parameters of freedom, security and justice while upholding the rule of law.

Recently, Douglas-Scott argued that the rule of law could be reflected in the justice paradigm in the EU if adopting a critical legal model of 'justice'.[13] The key to understanding justice is to take an holistic view of it which makes it more than an empty notion, and which substantiates the democratic European values it embodies.[14] Commentary points to the current injustice within the EU and the AFSJ in particular.[15] A persistent question is the extent to which the notion of justice, which in itself is difficult to define, is an EU constitutional principle as such or an objective of the EU?[16] Justice would then form a core part of the rule of law and is of crucial importance in the context of what it means to speak about constitutional principles in an AFSJ that is constitutional.[17] Accordingly, it can be concluded that the rule of law, encompassing the broader notion of 'justice', is the basic constitutional principle on which other EU principles are based on.

B. Mutual Trust and Mutual Recognition in the AFSJ

Much of the EU's cooperation in the AFSJ has been built on the principle of mutual recognition as underpinning cooperation in justice and home affairs matters.

[10] A von Bogdandy, 'Founding Principles' in Von Bogdandy and Bas (eds), *Principles of European Constitutional Law* (Oxford, München, Hart/Beck, 2010) 11.

[11] See Pech, 'The Rule of Law' (n 9). See also C Murphy, *EU Counter Terrorism Law* (Oxford, Hart Publishing, 2012) ch 2.

[12] In counter-terrorism law see Murphy, ibid, ch 2.

[13] S Douglas-Scott, 'The Problem of Justice in the European Union' in Dickson and Eleftheradis (n 4) ch 16.

[14] ibid.

[15] See A Williams, *The Ethos of Europe* (Cambridge, Cambridge University Press, 2010).

[16] Art 67 TFEU and Art 3 TEU indicate it is an objective.

[17] I have previously tried to analyse the different parameters of freedom, security and justice against the notion of mutual trust, in E Herlin-Karnell, 'The Integrity of European Criminal Law Cooperation: The Nation State, the Individual and the Area of Freedom, Security and Justice' in F Amtenbrink and P Van den Bergh (eds), *The Constitutional Integrity of the European Union. Assessing the Integrative Function of National Constitutions for the European Constitutional Legal Order* (The Hague, Asser Press, 2010) ch 10.

Indeed, the concept of mutual recognition constitutes the main rule in the structure for criminal law provided by Article 82 TFEU following the Treaty of Lisbon as well as in immigration and asylum law where trust plays an increasingly important role.[18] The principle of mutual recognition is based on the concept of mutual trust. Of course, before the Treaty of Lisbon there was very little power in the former third pillar to enact legislation in the field of criminal law and criminal justice.[19] The concept of mutual trust was therefore the subject of little use until recent years when the European Arrest Warrant became its flagship measure.

The idea of trust in this area has in many ways been used to overcome the lack of uniformity in national criminal justice systems. In the *NS* case the Court held that the area of freedom, security and justice was the raison d'être of the EU. The creation within that area of a Common European Asylum System was based on mutual confidence amongst the Member States. There must also be a presumption of compliance with fundamental rights standards by the Member States.[20] Of course, in *NS*, that presumption was the subject of rebuttal on the facts.

The *ne bis in idem* jurisprudence is also illuminating as it pioneers the creation of a European criminal law space based on mutual recognition and therefore reliant on mutual trust. In *Gözütok and Brügge*[21] the Court stated that it is a necessary implication of EU law that the Member States must have mutual trust in their criminal justice systems and that each of them recognises the criminal law in force in other Member States even when the outcome of a case would be different if its own national law were applied.

Thus, mutual recognition of judicial decisions across the Member States presupposes a level of trust between the national legal systems that appears particularly difficult to achieve in an area as sensitive as criminal justice. In general, criminal law deals with the deprivation of liberty, which strikes a contrast with the cornerstone of EU integration: free movement. The key problem that arises when discussing the notion of EU criminal law cooperation is that there is no articulation of what 'mutual trust' actually means in the field of criminal law.[22] This lack of conceptualisation is a significant lacuna in EU criminal law cooperation. Despite this there is a common perception that there is insufficient mutual trust at present between the Member States and no adequate protection of human rights for action within the former third pillar to justify such an analogy with the inter-

[18] Convention Determining the State Responsible for Examining Applications for Asylum Lodged in One of the Member States of the European Communities – Dublin Convention, OJ 1997 C254/1. On trust in V Moreno-Lax, 'Dismantling the Dublin System: MSS v Belgium and Greece' (2012) 14 *European Journal of Migration and Law* 1.

[19] See former Arts 29–31 EU.

[20] Case C-411/10 *NS*, judgment of 21 December 2011 nyr.

[21] C-187/01 and C-385/01 *Gözütok and Brugge* [2003] ECR I-1354. See also C-436/04 *Van Esbrock* [2006] ECR I-2333.

[22] For a discussion of the notion of trust see, eg V Mitsilegas, *EU Criminal Law* (Oxford, Hart Publishing, 2009) ch 3, see also N Walker, 'The Problem of Trust in an Enlarged Area of Freedom, Security and Justice: A Conceptual Analysis' in M Anderson and J Apap (eds), *Police and Justice Cooperation and the New European Borders* (The Hague, Kluwer Law International, 2002) 22.

nal market and mutual recognition.[23] The problem is that the concept of mutual trust and what constitutes it has always been fairly vague.[24]

Notwithstanding the lack of understanding as to what mutual trust entails it has since the Tampere Programme been seen as key to achieving an AFSJ. Thus, even if mutual trust does not strictly speaking qualify as a fully-fledged concept of constitutional law, but rather a quasi-constitutional axiom, it has been the foundation for many instruments such as the European Arrest Warrant.[25] The enduring problems of trust has seen several national courts, among them the German Federal Constitutional Court, question the loyalty obligation within the former third pillar. This obligation rests on a rather thin judicial ruling in *Pupino* in 2005 where a loyalty commitment was found to also apply in the third pillar.[26]

Indeed, several post-Lisbon Treaty cases on the limits to mutual recognition in the AFSJ such as the *NS*, *Wolzenburg*, *IB* and *Mantello* judgments demonstrate the concept of mutual trust is not an absolute precept of justice and home affairs but rather a presumption subject to rebuttal if necessary for the adequate protection of human rights.[27] In the *NS*[28] case in EU asylum law, the Court of Justice asserted that if there are substantial grounds for believing that there are systematic flaws in the asylum procedure in the Member State responsible then the transfer of asylum seekers to that territory would be incompatible with the Charter of Fundamental Rights. In *Radu*, concerning whether an arrest breaches a person's right to liberty in EU law, AG Sharpston went as far as to suggest that the Charter should constitute the template for deciding on the extent of mutual recognition.[29] According to AG Sharpston, the attribution of binding force to the Charter of Fundamental Rights is an expression of a political move towards enhancing the visibility of human rights and merely confirms the human-rights oriented approach which had already been enshrined in the Framework Decision on the EAW prior to the entry into force of the Treaty of Lisbon.[30] The Court of Justice did not elaborate on this aspect in its judgment.[31]

Accordingly, while mutual recognition plays a key role in the establishment of an AFSJ, it is no longer a blind insistence on mutual trust but rather it must fit within what is acceptable from a fundamental rights perspective.

[23] Peers, *EU Justice and Home Affairs* (n 1) ch 9.

[24] It is noteworthy that it is not only in EU asylum law and criminal law that mutual trust plays a role. The notion of trust has played an important function in the civil law area too. For example, in *Gasser*, in connection with the Lugano Convention, the Court concluded that reliance on mutual trust must prevail over conflicting considerations. See Case C-116/02 *Gasser* [2003] ECR I-14693.

[25] Framework Decision, *2002*/584/JHA, OJ 2002 L190/1, on the EAW.

[26] Case C-105/03 *Pupino* [2005] ECR I-5285, see eg G Cloots, 'Germs of Pluralist Judicial Adjudication on the EAW' (2010) 47 *CML Rev* 645.

[27] C-411/10 and C-493/10 *NS*, judgment of 21 December 2011 nyr; Case C-123/08 *Wolzenburg* [2009] ECR I-9621; Case C-306/09, *IB*; and Case C-261/09 *Criminal proceedings against Mantello* [2011] 2 CMLR. 5.

[28] C-411/10 and C-493/10 *NS*, judgment of 21 December 2011 nyr.

[29] Case C-396/11 *Radu*, Opinion delivered on 18 October 2012, judgment of 29 January 2013 nyr.

[30] ibid.

[31] Case C-396/11 *Radu*, judgment of 29 January 2013 nyr.

III. EFFECTIVENESS AS A CONSTITUTIONAL PRINCIPLE

The effectiveness principle has attracted renewed attention as a principle of fundamental importance to the Union project – in particular in the AFSJ sphere. The force of the idea of effectiveness was evident from early on in the EU's history where a number of foundational cases furthered the development of EU law. The very idea of effective judicial protection helped establish a new legal order.[32] The basic message was that otherwise, EU law would be deprived of its effectiveness. Further judgments, such as in *Mangold*[33] and *Kükükdeveci*,[34] demonstrate that the doctrine of effectiveness is still very much a vital EU law concept.

EU criminal law has played a key role with regard to the use of effectiveness.[35] The judgment in *Commission v Council*,[36] the *Environmental Crimes* case, saw the initiation of this line of jurisprudence. The EU had of course early on insisted on effective sanctions against breaches of EU law. The 'effective, proportionate and dissuasive' criteria were first stipulated in *Greek Maize* and later applied in other cases.[37] In the *Environmental Crimes* case the EU legislator concluded that criminal law could fall within the EU sphere of competence if it was necessary for the full effectiveness of EU law. This case opened up a vague and ill-defined competence in this judicial area, which fuelled a debate concerning the exact limits of competence.[38] This represented a new step in the development of EU criminal law as it placed weight on the effectiveness of EU law as a decisive factor for deciding on competence.

In the case of *Da Silva Jorge*, the ECJ stretched the reach of the classic effectiveness test to the EAW.[39] The ECJ also emphasised the importance of the full effectiveness of the operation of the EAW in the context of a possible opt-out from this measure under certain circumstances. In *Stefano Melloni*,[40] on the validity of the amendments made to the EAW by Framework Decision 2009/299/JHA,[41] and addressing the application of the principle of mutual recognition to trial *in absentia*, AG Bot provided an interesting account of the relationship between the EAW and the Charter of Fundamental Rights. The Advocate General focused on Article 53 of the Charter, which provides for the highest relevant human rights standard to be

[32] Case C-6/64 *Costa v ENEL* [1964] ECR 585.

[33] Case C-144/04 *Mangold v Helm* [2005] ECR I-9981.

[34] Case C-555/07 *Kükükdeveci* [2010] ECR I-5769.

[35] E Herlin-Karnell, *The Constitutional Dimension of European Criminal Law* (Oxford, Hart Publishing, 2012) ch 2.

[36] Case C-176/03 *Commission v Council* [2005] ECR I-7879.

[37] Case C-68/88 *Commission v Greece* (*Greek Maize*) [1989] ECR 1-2965, para 24.

[38] eg V Mitsilegas, 'The Transformation of Criminal Law in the Area of Freedom, Security and Justice' (2007) 26 *Yearbook of European Law* 1; S Peers, 'EU Criminal Law and the Treaty of Lisbon' (2008) 33 *EL Rev* 507.

[39] Case C-42/11 *Joao Pedro Lopes Da Silva Jorge*, judgment of 5 September 2012 nyr.

[40] Case C-399/11 *Criminal proceedings against Stefano Melloni*, Opinion of AG Bot delivered on 2 October 2012.

[41] Framework Decision, 2009/299/JHA, 2009 OJ L81/24.

applied. In doing so, he argued that the Charter is not, in any event, a primacy-restricting measure and does not empower the Member States to 'opt-out' from EU law obligations. The ECJ agreed and held that such an interpretation of Article 53 of the Charter would undermine the principle of the primacy of EU law. Specifically, the Court stated that where an EU legal act calls for national implementing measures, national authorities and courts remain free to apply national standards of protection of fundamental rights, providing that the level of protection in the Charter, as interpreted by the Court, and the primacy, unity and effectiveness of EU law are not thereby compromised.[42]

Furthermore, in *El Dridi*,[43] the principle of effectiveness was relied upon by the ECJ to define the competence and margin of appreciation of Member States concerning the coercive measures that they can implement in the context of the procedure for the return of illegally staying third-country nationals.[44] Here the effectiveness principle was employed as a way of restricting competences in the sense that the Member State must not prevent the achievement of the objectives of the Returns Directive,[45] as regards the implementation of an efficient policy of removal and repatriation of illegally staying third-country nationals.[46] There are thus good reasons to believe that the effectiveness principle will continue to play an important role in this area and help shape the constitutional contours of an AFSJ.

IV. PROPORTIONALITY: THE ART OF BALANCING AND THE NEED FOR IT

It is often said that the concept of proportionality constitutes the doctrinal core of transnational constitutionalism.[47] Generally, proportionality in EU law is taken to mean balancing means and ends with 'appropriateness'. It is seen as the golden thread for deciding on the desirability and need for EU action in a given area. Proportionality was referred to in the early days by the ECJ and was closely associated with the creation of human rights protection in the EU.[48] Alongside the principle of non-discrimination it is one of the most important principles for the law

[42] Case C-399/11 *Criminal proceedings against Stefano Melloni*, judgment of 26 February 2013, para 60.

[43] Case-C-61/11 *El Dridi*, judgment of 28 April 2011 nyr. See also Case C-430/11 *Sagor*, judgment of 6 December 2012.

[44] On the interpretation of this Directive, see D Acosta Arcarazo, 'The Returns Directive: Possible Limits and Interpretation' in K Zwaan (ed), *The Returns Directive: Central Themes, Problem Issues, and Implementation in Selected Member States* (Nijmegen, Wolf Legal Publishers, 2011) 7–24. Directive 2008/115/EC of the European Parliament and of the Council of 16 December 2008 on common standards and procedures in Member States for returning illegally staying third-country nationals, 2008 OJ L348/98.

[45] Directive 2008/115/EC, 2008 OJ L348/98.

[46] Case C-61/11 *El Dridi*, judgment of 28 April 2011 nyr, paras 41–43.

[47] A Stone Sweet, 'All Things in Proportion? American Rights Doctrine and the Problem of Balancing' available at: works.bepress.com/cgi/viewcontent.cgi?article=1034&context=alec_stone_sweet (last accessed January 2012). Also discussed in E Herlin-Karnell, *The Constitutional Dimension of European Criminal Law* (Oxford, Hart Publishing, 2012) ch 4.

[48] Case 11/70 *Internationale Handelsgesellschaft* [1970] ECR 1125. P Craig, *EU Administrative Law* (Oxford, Oxford University Press, 2012) 670–72.

of free movement.[49] It requires relevant interests to be identified. The Court will enquire whether the measure was suitable or appropriate to achieve the desired result or whether this could have been attained by a less onerous method. The assumption is that interference with EU law rights should be kept to a minimum and the test is whether it has been manifestly disproportionate to interfere with those rights.[50]

Moreover, in classic free movement law the concept of proportionality controls the degree to which the Member States can derogate from their EU law obligations. It also constitutes one of the leading principles for deciding whether EU legislative competence is warranted. In this regard any legislative action must be reasonably effective to achieve the aim for which the competence has been granted, the exercise of the competence has to be necessary and indispensable, and, finally, such exercise of competence has to be proportionate in the strict sense – the adverse effect on other interests must be weighed against the positive effect that the exercised competence entails for the objective pursued by it.[51] Yet the Court's approach to the proportionality analysis remains peculiarly abstract with general invocations of the limits of judicial review and the political nature of social and economic choices.[52] This becomes of course all the more complex in sensitive areas such as those pertaining to the AFSJ.

The problem is that the AFSJ seems to have been largely exempted from this golden rule of balancing. Remarkably the proportionality principle has not been applied to any greater extent in this legally thorny terrain, with complex ties between the EU, the Member States and their citizens, despite this being an area closely connected to national sovereignty and protection of human rights. Important legal measures in this area on arrest warrants which introduced the concept of mutual recognition to the fight against crime seemed to exclude such a proportionality test.[53]

Therefore in an attempt to address this deficit the Commission published an evaluation of the implementation since 2007 of the Framework Decision on the EAW.[54] The Commission notes that the systematic issue of EAWs for the surrender of persons had undermined the application of the EAW in respect of often very minor offences. In addition, the Commission states that there is a need to apply a proportionality test to curb the use of the EAW for offences which are not serious enough to merit it – even if they fall within the scope of Article 2(1) of the Framework Decision.[55] In particular, the Commission stipulates that the hand-

[49] eg T Tridimas, *General Principles of EU Law* (Oxford, Oxford University Press, 2006) chs 3–5.

[50] eg P Craig, 'Proportionality, Rationality and Review' (2010) *New Zealand Law Review* 265.

[51] L Senden, *Soft Law in the EU* (Oxford, Hart Publishing, 2004) 88.

[52] P Craig, *EU Administrative Law* (Oxford, Oxford University Press, 2012) chs 19 and 20 for an extensive overview of the notion of proportionality in EU law.

[53] See, eg J Spencer and J Vogel, 'Proportionality and the European Arrest Warrant' (2010) 6 *Crim LR* 474.

[54] 'On the implementation since 2007 of the Council Framework Decision of 13 June 2002 on the European Arrest Warrant and the surrender procedures between Member States' COM(2011) 175 final.

[55] ibid.

book on the EAW needs to be adjusted in order to comply with proportionality. The amended handbook now sets out the factors to be assessed when issuing an EAW and possible alternatives to be considered before adopting one.[56] This is thus an example of where the proportionality principle could have crucial impact.

Nonetheless, in the ruling in *Da Silva Jorge*[57] concerning the operation of the EAW, AG Mengozzi focused more on the imperative of non-discrimination than on the principle of proportionality as such. In particular, the Advocate General recognised the importance of a case-by-case approach in this area since circumstances may vary. The Court in turn confirmed this view by focussing on non-discrimination but at the same time giving extra weight to the importance of indirect effect of existing third pillar measures. It remains the case that such an *ad hoc* approach provides very little guidance for the national courts when applying the EAW in practice. Despite this there is no doubt that the application of a general proportionality test to AFSJ law is appropriate. There remains, however, the difficulty of pinning down the exact contours of proportionality within the context of criminal law cooperation.

Furthermore, in the *NS*[58] case, as noted above, the appellant challenged the decision of the UK Secretary of State for the Home Department to transfer him to Greece, on the grounds that the transfer would violate his fundamental rights under EU law. One of the main reasons for this allegation is that the European Court of Human Rights (ECtHR) and some national constitutional courts have considered that the Greek asylum system fails to uphold fundamental rights.[59] According to the Court of Justice there was no doubt that, where there is a serious risk that the applicant's rights, as guaranteed by the Charter of Fundamental Rights, may be breached, Member States should enjoy a wide 'margin of discretion'. This permits the Member State in which the application was lodged to examine it even when the criteria set out by Chapter III of the Dublin II Regulation do not apply, in particular when the state that should be responsible is to be deemed 'dangerous'. The question is the extent to which this margin of discretion should operate, in light of potential political or ideological conflicts.[60]

It is clear that the Charter impacts upon the principle of proportionality's future scope as a constitutional principle in the AFSJ.[61] Specifically, it has an impact on the emerging principles of EU criminal procedure law. In respect of

[56] ibid.

[57] Case C-42/11 *Da Silva Jorge*, Opinion delivered by AG Mengozzi on 20 March 2012, judgment of 5 September 2012 nyr.

[58] C-411/10 and C-493 *NS*, judgment of 21 December 2011.

[59] *MSS v Belgium and Greece* (30696/09) (2011) 53 EHRR 2 (ECtHR); Austrian Constitutional Court Decision No U 694/10-19, 7 October 2010. For a discussion of this case see, M Fichera and E Herlin-Karnell, 'The Margin of Appreciation Test and Balancing in the Area of Freedom Security and Justice: A Proportionate Answer for a Europe of Rights?' (2013) 4 *European Public Law* (forthcoming).

[60] ibid.

[61] On the Charter see, eg F Jacobs, 'The Lisbon Treaty and the Court of Justice' and D Anderson and CC Murphy, 'The Charter of Fundamental Rights' in A Biondi, P Eeckhout and S Ripley (eds), *EU Law after Lisbon* (Oxford, Oxford University Press, 2012) chs 7 and 9.

due process rights, Article 49 provides a requirement of legality and proportionality in a more extensive way than the European Convention on Human Rights (ECHR). Also, Article 47 of the Charter guarantees the right to an effective remedy, while Articles 48–49 stipulate the presumption of innocence and the right of defence.[62] The latter provision also makes it clear that the severity of penalties must not be disproportionate to the criminal offence. It is therefore likely that the binding status of the Charter will have both a significant symbolic importance and a real substantive impact on criminal law. Moreover, Article 50 of the Charter guarantees the right not to be tried twice for the same offence (*ne bis in idem*).

Nevertheless, Article 52(1) of the Charter sets out some important exceptions to the application of the Charter as a whole. This provision makes it clear that

> [a]ny limitation on the exercise of the rights and freedoms recognized by this Charter must be provided for by law and respect the essence of those rights and freedoms. Subject to the principle of proportionality, limitations may be made only if they are necessary and genuinely meet objectives of general interest recognized by the Union or the need to protect the rights and freedoms of others.

Admittedly, such a limitation is not unique to the EU: the ECHR (Article 5) has a similar limitation on the presumption of freedom based on necessity. The key point is that although it is necessary to maintain a secure society, there is a danger that the security agenda can be subject to manipulation to fit what is 'necessary in a democratic society'.[63]

Therefore, it could be argued that the scope of EU human rights protection under the Charter turns on the elasticity of the proportionality principle. After all, the Member States could invoke proportionality to derogate from the rights guaranteed in the Charter since Article 52 applies to all rights. The explanatory notes on the Charter confirm that these exceptions are based on the Court's well-established case law that restrictions may be imposed on the exercise of fundamental rights.[64] The explanatory notes also make it clear that the reference to the general interests recognised by the Union covers both the objectives mentioned in Article 3 TEU, and other interests protected by specific provisions of the treaties, provided that those restrictions in fact correspond to objectives of general interest of the EU. Moreover, these explanatory notes state that such restrictions may not, with regard to the aim pursued, be disproportionate or cause unreasonable interference undermining the very substance of any Charter rights.[65] So unlike the ECHR, which limits deroga-

[62] In her recent Opinion delivered on 18 October in Case C-396/11 *Radu,* para 103, AG Sharpston, discusses the boundaries of Art 49 of the Charter by stipulating that it would be interesting to explore the boundaries of these provisions in the context of Art 3 ECHR where the ECtHR has held that a sentence that is grossly disproportionate could amount to ill-treatment contrary to Art 3 ECHR. The Court did not elaborate on this issue.

[63] See, eg CC Murphy, *EU Counter-terrorism Law: Pre-emption and the Rule of Law* (Oxford, Hart Publishing, 2012) 229–30.

[64] The Explanations relating to the Charter of Fundamental Rights, OJ 2007 C83/2, see also the discussion in P Craig, *EU Administrative Law* (Oxford, Oxford University Press, 2012) 473–74.

[65] ibid.

tions from certain rights, the Charter does not appear to recognise absolute rights in the sense that all rights may be derogated from in accordance with Article 51(1) of the Charter.[66] Yet, the Charter refers to the ECHR in Article 52(3) in pointing out that the ECHR is always the minimum standard of protection.

An example of use of the Charter in the context of strict liability and the question of proportionality is found in *Åkerberg Fransson* concerning the compatibility with the *ne bis in idem* principle of a national system involving two separate sets of proceedings to penalise the same wrongful conduct.[67] Advocate General Cruz Villalon stated in his Opinion that Article 50 of the Charter did not preclude the Member States from bringing criminal proceedings relating to conduct in respect of which a final penalty has already been imposed in administrative proceedings, provided that the national criminal court was in a position to take into account the existence of an administrative penalty in mitigation.[68] The Advocate General therefore puts his trust in the hands of a stringent application of proportionality here in the national courts. The ECJ did not elaborate on this aspect of proportionality, but adopted a very broad reading of the Charter.[69] It held that although the national rules in question did not *stricto sensu* involve any implementation, it was clear from Article 325 TFEU that the Member States are required to fight fraud against the EU and thereby supply the same level of penalties for EU fraud and domestic fraud respectively. Moreover, the Court observed that EU law precludes a judicial practice which makes the obligation for a national court to disapply any provision contrary to a fundamental right guaranteed by the Charter conditional upon that infringement being clear from the text of the Charter or the case law relating to it. According to the Court such an interpretation would withhold from the national court the power to assess fully whether that provision in question is compatible with the Charter.[70]

The crucial point here is that the proper application of proportionality functions as a rebuttal of the previous assumption that there were no, or very few limits, on mutual recognition in this area. Non-discrimination and proportionality in the context of EU criminal law (at least) should therefore be seen as intertwined principles.

V. SUBSIDIARITY

Subsidiarity has been part of the constitutional landscape for some time but remains a contested concept due to its political nature.[71] Protocol 2 on the Application of the

[66] See also Fichera and Herlin-Karnell, 'The Margin of Appreciation Test' (n 59).

[67] Case C-617/10 *Åkerberg Fransson,* judgment of 26 February 2013 nyr.

[68] Opinion of AG Cruz Villalon delivered on 12 June 2012.

[69] Case C-617/10 *Åkeberg Fransson,* judgment of 26 February 2013 nyr.

[70] ibid, para 48 of the judgment.

[71] For recent accounts of subsidiarity see, eg A Biondi, 'Subsidiarity in the Courtroom' in A Biondi, P Eeckhout and S Ripley (eds), *EU Law After Lisbon* (Oxford, Oxford University Press, 2012) ch 10; and P Craig, 'Subsidiarity a Political and Legal Analysis' (2012) 50 *Journal of Common Market Studies* 72.

Principles of Subsidiarity and Proportionality is attached to the Lisbon Treaty. This important Protocol declares that the Commission must consult widely when proposing legislation and that it must furnish reasons as to why an objective is better achieved at the EU level which are supported by qualitative and, wherever possible, quantitative indicators.[72] Furthermore, the Protocol makes it clear that subsidiarity applies when checking whether a measure is still needed. In addition, Protocol 1 on the Role of the National Parliaments in the European Union reaffirms the increase in importance of subsidiarity if interpreting the Treaty. Indeed, one of the most important innovations in the Lisbon Treaty regarding subsidiarity is that the Treaty imposes an obligation on the Commission to send legislative initiatives to the national parliaments at the same time as to the EU institutions.[73] Thereafter, the national parliaments have eight weeks to draft a statement of any objection as to why the proposed legislation does not comply with subsidiarity. If the national parliaments expressing concern about non-compliance represents one-third of the votes – or one-quarter for proposals in the AFSJ allocated to these parliaments – there is a duty to review the proposal.

But is subsidiarity different here as compared to EU law in general? Article 69 TFEU emphasises the importance of subsidiarity in Chapters 4 and 5 of Title V of the AFSJ: EU criminal law cooperation and police cooperation. So does that mean that subsidiarity is not as important in the other policy fields of the AFSJ? The ordinary rules on subsidiarity monitoring including Protocols 1 and 2 apply to all legislation. At the very least Article 69 TFEU singles out the need for subsidiarity in criminal law and thereby confirms the sensitive nature of it. The need for delegation away from centralisation appears particularly important in this field. After all, criminal law can be understood as having its own principle similar to that of subsidiarity embedded in the '*ultima ratio*' concept.[74] Briefly, this means that criminal law should be the last resort as a means of control. According to this view, criminal law should be reserved for the most serious infringements of social rules since less serious misconduct is more appropriately dealt with by civil law or by administrative regulation.[75] Accordingly, when discussing criminalisation, one has to ask whether it is justifiable to undertake criminal justice action at all: that is, whether the consequences of legislative action in the area in question are sufficiently clear, effective and precise.[76] Moreover, application of subsidiarity is about ensuring quality of any enacted legislation and where any relocation from the local level needs to be justified. In any case, the national identity clause set out in

[72] Moreover, the Commission must submit an annual report to the Council, the European Council and the European Parliament.

[73] P Craig, *The Lisbon Treaty, Law, Politics and Treaty Reform* (Oxford, Oxford University Press, 2010) 184–86; P Kiiver, 'The Treaty of Lisbon: The National Parliaments and the Principle of Subsidiarity' (2008) 15 *Maastricht Journal of European and Comparative Law* 77.

[74] E Herlin-Karnell, 'Subsidiarity in the Area of EU Justice and Home Affairs – A Lost Cause?' (2009) 15 *European Law Journal* 351; J Turner, 'The Expressive Dimension of EU Criminal Law' (2012) *American Journal of Comparative Law* 555.

[75] See generally, A Ashworth, *Principles of Criminal Law* (Oxford, Oxford University Press, 2006).

[76] ibid.

Article 4(2) TEU is a novelty of the Lisbon Treaty. Arguably, the national identity clause is connected to the subsidiarity principle, as it insists on respect for Member State values. It is clear that this is particularly important in the AFSJ with regard to those national areas of law that are sensitive to national sovereignty.

A further question of importance is whether subsidiarity within EU asylum and immigration law is different when compared with subsidiarity reasoning within criminal law and police cooperation. Overall, it appears as if Member States have expressed concern with regard to EU activity in this area. More specifically, Article 70 TFEU makes it clear that the national parliaments should take part in the evaluation of EU policies in the AFSJ. This article states that the Council may, on a proposal from the Commission, adopt measures laying down the arrangements whereby Member States, in collaboration with the Commission, conduct objective and impartial evaluation of the implementation of the Union policies referred to in this Title by Member States' authorities, in particular in order to facilitate full application of the principle of mutual recognition. The European Parliament and national parliaments shall be informed of the content and results of the evaluation. As pointed out by Peers, these evaluation measures are non-legislative acts to be adopted by qualified majority voting (QMV) in the Council on a proposal from the Commission with no direct involvement of the European Parliament as it is only being 'informed'.[77] Indeed, though evaluation exercises and impact assessments are steps in the right direction towards a more sophisticated attitude to EU legislation,[78] it does not help much if their outcomes are not sufficiently explained or subject to analysis. Moreover, national parliaments shall be involved in the evaluation and scrutiny of Eurojust's activities (Articles 85 and 88 TFEU).[79] Accordingly, subsidiarity has been given weight here and expression in the evaluation process and promises an important function in the future. In other words, given the poor record of subsidiarity in the history of EU integration so far, it may be that things can only get better regarding how it is applied in the future.

VI. MANAGING THE OPT-OUTS: CHAOS OR CONSTITUTIONAL RICHNESS?

Despite the above principles which I have described as unifying, albeit embryonic, constitutional principles in the AFSJ, there are challenges as to how these principles are applied when one enters the 'flexibility' landscape of opt-outs and opt-ins. As is well known, the UK, Ireland and Denmark have negotiated particular approaches to the AFSJ project. This poses challenges not only for those trying to analyse the current state of play but also for national courts as well as the ECJ when

[77] Peers, *EU Justice and Home Affairs* (n 1) ch 2.

[78] See A Meuwese, *Impact Assessment in EU Lawmaking* (The Hague, Kluwer Law Publishing, 2008) 126–29.

[79] For a discussion of the national parliaments role in the AFSJ, see M van Keulen and F Mittendorff, 'Justice and Home Affairs at Home: Shaping the AFSJ at the National Level' in S Wolff et al (eds), *Freedom, Security and Justice after Lisbon and Stockholm* (The Hague, Asser Press, 2011) ch 4.

applying EU constitutional principles. These Member States have the opportunity to opt out of criminal law cooperation provisions as provided by the Lisbon Treaty and Protocol 21.[80] They can later opt-in under the conditions set out in the Protocol. Yet in some areas, such as anti-money laundering and counter-terrorist finance, opt-outs are less likely because of the international obligations beyond EU law and because the UK has been one of the leading proponents of further cooperation in this field. In addition, the Transitional Protocol 36 contains specific rules that apply only to the UK and under which the UK must decide by 2014 whether it wishes to participate in remaining third pillar measures at all and if it accepts the jurisdiction of the Court in this area.[81] The consequence of any opt-out by a Member State is that the ECJ will not have jurisdiction to monitor action by that Member State in that field. An opt-out also applies to any international agreement concluded by the Union in relation to the cooperation in question. In other words, an opt-out has serious consequences for the EU in general.

Needless to say this is a political decision and will be the cause of further complexity in the legal development of the AFSJ. Future case law must clarify what this means for the scope of application of the Charter. Will the Court develop the principles as recognised in the Charter to cover situations where the UK has opted out; for example a measure on legal safeguards (eg Articles 47–50 of the Charter)? Arguably, the opt-out area offers a fascinating yet complicating test of just what constitutional principles apply and how they work in the AFSJ. The position of Denmark in particular and Protocol 22 appears challenging. Protocol 22 to the Lisbon Treaty grants Denmark a special position by granting it the right to remain outside the AFSJ. This Protocol means that Denmark participates in Schengen related measures and pre-Lisbon third pillar instruments on the basis of international law which continue to be binding and applicable to Denmark as before, even if these acts are amended. Denmark may however notify the other Member States that it wishes to join the EU criminal law venture. Accordingly, Denmark could decide to opt-in to the whole package unlike the UK and Ireland that are opting in/or out with respect to each new criminal law measure in question.[82] The opt-out area and the concept of a multi-speed Europe is a testing ground for the AFSJ and the scope and function of the classic EU constitutional principles.

[80] See, eg Peers, *EU Justice and Home Affairs* (n 1); E Fahey, 'A Jagged-edged Jigsaw: The Boundaries of Constitutional Differentiation and Irish-British-Euro Relations after the Treaty of Lisbon' in L Rubini and M Trybus, *The Treaty of Lisbon and the Future of European Law and Policy* (Cheltenham Edward Elgar, 2012) ch 7; A Hinarejos, J Spencer and S Peers, 'Opting Out of Criminal Law: What is Actually Involved?' (2012) Centre for European Law Cambridge Working Paper 2012/1.

[81] See J Piris, *The Lisbon Treaty, A Legal and Political Analysis* (Cambridge, Cambridge University Press, 2010) 199–200; P Craig, *The Lisbon Treaty, Law, Politics and Treaty Reform* (Oxford, Oxford University Press, 2010) 341.

[82] See, eg A Suominen, 'EU Criminal Law Cooperation before and after the Lisbon Treaty – Aspects and Comments Especially in Relation to the Norwegian Position' JFT 6/2012 ss 573–604.

VII. CONCLUSION: CONSTITUTIONAL INS AND OUTS OF THE AFSJ

The recent history of the AFSJ tests the feasibility of EU constitutional principles that were developed within classic first pillar law and poses questions as to their effective operation in the field of security and criminal justice. This chapter set out the rule of law, mutual recognition and trust, effectiveness, proportionality, and subsidiarity as classic constitutional concepts and principles. Yet when these principles are applied in the novel context of the AFSJ it is necessary to be aware of the potential pitfalls of translating ordinary EU law principles to the particular context of the AFSJ. In addition, the chapter tentatively discussed the complex regime of the opt-outs and opt-ins and stressed the peculiar situation of Denmark (which stays out of all AFSJ law). The constitutional framework of an AFSJ rests on the rule of law as an anchoring principle. The importance of the rule of law is evident as a substantial meaning and application of it adds to the integrity of the AFSJ.

4

Institutions and Agencies: Government and Governance after Lisbon

JORRIT J RIJPMA

I. INTRODUCTION

WITH THE ENTRY into force of the Lisbon Treaty, competences in justice and home affairs (JHA) were reunited under a single institutional framework under Title V of Part III of the Treaty on the Functioning of the Union (TFEU). With the demise of the pillar system and the extension of the ordinary legislative procedure throughout most of the area of freedom, security and justice (AFSJ), the Lisbon Treaty hailed the final step towards full 'communitarisation' of this policy field.[1]

It is no surprise that integration in this area has taken place incrementally. Powers related to Member States' competences in the field of migration and asylum, as well as criminal law and police cooperation touch upon core understandings of sovereignty. Cooperation between the Member States originated in the 1970s when outside the EU framework a range of relatively informal and secretive working groups was set up at ministerial level, the most prominent being TREVI.[2] This cooperation was brought within the EU constitutional structure by the inclusion of competences in JHA as 'areas of common interest' under the Treaty of Maastricht. The Treaty of Amsterdam supra-nationalised parts of the field, locating powers in the area of migration, asylum, borders and visa within the Community pillar of the EU. Competences in the field of justice and police cooperation in criminal matters remained within the supranational third pillar. Notwithstanding this division, the establishment of an area of freedom, security

[1] Of course the term 'communitarisation' is at odds with the fact that the Community has been usurped by the Union, however it best describes the mainstreaming or supranationalisation of policies under what was formerly known as 'the Community method'.

[2] The Rome European Council of 1975 created the TREVI group, which was a network of national officials from Ministries of Justice and the Interior. It developed a range of working groups that reported to occasional ministerial meetings. See S Lavenex and W Wallace, 'Justice and Home Affairs: Towards a 'European Public Order?' in H Wallace et al (eds), *Policy Making in the European Union* (Oxford, Oxford University Press, 2005) 459.

and justice (AFSJ) became an overarching and self-standing Union objective, alongside the internal market (Article 3 TEU).

This chapter will scrutinise the degree to which the *institutional settlement* of the AFSJ continues to reflect the particular origins and specificities of JHA cooperation. This requires assessing not only the treaty provisions, but also institutional practices following the entry into force of the Lisbon Treaty. In addition, the sub-institutional actors and 'light' institutional governance structures, which have always played an important role in the AFSJ must be studied.

II. THE INSTITUTIONAL SETTING: SAME PLAYERS, NEW RULES

The application as a general rule of the ordinary legislative procedure (extension of qualified majority voting in the Council and co-decision with the European Parliament) confirms the shift away from intergovernmental law and policy-making in this area, in particular as regards the former third pillar.[3] Specific third pillar instruments (common positions, framework decisions, decisions and conventions) have been abolished, leaving 'classic' EU instruments at the legislator's disposal: directives, regulations and decisions.

Overall inter-institutional relations have been rebalanced in favour of the European Commission and the Parliament, at the expense of the Member States represented in the Council and the European Council. The powers of the Court of Justice of the European Union (ECJ) have been significantly enhanced by giving it compulsory jurisdiction to hear preliminary rulings from national courts at all levels of the domestic court system.[4]

Nonetheless, the institutional framework of the AFSJ retains a number of distinctive, mainly intergovernmental features. Some of these are temporary and linked to the transitional arrangements that apply to the field of police and judicial cooperation in criminal matters.[5] Others are of a more permanent and also more fundamental nature, responding to (specific) Member States' sovereignty concerns.

The United Kingdom, Ireland and Denmark continue to opt-out of cooperation on borders, migration, visa and asylum.[6] Their opt-outs have been extended

[3] See in particular, M Fletcher, 'EU Criminal Justice: Beyond Lisbon' in C Eckes and T Kostadinides, *Crime within the Area of Freedom, Security and Justice: A European Public Order* (Cambridge, Cambridge University Press, 2011) 10–42 and JW De Zwaan, 'The New Governance of Justice and Home Affairs: Towards Further Supranationalisation' in S Wolff, F Goudappel and JW de Zwaan (eds), *Freedom, Security and Justice after Lisbon and Stockholm* (The Hague, TMC Asser Press, 2011) 7–26.

[4] Under Art 68 of Title IV EC only last instance courts could refer to the Court. Under Art 30 TEU, Member States could accept the jurisdiction of the Court for preliminary references on third pillar acts, but could limit this to last instance courts.

[5] Art 10 of Protocol 36. The period will end five years after the entry into force of the Lisbon Treaty, ie 30 November 2014. See further the discussion in ch 2.

[6] Protocol 19 on the Schengen *acquis* integrated into the Framework of the European Union, Protocol 21 on the position of the United Kingdom and Ireland in respect of the area of freedom, security and justice and Protocol 22 on the position of Denmark.

to the whole AFSJ, hence also covering police and judicial cooperation in criminal matters. Denmark does participate in the Schengen *acquis* and can opt-in to measures developing that *acquis* within six months. The UK and Ireland can in principle opt-in to parts of the Schengen *acquis* and the measures that develop these areas. Denmark does not have the possibility to opt-in to measures that do not develop the Schengen *acquis.* It may however unilaterally bring into effect the Annex to the Danish Protocol, which would allow it to do so.[7]

With respect to Member States that are bound by the AFSJ, Article 72 TFEU repeats what is already stated in Article 4(2) TEU: Member States remain ultimately responsible for their internal security. The ECJ does not have jurisdiction to review the validity or proportionality of operations carried out by the Member States' law enforcement services or the exercise of their responsibilities as regards safeguarding internal security.[8]

In the area of police and judicial cooperation in criminal matters, the Commission shares its right of initiative with a quarter of the Member States.[9] The European Council continues to define the strategic guidelines for legislative and operational planning in the AFSJ as a whole, as it has done since the Tampere Agenda.[10] One may however question whether in the spirit of the Lisbon Treaty, it would not be better if the European Council were to limit itself to more general guidelines, rather than the detailed policy plans that have guided the development of the AFSJ so far (Tampere, The Hague, Stockholm).[11]

National parliaments are involved to a greater extent than in other areas of EU competence in monitoring the policy area,[12] in particular also as regards the respect for the principle of subsidiarity.[13] An emergency break procedure foreseen in Articles 82(3) and 83(3) TFEU (criminal law and criminal procedure) allows Member States to block the adoption of a legislative proposal and refer it to the European Council if a fundamental aspect of their criminal justice system would be affected.[14] In case of continuing disagreement, the option of enhanced coopera-

[7] E Fahey, 'Swimming in a Sea of Law: Reflections on Water Borders, Irish (–British) –Euro Relations and Opting-out and Opting-in after the Treaty of Lisbon' (2010) 47 *CML Rev* 673. See in more detail, T Gammeltoft-Hanssen and R Adler-Nissen, 'Straightjacket or Sovereignty Shield? The Danish Opt-out on Justice and Home Affairs and Prospects after the Treaty of Lisbon' in N Hvidt and H Mourtizen (eds), *Danish Foreign Policy Yearbook 2010* (Copenhagen, DIIS, 2010) 137–61.

[8] Art 276 TFEU. Pre-Lisbon this provision was contained in Art 68(2) EC and Art 35(5) EU. Article 276 TFEU, however, only relates to police and judicial cooperation in criminal matters.

[9] Art 76 TFEU.

[10] Art 68 TFEU.

[11] See also, E Guild and S Carrera, who in addition argue that before adopting a new five-year plan, the Stockholm Programme should be implemented first: 'Does the Stockholm Programme Matter? The Struggles over Ownership of AFSJ Multiannual Programming' (2012) CEPS Working Paper 51, December 2012.

[12] Art 12(c) TEU.

[13] Art 7(2) of Protocol 2 on the application of the principles of subsidiarity and proportionality requires only a fourth of the votes allocated to national parliaments in case of a proposal made by a group of Member States under the AFSJ, where normally a third is required.

[14] In another sensitive policy area falling under the AFSJ – family law with a cross-border dimension – the unanimity risk was maintained (Art 81(3) TFEU). This is also the field in which enhanced co-operation was first used: Decision 2010/405, OJ 2010 L189/13.

tion would be open to at least nine Member States wishing to proceed with the proposal. Enhanced cooperation is also specifically mentioned as regards the establishment of a European Public Prosecutor's Office (EPP) and police cooperation.[15]

The transitional arrangements provide that only after a five-year period from the entry into force of the Lisbon Treaty may the institutions fully exercise their powers under the Treaty as regards Union acts that were adopted under the former third pillar. This would mean that, for instance, the Commission could bring enforcement proceedings against Member States before the ECJ, which in turn would have jurisdiction to hear such cases.

The question remains whether this would also change the legal nature of these acts and whether principles of EU law such as supremacy and direct effect would automatically apply. A simple solution serving legal certainty would be to recast these instruments as soon as possible as Union instruments under the current treaties. Some have called for a judgment confirming the direct effect of all JHA measures, much as *Van Gend en Loos* did for the internal market.[16] Already the ECJ in the case of *Pupino* has declared the duty of loyal cooperation applicable to the former third pillar and deduced from that an obligation to interpret national law in conformity with framework decisions.[17]

The expiry of the transitional period raises another issue, namely the particularly broad opt-out that was negotiated by the UK in the wake of the rejection of the Constitutional Treaty. The UK will have to inform the Council whether it is willing to accept the consequences of the expiry of the transitional period as regards the powers of the institutions at least six months before that expiration. If it does not, these measures will cease to apply to the UK, after which it may however decide to opt-in again under the protocols applicable to the UK on the Schengen *acquis* and Title IV TFEU. At the time of writing there have been strong suggestions by British Prime Minister David Cameron that his government may indeed opt-out of the approximately 130 police and criminal justice measures by 1 November 2014.[18]

Although Denmark lacks the possibility to opt-in to new measures on police and justice cooperation in criminal matters, the Danish Protocol specifically stipulates that former third pillar measures remain binding on Denmark, even when subsequently amended.[19] Assuming therefore, the exclusion of Denmark in the

[15] Arts 86(1) and 87(3) TFEU.

[16] Case 26/62 *Van Gend en Loos* [1963] ECR 1. E Perilo, 'Le droit pénal substantiel et l'espace de liberté, de sécurité et de justice, deux ans après Lisbonne: une analyse de jure condito et quelques perspectives de jure condendo' (FIDE 2012 EU Institutional Report) in J Laffranque (ed), *The Area of Freedom, Security and Justice, Including Information Society Issues* (Tartu, Tartu University Press, 2012) 199ff.

[17] C-105/03 *Pupino* [2005] ECR I-5285. See, for further examples of a blurring of the pillar divide pre-Lisbon, J Monar, 'The Institutional Framework of the AFSJ: Specific Challenges and Dynamics of Change' in J Monar (ed), *The Institutional Dimension of the European Union's Area of Freedom, Security and Justice* (Brussels, PIE Lang, 2010) 43–45.

[18] See on the consequences, A Hinarejos, J Spencer and S Peers, 'Opting out of EU Criminal Law: What is Actually Involved?' (2012) CELS Working Paper, New Series, No 1, September 2012.

[19] Art 2 Danish Protocol.

proposal for a regulation on Europol, would mean that Denmark's continued participation in the Agency would have to take place on the terms of the 2009 Decision.[20] However, the Protocol does not seem to provide a solution where this would lead to an inoperable situation.[21] It could, moreover, be argued that the new regulation does not constitute an amendment but rather a new piece of legislation excluding Denmark from future cooperation in Europol.

III. INSTITUTIONAL PRACTICE: AFFIRMING NEW POWERS AND HOLDING ON TO OLD ONES

The Lisbon Treaty entered into force on 1 December 2009 and a month later the European Council adopted a new multi-annual agenda for the AFSJ: the Stockholm Programme.[22] In early 2010, the second Barroso Commission took office and the responsibility for the AFSJ was divided between two Commissioners: Home Affairs (Cecilia Malmström) and Justice (Viviane Reding). The AFSJ Directorate General (JLS) was eventually split up in a DG Home and DG Justice. This move was much favoured by Reding allowing her to enhance the fundamental rights profile of the AFSJ.[23] The division also mirrors the situation in many Member States, where justice and home affairs is divided over two ministries.[24]

Following the adoption of the Stockholm Programme, the Commission presented an ambitious Action Plan for its implementation.[25] The Council was not amused, with some officials calling it 'an act of provocation' which went far beyond the policy agenda set out in the Programme itself.[26] Indeed, the plan refers to the need for 'greater ambitions' and the use of the new institutional framework 'to the fullest extent possible'. Not surprisingly, the JHA Council Conclusions recall that the Stockholm Programme is 'the only guide frame of reference', a clear sign of disapproval.[27]

[20] 'Proposal for a regulation of the European Parliament and of the Council on the European Union Agency for Law Enforcement Cooperation and Training (Europol) and repealing Decisions 2009/371/JHA and 2005/681/JHA' COM(2013) 173 final, Recital 61.

[21] Unlike Art 5 of the Annex to the Protocol, which – once in force – would allow the Council to exclude Denmark from further application of an existing measure if that measure in an amended form would become inoperable and Denmark would refuse to use its opt-in to the amended measure.

[22] The Stockholm Programme – An Open and Secure Europe Serving and Protecting Citizens, OJ 2010 C115/1.

[23] It was for that reason also assessed as a positive development: J Jeandesboz, A Scherrer and E-P Guittet, *Developing an EU Internal Security Strategy, Fighting Terrorism and Organised Crime*, LIBE Committee of the European Parliament, Study, PE 462.423, November 2011, 37.

[24] However, the difficult working relationship between the two Commissioners is likely to have played an important role as well: *European Voice*, 10 June 2010: www.europeanvoice.com/article/imported/a-departmental-split-to-end-turf-wars-/68186.aspx (last accessed 15 May 2013).

[25] Commission, 'Delivering an area of freedom, security and justice for Europe's citizens: Action Plan implementing the Stockholm Programme' (Communication) COM(2010) 171 final.

[26] E Guild and S Carrera (n 11) 3 and S Carrera, 'The Impact of the Treaty of Lisbon over EU Policies on Migration, Asylum and Borders: The Struggles over the Ownership of the Stockholm Programme' in E Guild, P Minderhoud and R Cholewinski (eds), *The First Decade of EU Migration and Asylum Law* (Leiden, Martinus Nijhoff Publishers, 2012) 229–54.

[27] Draft Council Conclusions, Council Document 9935/10, 19 May 2010.

It is understandable that the Commission would want to assert its new role under the Lisbon Treaty and indeed a more hands-off approach by the Council would eventually be justified. Still, the Commission may be wise to acknowledge the intergovernmental origins of the AFSJ and recognise that under the new Treaty Framework the Council remains an important policy driver. After the Amsterdam Treaty came into force the ECJ showed a considerable sensitivity for the specific nature of competences in the field of borders and visa, and the gradual transfer of powers, allowing the Council to maintain certain implementing powers in this field.[28] Interestingly, a much less contentious division of work seems to have emerged as regards the formulation of a Fundamental Rights Strategy – in which the Commission took the lead – and the EU's Internal Security Strategy, for which the Council took the initiative.[29]

The European Parliament's LIBE Committee has become one of the most active and busy parliamentary committees. Experience under the former first pillar, which saw the European Parliament develop towards an equal footing with the Council in the legislative process, has allowed it to grow into its role as co-legislator in the AFSJ. The trend towards reaching agreements on AFSJ legislation on first reading has consolidated after the entry into force of the Lisbon Treaty.[30] This may be interpreted as a sign of trust between the institutions. It also seems to prove wrong those who expected the European Parliament to become a more difficult partner in the legislative process, especially as a champion of fundamental rights.[31] Where necessary however, the Parliament will flex its muscles as it did successfully in bringing a case against the Council for exceeding its implementing powers on guidelines for joint border control operations at sea.[32]

The ECJ has seen a steady rise in cases pertaining to the AFSJ. First of all, the Commission has brought an important number of infringement proceedings against Member States.[33] This may indicate that it feels increasingly comfortable with its role as 'Guardian of the Treaties' in this policy field. It will be interesting to see whether the expiry of the transitional period and the progressive recast of

[28] Case C-257/01 *Commission v Council* [2005] ECR I-345.

[29] Commission, 'Strategy for the effective implementation of the Charter of Fundamental Rights by the European Union' (Communication) COM(2010) 573 final and the Internal Security Strategy for the European Union: Towards a European Security Model, Council document 5842/2/2010, 23 February 2010 (see below).

[30] A Ripoll Servent, 'Playing the Co-decision Game? Rules, Changes and Institutional Adaptation at the LIBE Committee' (2012) 34 *Journal of European Integration* 55 and E De Capitani, 'The Evolving Role of the European Parliament in the AFSJ' in J Monar (ed), *The Institutional Dimension of the European Union's Area of Freedom, Security and Justice* (Brussels, PIE Lang, 2010) 139.

[31] See, eg on the adoption of the Return Directive (Directive 2008/15), D Acosta, 'The Good, the Bad and the Ugly in EU Migration Law: Is the European Parliament Becoming Bad and Ugly?' (2009) 11 *European Journal of Migration and Law* 19. The picture is however mixed: it was for instance at the instigation of the European Parliament that many human rights safeguards were included in the amended legal basis of the European Border Agency Frontex (see below).

[32] See Case 355/10 *European Parliament v Council*, judgment of the Court (Grand Chamber) of 5 September 2012 nyr. Note that this case essentially constituted an institutional battle of power, rather than being out of the Parliament's concern with the content of the decision from a fundamental rights perspective.

[33] E Guild and S Carrera (n 11) 13.

former third pillar instruments into 'ordinary' instruments of EU law will result in a further increase in infringement proceedings. In any case, as more legislation is adopted and the jurisdiction of the Court extended to criminal matters, one may expect an increase in preliminary references, as may already be observed in the area of migration and asylum. Because many of these cases are likely to involve people in custody, one may also expect more extensive use of the urgent preliminary ruling procedure.[34]

Finally, more cases are likely to reach the Court as a result of the binding force of the Charter of Fundamental Rights post-Lisbon. Many of the competence areas of the AFSJ have the potential of affecting individual fundamental rights. In this respect it has been pointed out that the Court's role in criminal matters is much less that of a motor of (negative) integration, than that of a check on (positive) integration.[35] This observation holds stake more generally for the AFSJ, as shown by the *NS* and *ME* case.[36] Here, the Court obliged Member States not to transfer asylum seekers under the rules of the Dublin Regulation if this would expose them to a risk of inhumane treatment. At the same time, the Court does consistently reaffirm the importance of the principle of mutual trust and mutual recognition as the cornerstone of cooperation in the AFSJ, as it also did in the *Melloni* case.[37]

The post-Lisbon AFSJ remains susceptible to institutional battles and Member States' wishes to retain or even retrieve powers in this area. This is clearly demonstrated by events in the Schengen area. In 2011, the Arab Spring resulted in a considerable inflow of third-country nationals, mainly Tunisians, in Malta and Italy. With reception centres running out of capacity, the Italian Government granted around 20,000 temporary residence permits, which being valid as a Schengen visa allowed these people to travel onwards.[38] France responded by increasing controls in its border area with Italy, threatening to reintroduce border controls, as did other Member States. In a joint letter French President Sarkozy and Italian Prime Minister Berlusconi asked the President of the Commission and the President of the European Council to consider measures allowing for a reinstatement of internal border controls in case of exceptional problems at the external borders.[39]

[34] Art 267 TFEU and Ch III of the Court's Rules of Procedure, OJ 2012 L265/5.

[35] A Hinarejos, 'Integration in Criminal Matters and the Role of the Court of Justice' (2011) 36 *EL Rev* 428.

[36] Joined Cases C-411/10 and C-493/10 *NS* and *ME*, judgment of the Court (Grand Chamber) of 21 December 2011 nyr, para 83.

[37] Case C-399/11 *Melloni*, judgment of the Court (Grand Chamber) of 26 February 2013 nyr, para 63.

[38] Decreto del Presidente del Consiglio, 5 April 2011, Misure di protezione temporanea per i cittadini stranieri affluiti dai Paesi nordafricana, *GU* No 81, 8 April 2011.

[39] Joint Letter of 26 April 2011, available in English at: www.elysee.fr/president/root/bank_objects/Lettre_conjointe_FRITavril11%5B1%5D.pdfwww.ambafrance-uk.org/Letter-from-French-and-Italian. See for President Barosso's response, dated 29 April 2011: ec.europa.eu/commission_2010-2014/president/news/letters/pdf/20110502_fr.pdf (last visited 15 May 2013).

In May 2011, the Commission responded with its Communication on Migration in which it announced proposals for improved 'Schengen governance', followed by a Communication on the issue and two proposals for legislation later that year: the Schengen Governance Package.[40] The first proposal provides for a mechanism allowing for a decision on reintroducing border checks at EU level, with a predominant role for the Commission.[41] The second proposal would replace the intergovernmental system of peer reviews evaluating Member States' application of the Schengen rules with a system under which evaluations would be carried out by the Commission and Frontex.[42] The proposals were based on Article 77(2)(e) TFEU, which provides for the adoption of measures abolishing internal borders and using the ordinary legislative procedure. The Council, however, amended the legal basis on the Schengen evaluation mechanism to Article 70 TFEU allowing the Council to adopt measures for the objective and impartial evaluations of JHA policies.[43] Under this legal basis Parliament would only have to be consulted.

Although it could well be argued that indeed Article 70 TFEU was the correct legal basis, the Council's move led to a months-long stand-off between the Parliament and Council, freezing negotiations also on other legislative proposals in the AFSJ. Only in May 2013 was an agreement reached between the Council and Parliament under which the Commission and not the Council would adopt the evaluation reports of the Schengen evaluation under comitology.[44] Moreover, a linking clause in the Schengen Border Code would refer to the Schengen evaluation mechanism and a joint declaration of the institutions stated that the European Parliament would be consulted on the amendment of the Schengen evaluation mechanism.

The dispute on the Schengen Border Package was not only one between the EU institutions, but also between the Member States and the EU over the level at which decisions over borders ought to be taken. The Council thus also proposed amendments to limit the role of the Commission in the decision on the reintroduction of internal border controls.[45] The Commission received six reasoned opinions on the proposal for temporary reintroduction of border controls at internal borders (the Schengen Area) in exceptional circumstances, arguing that Member States are in a better position to monitor border controls and that compliance with the

[40] Commission, 'Communication on Migration' COM(2011) 248 final, 8; Commission, 'Schengen Governance – Strengthening the area without internal border controls' (Communication) COM(2011) 561 final.

[41] Commission, 'Proposal for a regulation amending Regulation (EC) 562/2006 in order to provide for common rules on the temporary reintroduction of border control at internal borders in exceptional circumstances' COM(2011) 560 final.

[42] Commission, 'Proposal for a regulation on the establishment of an evaluation and monitoring mechanism to verify the application of the Schengen *acquis*' COM(2011) 559 final. See, for an extensive discussion, S Carrera, 'An Assessment of the Commission's 2011 Schengen Governance Package Preventing Abuse by EU Member States of Freedom of Movement?' (2012) CEPS Working Paper No 47, March 2012.

[43] Council Document 11588/12, 19 June 2012.

[44] Council Document 9606/13, 22 May 2013.

[45] Council Document 6161/4/12, 4 June 2012.

subsidiarity principle was not sufficiently justified.[46] The Commission's response to national parliaments argued that as the rules governing the Schengen Area were subject to EU legislation, it was appropriate for decisions derogating from the freedom to move freely across internal borders to be made at EU level.[47]

Overall institutional practice in the AFSJ reflects the alignment with other areas of EU competence. The Commission and the European Parliament are increasingly able to fulfill the role that was originally assigned to them in the treaties under the Community pillar. Of course the AFSJ retains a number of intergovernmental traits, which are especially prominent during the transitional phase. Moreover, the political turmoil on the Schengen Governance Package shows that institutions are either eager to assert their new position under the Lisbon Treaty, or rather try to cling on to old prerogatives. The transition to a post-Lisbon reality is therefore not entirely a smooth one. The institutions will need to acknowledge this and work together in a spirit of loyal cooperation in order to avoid political blockage.

IV. EXECUTIVE POWERS: OPERATIONAL COOPERATION IN THE AFSJ

So far, the focus has been on the role of the institutions in the legislative and adjudicative processes. As successive treaty amendments have aligned the institutional framework and legislative procedures of the AFSJ with other areas of Union competence, there has been a noticeable increase in legislative activity. However, this legislation is largely based on the mutual recognition of Member States' legal systems, without a concomitant harmonisation of substantive rules. One category has established procedural rules, such as determining the responsibility for an asylum claim or the rules for surrender on the basis of an EAW. Another category of legislation aims to facilitate the practical cooperation between Member States' competent authorities. This may be in the form of financing instruments or by allowing the deployment of law enforcement staff of one Member State in another. Importantly, legislation has given a more structural basis to previously existing cooperation arrangements in the form of semi-autonomous agencies charged with coordination and facilitating operational activity.

Member States' weariness of substantive harmonisation in the AFSJ and the intrinsic operational nature of law enforcement cooperation reinforce the AFSJ's executive dimension. This executive dimension should not be understood as executive rule-making (delegation and implementation) but rather the factual involvement of the EU with on the ground cooperation of Member States' competent authorities. At a practical level, both the Council and JHA agencies have played an important role in promoting operational activity and integrating

[46] www.ipex.eu/IPEXL-WEB/dossier/document/COM20110560.do#dossier-COD20110242 (last visited 15 May 2013).

[47] Commission, 'Subsidiarity and Proportionality' (Report) COM(2012) 373 final, 9.

Member States' competent authorities.[48] It is however important to stress that neither the EU, nor its bodies and agencies have been endowed with public authority in matters of JHA. Operational activity at EU level is limited to the *coordination* and *facilitation* of operational activities of national authorities. The Lisbon Treaty, and in particular the Stockholm Programme, give a new impetus to this operational dimension with the establishment of a Standing Committee on Internal Security under the Council (COSI), the development of an Internal Security Strategy and the reinforcement of the various agencies in this field. The question arises to the extent to which the 'communitarisation' of the AFSJ is also reflected at the level of operational cooperation in the AFSJ.

A. JHA Agencies

JHA agencies resemble in many of their tasks 'classic' regulatory agencies in other policy areas for the way in which they contribute to the implementation of an EU policy through the provision of technical and informational assistance. A subtle yet important difference is that this assistance is geared toward the Member States rather than the EU institutions. This again bears witness to the intergovernmental origins of JHA and the fact that executive powers remain in the hands of the Member States.

The currently existing JHA agencies are Europol, Eurojust, the European Police College (CEPOL), the European Agency for the Coordination of Operational Cooperation at the External Borders of the EU (Frontex) and the European Asylum Support Office (EASO).[49] The Agency for Management of Large Scale IT systems (EU-LISA) administers the centralised databases EURODAC, the Schengen Information System II (SIS II) and the Visa Information System (VIS).[50] Two agencies are linked more to the justice dimension of the AFSJ: the Fundamental Rights Agency (FRA) and the European Institute for Gender Equality (EIGI).[51] The FRA's remit was originally limited to matters covered by the Community pillar, specifically excluding police and justice cooperation. Despite the 'communitarisation' of the third pillar, there is still resistance – in particular from the UK – against the FRA also covering this policy field.[52] Finally, the European Monitoring Centre for Drugs

[48] J Monar, 'Specific Factors, Typology and Development Trends in Modes of Governance in the EU JHA Domain' (New Gov Project, Strasbourg, 2006) 19, available at: www.eu-newgov.org/database/DELIV/D01D17_Emergence_NMG_in_JHA.pdf. See for an overview of powers and tasks of agencies in the field of criminal law: V Mitsilegas, *EU Criminal Law* (Oxford, Hart Publishing, 2005) 161ff.

[49] Europol: Council Decision 2009/371/JHA, OJ 2009 L121/37; Eurojust: Council Decision 2009/426/JHA, OJ 2009 138/14; CEPOL: Council Decision 2005/681/JHA, OJ 2005 L256/63; Frontex: Council Regulation (EC) 2007/2004, OJ 2004 L 349/1; EASO: Regulation (EU) 439/2010, OJ 2010 L132/11.

[50] EU-LISA: Regulation (EU) 1077/2011, OJ 2011 L286/1.

[51] FRA: Council Regulation (EC) 168/2007, OJ 2007 L53/1; EIGI: Council Regulation (EC) 1922/2006, OJ 2006 L403/9.

[52] The multi-annual policy framework does include access to justice and victims of crime as thematic areas: Art 2, Council Decision 252/2013/EU establishing a Multiannual Framework for 2013–17 for the European Union Agency for Fundamental Rights, OJ 2013 L79/1.

and Drug Addiction (EMCCDDA), established in 1993 to provide information on drugs and drug addiction, is considered a JHA agency.[53] Although established on the basis of Article 114 TFEU (internal market) the European Network and Information Security Agency (ENISA) is also sometimes classified as such.[54]

Europol, Eurojust and CEPOL originate under the former third pillar of the EU.[55] With the entry into force of the Lisbon Treaty, Eurojust and Europol were given a special position within the EU's institutional framework, as the TFEU contains an explicit legal basis for their establishment in Articles 85 and 88 TFEU. Other agencies have been established on the legal basis for the respective policy field in which they operate. This has often been done in an *ad hoc* fashion, resulting in their proliferation and an overlap in competences. Recently, the EU legislator has taken a more critical approach towards the creation of agencies in general, aiming also at the rationalisation of agencies' tasks and the creation of synergies.[56] This is certainly reinforced by the current crisis and ensuing budgetary constraints. A clear sign of this new approach is the proposal to incorporate CEPOL into EUROPOL, preventing an overlap in training activities of law enforcement staff.[57]

A distinctive feature of the four most prominent JHA agencies – Europol, Eurojust, Frontex and EASO – is their role in the coordination of operational activity of the Member States' authorities competent in their field. In contrast to conventional wisdom that coordinating agencies protect the prerogatives of national administrations and Member States' sovereignty, there is great transformative potential in the way in which JHA agencies coordinate cooperation between national administrations.

First, the network structure of these agencies forces Member States to coordinate the activities of their competent authorities and to establish single national contact points for their dealings with the agencies. Secondly, joint operations may involve the deployment of public officials exercising executive powers outside their own Member State in the framework of Joint Investigation Teams (JITs), European Asylum Emergency Teams or European Border Guard Teams.[58] The powers of visiting border guards can be especially far-reaching, including the power to use force and carry weaponry.[59] In the case of JITs Europol officials may

[53] EMCCDDA: Regulation (EC) 1920/2006, OJ 2006 L376/1.

[54] ENISA: Regulation (EC) 460/2004, OJ 2004 L77/1.

[55] Eurojust: Council Decision 2002/187/JHA, OJ 2002 L63/1; Europol: Council Act drawing up the Convention based on Art K.3 of the Treaty on European Union, on the establishment of a European Police Office, OJ 1995 C316/1.

[56] Joint Statement and Common Approach to the EU Agencies adopted by the European Parliament, Commission and Council in July 2012, Council Document 11450/12, 18 June 2012.

[57] Commission, 'Proposal for a regulation of the European Parliament and of the Council on the European Union Agency for Law Enforcement Cooperation and Training (Europol)' COM(2013) 713 final. See for the disproving reaction of CEPOL its position paper: www.statewatch.org/news/2013/may/eu-cepol-position-paper-europol-merger.pdf (accessed 15 May 2013). Note that the training of border guards would remain in the hands of Frontex in line with its founding regulation.

[58] Council Framework Decision of 13 June 2002 on joint investigation teams, OJ 2002 L162/1; Ch 3 EASO Regulation Art 3(1b) Frontex Regulation.

[59] Art 10, Frontex Regulation.

participate within the limits provided for by the host Member State's national law, although they are not allowed to take part in any coercive measures.[60] Thirdly, the founding regulation of EASO and Frontex provides for the establishment of a pool of border guards and asylum experts respectively.[61] In the case of Frontex, the latest amendments to its founding regulation even allows national border guards seconded to the Agency as national experts to become part of this pool, hence putting them at the full disposal of the agency for a period of a maximum of six months per year.[62] This contributes even more to the creation of an embryonic 'European Corps of Border Guards'.[63]

Finally, there may be possibilities for a transfer of genuine executive power found in the Lisbon Treaty. In as far as Europol is concerned the Treaty clearly provides that the application of coercive measures remains the exclusive responsibility of the competent national authorities.[64] The broadly formulated Article 77(1)(c) TFEU which provides the legal basis for the gradual introduction of an 'integrated management system for external borders' does not necessarily exclude this possibility for Frontex. Both the Frontex Regulation and the Stockholm Programme call for a study into the feasibility of a European *System* of Border Guards.[65] Although reference is no longer made to a European *Corps* of Border Guards the establishment of an independent corps having (limited) independent executive powers will certainly be an option to be examined.

As regards public prosecution, the Lisbon Treaty clearly goes further than the current legal framework. Article 85 TFEU allows for a transformation of Eurojust 'from a simple mediator at a horizontal cooperation level to a player with binding operational powers at a vertical integration level'.[66] Nevertheless, the centre of gravity for investigations and prosecutions would not be transferred to EU level.[67] Article 86 TFEU, however, paves the way for the establishment, by means of regulations, of a prosecutor's office – the EPP. The creation of Eurojust had always been intimately connected to the EPP, which has its origins in the *Corpus Iuris* Project.[68] The EPP resurfaced in the Constitutional Treaty and eventually made its way into the Lisbon Treaty. It may only address 'offences against the Union's financial interests'. An extension of the Prosecutor's remit to 'serious

[60] Art 6, Europol Decision.

[61] Art 3(1b), Frontex Regulation and Art 15, EASO Regulation.

[62] Art 3b(3), Frontex Regulation.

[63] The reference to the establishment of such a corps was made in 2002: Commission, 'Towards integrated management of the external borders of the Member States of the European Union' (Communication) COM(2002) 233 final, but has been omitted since.

[64] Art 88(3) TFEU.

[65] Point 5.1, Stockholm Programme; Art 33(2a), Frontex Regulation.

[66] 'Eurojust and the Lisbon Treaty: Towards more effective action' (Conclusions of the strategic seminar organised by Eurojust and the Belgian Presidency, Bruges, 20–22 September) Council Document 17625/10, 9 December 2010.

[67] ibid.

[68] C Van den Wyngaert, 'Eurojust and the European Public Prosecutor in the Corpus Iuris Model: Water and Fire?' in N Walker (ed), *Europe's Area of Freedom, Security and Justice* (Oxford, Oxford University Press, 2004) 201–39. See also K Ligeti and M Simonato, 'The European Public Prosecutor's Office: Towards a Truly European Prosecution Service' (2013) 4 *New Journal of European Criminal Law* 7.

crime having a cross-border dimension' would be possible but would again require unanimity. As the competence of the EPP, at least in the beginning, will be limited, Eurojust will continue to exist in a (possibly amended) structure.

Article 86 TFEU provides that the EPP will be created '*from* Eurojust'. There are different scenarios as to how both bodies could function alongside one another.[69] The EPP could become a 29th national member and sit in the College every time the protection of the financial interests of the Union is discussed. An alternative option would be for the College of Eurojust to become the EPP. The Commission work plan for 2013 foresaw the publication of the proposal for an EPP later that year. In order to convince hesitant Member States, the proposal would have to make a strong case for the establishment of an EPP and clearly define the relation between the EPP and Eurojust, as well as the EU's anti-fraud office (OLAF), national prosecuting authorities and JHA agencies such as Europol.

The post-Lisbon environment has seen the establishment of three new agencies (EASO, EU-LISE and EIGE), as well as the amendment of the Frontex Regulation. Articles 85 and 88 TFEU provide that the founding acts of Eurojust and Europol should be recast as regulations. A proposal for a Europol Regulation was presented in March 2013; the proposal for Eurojust was expected later that year.

Despite the more critical approach to agency creation, there is a consolidation and fortification of JHA agencies' role, coupled with increased accountability mechanisms being put in place. This is a consequence of the call for decisive EU action in the AFSJ resulting in new tasks and powers for JHA agencies as well as the concern for effective democratic scrutiny of their functioning and need to respect fundamental rights. The proposals for a regulation establishing Europol and Eurojust should include rules on scrutiny by the European Parliament and national parliaments. Both the importance of national parliaments as a source of legitimacy in the Treaty of Lisbon and the nature of JHA competences justify a joint supervision of JHA policies and agencies.[70]

In 2010, the Commission published its Communication on procedures for the democratic scrutiny of Europol, in which it argued that most of the European Parliament's concerns as regards its role in scrutinising Europol had been addressed by the 2009 Europol decision.[71] Outstanding issues related primarily to the role of national parliaments' involvement in the democratic scrutiny of Europol. National parliaments have experienced difficulty in scrutinising Europol's work through the national representatives on the Management Board, in finding information and in

[69] H Nilsson, 'Judicial Cooperation in the EU: Eurojust and the European Public Prosecutor' in E Guild, S Carrera and A Eggenschwiller (eds), *The Area of Freedom, Security and Justice Ten Years On: Successes and Future Challenges Under the Stockholm Programme* (CEPS, Brussels) 73–78. See also, S White and N Dorn, 'Towards a Decentralized European Public Prosecutor's Office?' (2012) 89 *Amicus Curiae* Spring 2.

[70] V Mitsilegas, 'Interparliamentary Cooperation in EU Justice and Home Afffairs' (Fifty Years of Interparliamentary Cooperation Conference, Stiftung Wissenschaft und Politik, Berlin, 13 June 2007).

[71] Commission, 'Procedures for the scrutiny of Europol's activities by the European Parliament, together with national Parliaments' (Communication) COM(2010) 776 final.

coordinating their efforts, internally amongst national parliaments and with the European Parliament.[72] The same holds true for Eurojust and Frontex.[73]

The Europol proposal aligns Europol's structure and accountability mechanisms further with those of other agencies. The proposal does not give far-reaching new rights to national parliaments or to the European Parliament. It does, however, reinforce reporting obligations extending them to national parliaments as well. Importantly, it provides for the conclusion of a working arrangement between Europol and the European Parliament to govern the access of MEPs and their representatives to classified and sensitive non-classified information.[74]

The 2011 Regulation amending Frontex's founding instrument introduced frequent references to fundamental rights.[75] It strengthens accountability mechanisms aimed at ensuring that in the course of joint operations fundamental rights are respected. It created the position of Human Rights Officer and a Consultative Forum bringing together stakeholders such as UNCHR, Amnesty and the European Council for Refugees. The Agency is under an obligation to adopt a Code of Conduct, a Common Core Curriculum and a Fundamental Rights Strategy. The Executive Director has the duty to suspend joint operational activity if he becomes aware of serious human rights violations.[76] The question that arises in relation to these amendments is the extent to which they are soft law obligations in the guise of hard law. Their main value appears to lay in the awareness-raising and mainstreaming of fundamental rights in the work of the agency and national authorities, rather than giving wronged individuals an effective tool for redress against the agency.

Although the amendment of the Frontex Regulation and the proposed Europol Regulation both expand the powers of these agencies to support the operational activity of national authorities, the most important increase in their powers can be found in a reinforcement of their intelligence gathering and processing role. This includes the exchange of data with third countries supporting the external dimension of the AFSJ. This expansion does not merely take place in the founding regulations, but also by granting these agencies tasks under other legislation.

The Europol proposal reinforces the obligations of Member States to provide information to the agency, thereby strengthening the Agency's role as a hub in information exchange and analysis.[77] It no longer refers specifically to the Europol Information System but instead lays down the framework within which Europol may process and collect data.[78] The proposal at the same time reinforces the

[72] See also, D Ruiz de Garibay, 'Interparliamentary Cooperation in the EU: A Case Study of Justice and Home Affairs' (60th Political Studies Association Annual Conference, Sixty Years of Political Studies: Achievements and Futures, Edinburgh, 29 March to 1 April 2010).

[73] B de Witte and JJ Rijpma, *Oversight of the European Union's Area of Freedom, Security and Justice (AFSJ) Bodies: Parliamentary Scrutiny of Justice and Home Affairs Agencies*, LIBE Committee of the European Parliament, Thematic Study, PE 315.283, November 2011, 385.

[74] Art 54, COM(2013) 173 final.

[75] Reg (EU) 1168/2011, OJ 2011 L304/1.

[76] Art 3(1a), Frontex Regulation.

[77] Art 7(5)(a), Europol Proposal.

[78] Art 24, Europol Proposal.

autonomous data protection regime that is applicable to Europol.[79] It grants the European Data Protection Supervisor (EDPS) competence over the processing of personal data by Europol and limits direct access of Member States to the information stored and prohibits the processing of data of victims.

The Commission seems to live up to its promise in its 2012 Communication on the European Information Exchange Model that it would not establish new EU level law enforcement databases or information exchange instruments, but that 'existing EU instruments could and should be better implemented, and the exchanges should be organised more consistently'.[80] However, this has meant that both national law enforcement authorities and Europol and Eurojust have been increasingly granted access to JHA database systems. Europol and Eurojust were given access to the SIS in 2005.[81] In addition, Europol was granted access to the VIS, alongside national enforcement authorities, in 2008.[82] The European Parliament has reached a deal with the Council on granting the law enforcement authorities, including Europol, access to EURODAC.[83] A proposal for the establishment of an entry–exit system that registers all third-country nationals crossing external Schengen borders contemplates access for law enforcement staff – presumably including Europol.[84]

Also Frontex, which previously did not have the power to collect and exchange personal data, has now been given a limited power to do so in the framework of return operations and during joint operational activity as regards persons suspected of cross-border crime, including human smuggling and trafficking.[85] In doing so, Frontex is subject to the EU Data Protection Regulation currently in force.[86] Of much greater importance is, however, Frontex's role as information hub in the new EUROSUR system.[87] EUROSUR should form an overarching 'system of systems' allowing Member States' border-control authorities access to a secure and decentralised information-sharing network increasing situational awareness at the external borders. The management of this system and the responsibility of compiling situational pictures falls on Frontex. Although one could consider this as a primarily technical measure, EUROSUR is rather a 'business model', once more forcing the authorities of different Member States to exchange information with Frontex and amongst themselves.

[79] Ch VII, Europol Proposal.

[80] Commission, 'Strengthening law enforcement cooperation in the EU: The European Information Exchange Model (EIXM)' (Communication) COM(2012) 735 final, 2.

[81] Council Decision 2005/211/JHA, OJ 2005 L68/44.

[82] Council Decision 2008/633/JHA, OJ 2008 L218/129.

[83] Commission, 'Proposal for a Council decision on requesting comparisons with EURODAC data by Member States' law enforcement authorities and Europol for law enforcement purposes' COM(2009) 344 final.

[84] Commission, 'Proposal for a regulation establishing an entry/exit system (EES) to register entry and exit data of third-country nationals crossing the external borders of the Member States of the European Union' COM(2013) 95 final, Art 46(5).

[85] Art 11b and 11c, Frontex Regulation.

[86] Reg (EC) 45/2001, OJ 2001 L8/1.

[87] Commission, 'Proposal for a regulation of the European Parliament and the Council establishing the European Border Surveillance System (EUROSUR)' COM(2011) 873 final, Art 6.

The way in which databases that were initially established for the purpose of managing migration and asylum are used as law enforcement tools forms, however, a worrisome textbook example of competence creep. There can be serious doubts as to necessity and proportionality, as well as the practical feasibility, of establishing large systems for information exchange such a EUROSUR and the entry–exit system.[88] Particularly disturbing is the fact that new systems are proposed whilst a new data protection regime is still to be adopted.[89] JHA agencies, in particular, seem to benefit from this increase in data and information processing and in fact play an important role in the preparation and testing of such systems.

B. The Internal Security Committee (COSI)

Operational coordination has not been the exclusive domain of JHA agencies. In fact, during the intergovernmental years of the AFSJ, the Council and its secretariat came to play an important executive role. Alongside Europol and Eurojust, it served as a forum for operational cooperation between Member States' law enforcement authorities, occasionally even taking on a coordinating role itself in the absence of powers in this regard for the Commission.[90] In its final report for the Constitutional Convention, the Working Group on the AFSJ proposed to separate the Council's operational and legislative role more clearly.[91] It proposed a merging of the various Council working groups dealing with internal security and removing the so-called Article 36 Committee (CATS) from the legislative process, limiting its role to that of coordinator of operational cooperation.[92] As did the Constitutional Treaty, Article 71 TFEU provides for the setting up of a Standing Committee on Internal Security (COSI) which should promote and strengthen operational cooperation on internal security and 'facilitate' the coordination of the activities of Member States' competent authorities.

COSI was established by a Council decision of November 2009, even though preparatory work had started already prior to the rejection of the Constitutional

[88] See also the various Opinions of the Standing Committee of Experts on International Immigration, Refugee and Criminal Law (Meijers Committee): www.commissie-meijers.nl/commissiemeijers/pagina.asp?pagnaam=english (last accessed 15 May 2013).

[89] Data Protection Reform Package: Commission, 'Proposal for a regulation on the protection of individuals with regard to the processing of personal data and on the free movement of such data (General Data Protection Regulation)' COM(2012) 11 final; Commission, 'Proposal for a directive on the protection of individuals with regard to the processing of personal data by competent authorities for the purposes of prevention, investigation, detection or prosecution of criminal offences or the execution of criminal penalties, and the free movement of such data' COM(2012) 10 final.

[90] D Curtin, *Executive Power of the European Union: Law, Pratices and the Living Constitution* (Oxford, Oxford University Press, 2009) 129.

[91] Interestingly, the Working Group seems to have included the implementation of legislation under the Council's legislative tasks: House of Lords Select Committee on the EU, *The Future of Europe: Constitutional Treaty – Draft Art 31 and Draft Articles from Pt 2 (Freedom, Security and Justice)* (HL Paper 81, Session 2002–03, 16th Report, 27 March 2003) 16.

[92] Final Report of Working Group X on Freedom, Security and Justice, CONV 426/02, 3.

Treaty.[93] COSI's founding decision excludes a role for the Committee in the legislative process. Its tasks are limited to the setting of priorities and coordination of operational cooperation. At the same time, the founding decision explicitly stipulates that the actual carrying out of law enforcement operations is left to the Member States.

Like the rest of the Council working groups, COSI's presidency rotates on a six-monthly basis. Its membership was initially contemplated to consist of residential, permanent members. This was eventually changed to a 'capitals-based' membership – non-fixed membership.[94] In practice there has been an imbalance in the representation of Member States in COSI, not only in rank, but also in background (ministries/law enforcement authorities/Brussels staff).[95] It is also interesting to note that the establishment of COSI meant the end of the Police Chiefs Task Force (PCTF). With no formal representation of police forces in COSI, this has been interpreted as the EU Member States placing the control over police coordination back in the hands of the political–administrative level.[96] At the same time the Chiefs of Police did decide during the Belgian Presidency of the EU on 25 and 26 October to continue informal meetings once or twice a year as a forum for dialogue.[97] COSI's position in relation to the Counter-terrorism Coordinator and SitCen, which has now been brought under the European External Action Service, remains ill-defined. Interestingly, the decision that is to implement the Solidarity Clause, Article 222 TFEU, would give a leading role to the EEAS.[98] JHA agencies are not members of COSI, but may be invited where appropriate. In particular Europol and Frontex have been the main interlocutors of the Committee, second to CEPOL and Eurojust. Justice agencies such as the FRA, but also the EDPS do not seem to be included in COSI's work in a systematic manner. This of course carries a danger that the Committee loses sight of the important implications its work may have on fundamental rights and data protection.[99]

A rationalisation of working groups and parties in the Council has taken place, reflecting more closely organisation structures in other EU policy fields.[100] For the time being, however, the four-level working structure in EU law-making in the AFSJ is maintained. This means that CATS (on police and criminal cooperation) and SCIFA (on asylum and migration) remain in place for now. This additional

[93] Council Decision 2010/131/EU, OJ 2010 L52/50. Discussion paper on the future Standing Committee on Internal Security (COSI), Council Document 6626/05, 21 February 2005.

[94] Council Document 5949/10, 5 February 2010.

[95] J Jeandesboz et al (n 23) 41 and M Busuioc and D Curtin, *The EU Internal Security Strategy, The EU Policy Cycle and the Role of (AFJS) Agencies: Promises, Perils and Pre-requisites*, LIBE Committee of the European Parliament, Study, PE 453.185, May 2011, 11.

[96] J van Buuren, 'Runaway Bureaucracy? The European Police Chiefs Task Force' (2012) 6 *Policing* 288.

[97] W Bruggeman and M Den Boer, 'Policing and Internal Security in the Post-Lisbon Era: New Challenges' in S Wolff, F Goudappel and JW de Zwaan (eds), *Freedom, Security and Justice after Lisbon and Stockholm* (The Hague, TMC Asser Press, 2011) 144.

[98] Joint Proposal for a Council Decision on the arrangements for the implementation by the Union of the Solidarity Clause, JOIN(2012) 39 final.

[99] J Jeandesboz et al (n 23) 9 and M Busuioc and D Curtin (n 95) 13.

[100] See the List of Council preparatory bodies, Council Document 5581/13, 22 January 2013.

layer within the legislative process within the Council is situated between working group level and COREPER and was intended to allow national ministries for JHA affairs to retain influence over these policy fields.[101] The Council Secretariat seems inclined to favour a continued role for both CATS and SCIFA, as a forum for more specialised, high level debates in politically sensitive areas.[102]

COSI has been criticised as an EU interior ministry in the making,[103] or as a toothless standing committee[104] and some have asked whether it would be necessary at all to formally provide for such a committee.[105] It still remains too early to render judgment on the functioning of COSI, although it does already appear to struggle to define its role. Its rotating presidency and disparate membership carries the risk of a lack of focus and continuity, allowing other actors, such as the Council's secretariat and the JHA agencies, to exercise considerable influence over the Committee. So far, COSI has been mainly involved in the implementation of the European Internal Security Strategy.

C. The Internal Security Strategy and the Policy Cycle

The Stockholm Programme called upon the Council and the Commission together to draw up an Internal Security Strategy (ISS) 'aimed at strengthening cooperation in law enforcement, border management, civil protection, disaster management as well as judicial cooperation in criminal matters'. Before Lisbon various JHA Council Conclusions had already taken steps towards closer cooperation between the Member States in the field of internal security. Although this may explain why the Council was able to take the lead in the formulation of the Strategy, the absence of the Commission and Parliament from the drafting of the ISS shows how the third pillar regime continues to cast a shadow over operational cooperation. A working document of the LIBE Committee considered the exclusion of the Parliament from the process 'inexplicable'.[106]

The ISS was adopted in February 2010 and subsequently endorsed by the European Council.[107] The European Parliament's resolution on the ISS underlined that in the post-Lisbon constellation the Parliament ought to have been

[101] This fourth level between working parties and COREPER was initially introduced so as to allow the ministries of the interior to retain influence over the area, considering that the Member State's representatives in COREPER originate from the Member States' foreign ministries.

[102] Council Documents 17187/11 and 17182/11, 18 November 2011.

[103] T Bunyan, 'The Creation of an EU Interior Ministry', *Statewatch News*, April 2003, 3: www.statewatch.org/news/2003/apr/TBART.pdf (last accessed 15 May 2013).

[104] A Townsend, 'Can the EU Deliver in the Area of Freedom, Security and Justice?' (2003) Brussels, EPIN Working Paper No 9, September 2003, 11.

[105] J Monar, 'A New "Area of Freedom, Security and Justice" for the Enlarged EU? The results of the European Convention' in K Henderson, *The Area of Freedom, Security and Justice in the Enlarged Europe* (Hampshire, Palgrave MacMillan, 2005) 127.

[106] LIBE Committee of the European Parliament, Working Document on the European Union's Internal Security Strategy, Rapporteur Borsellino, PE458.598v01-00, 4.

[107] EU Internal Security Strategy, above (n 29).

'part of the process as regards policy guidance, implementation and evaluation of results'.[108] The influence that the JHA agencies Europol, Eurojust and Frontex had in the preparation of the ISS is also important.[109] In the ISS, the Council tasked the Commission to come forward with an action-oriented plan. The Commission identified five strategic objectives and proposed specific actions for each of them.[110] While the Commission's Action Plan emphasised the shared responsibility of institutions, agencies and Member States for the implementation of the ISS, the Council in its conclusions on the Communication underlined the primacy of COSI 'in line with the Stockholm Programme'.[111]

One way in which the ISS is implemented is through the establishment of the 'policy cycle' for serious and organised international crime. Following the failure of the Constitutional Treaty, the Council adopted the Architecture of Internal Security.[112] Rather than an institutional blue print, this document introduced the outline for what was to become a 'reference framework' for internal security: the policy cycle. The policy cycle is a model that must ensure a coherent and methodological approach to the setting of priorities in this area and the translation of these priorities into concrete action.[113] It contains four phases: first, policy preparation on the basis of risk assessment; second, policy setting by the Council and development of multi-annual strategic plans (MASPs) for each priority; third, development and implementation of annual operational action plans (AOPs) in line with the objective set in the MASPs; and fourth, evaluation.

COSI is the main body tasked with overseeing the development and implementation of the policy cycle. The first (reduced) policy cycle (2011–13) is carried out on the existing Organised Crime Threat Assessment by Europol (OCTA 2011).[114] Again the limited role for both Commission and Parliament is striking. Whereas the Commission would be responsible for drawing up the MASPs, there were no fully-fledged MASPs during the first policy cycle. Instead strategic goals were formulated per crime priority by an expert group of Member States and agencies. The Member States, together with the agencies, translated these goals into AOPs, which were subsequently validated by COSI. This predominance of COSI and the Member States may explain that only one of the key internal security threats, identified by the Commission in its ISS in Action Communication, is also covered by the policy cycle, namely the disruption of international criminal networks.[115]

[108] European Parliament resolution of 22 May 2012 on the European Union's Internal Security Strategy (P7_TA-PROV(2012)0207), Rapporteur Borsellino.

[109] See, eg the Joint Report by EUROPOL, EUROJUST and FRONTEX on the State of Internal Security in the EU, Council Document 9359/10, 7 May 2010.

[110] Commission, 'Implementation of the Internal Security Strategy (ISS): The ISS in Action' (Communication) COM(2010) 673 final.

[111] JHA Council Conclusions of 24 and 25 February 2011.

[112] Council Document 9596/1/06 REV 1, 22 May 2006.

[113] JHA Council conclusions on the creation and implementation of an EU policy cycle for organised and serious international crime, 8 and 9 November 2010.

[114] A new four-year policy cycle should be established on the basis of the new EU SOCTA 2013 by Europol (EU Serious Organised Crime Threat Assessment).

[115] M Busuioc and D Curtin, above (n 95) 12.

Also interesting is the role of the JHA agencies in formulating the strategic goals, which again comes close to policy-making.[116] Both Europol and Frontex have gained influence as a result, the latter as 'co-driver' for the priority on irregular migration and participant in the priority on human trafficking.[117]

The European Parliament does not have any role in the policy cycle. It quite rightly called upon the Council to revise its conclusions on the policy cycle to do justice to the Parliament's new position as co-legislator in this field.[118] Not only does the Parliament lack a role in the setting of operational priorities in this field, there are also no structural mechanisms put in place to ensure that it can satisfactorily exercise parliamentary control. Article 71 TFEU and Article 6(2) of the COSI Decision provide that the European Parliament (as well as national parliaments) shall be kept informed of the proceedings of COSI. So far two reports on its functioning have been sent to the European Parliament and national parliaments. It is doubtful whether this suffices to ensure an effective democratic scrutiny of operational cooperation in the AFSJ.

D. Inter-Agency Cooperation

The Stockholm Programme defined 'stringent cooperation between the Union agencies, including improving their information exchange' as one of the principles underlying the ISS. The Council's ISS specifically referred to COSI in this regard. Although not explicitly mentioned, COSI's responsibility for overseeing operational cooperation of course also implies a role as 'coordinator of the coordinators' in internal security. In fact, inter-agency cooperation has been one of the Committee's priorities from the outset. The COSI Decision states that it shall exercise its coordinating role without prejudice to the powers of the agencies, yet it risks drawing these agencies back into the sphere of influence of the Council, despite the entry into force of the Lisbon Treaty.[119]

The cooperation between JHA agencies precedes COSI's establishment. That cooperation received a boost when the establishment of COSI was postponed due to the failure of the Constitutional Treaty.[120] Since 2005, the heads of JHA agencies have been meeting on an annual basis. The secretariat of these meetings rotates amongst the agencies annually. Many agencies have developed bilateral relations in the form of working arrangements – also with non-JHA agencies – which allow for practical cooperation and information exchange.

An important principled decision was taken as early as 2008, when the heads of the EU JHA agencies agreed that they would consider each other's confidentiality

[116] J Parkin, 'EU Home Affairs Agencies and the Construction of EU Internal Security' (2012) CEPS, Working Paper No 53, December 2012.

[117] EU Policy Cycle: Implementation Monitoring, Council Document 11246/1/12, 19 June 2012, 7.

[118] European Parliament resolution of 25 October 2011 on organised crime in the European Union (PE 454.687v04-00), rapporteur Alfano.

[119] Art 3(1), COSI Decision.

[120] Council Document 9596/1/06, 22 May 2006.

rules/security regulations as equivalent.[121] In practice, however, the exchange of information has been hampered by Member States' reluctance to allow the onward sharing of information from one agency to another.[122] The exchange of classified information between JHA agencies and the institutions – as well as between JHA agencies themselves – has often required administrative agreements to this effect, as well as secured communication lines.

The 2013 Europol proposal illustrates the legal complexities of data exchange, although for the first time providing a clear legal basis for such exchange. The proposal regulates the access of OLAF, the Commission's Anti-fraud Office, as well as EUROJUST to the data it holds.[123] Data, including personal data, can in principle be freely exchanged with other JHA agencies,[124] subject to the originators' possibility to limit the exchange.[125] The Agency must ensure the security of processing of personal data,[126] and establish its own security rules on classified information following the basic principles and minimum standards of the Council's security rules for protecting EU classified information.[127]

In October 2009 the Swedish Presidency made a request to four agencies – Eurojust, Europol, CEPOL and Frontex – to evaluate and improve their cooperation. In June 2010 a final report was adopted and submitted to COSI, containing a list of areas for improvement.[128] A contact group was established, overseeing its implementation, and a score board developed to monitor the follow-up.[129] This score board is a 'living document' and is regularly updated.[130] It lists, amongst others, common approaches towards rules such as data protection, the mutual consultation on work programmes and possible joint operational activities or training on shared thematic priorities.

The cooperation between agencies is likely to receive a new boost as a result of the new approach towards agencies and the aim to improve their governance, efficiency, accountability and overall coherence.[131] COSI has argued that it has the remit and competence to promote operational cooperation and to facilitate coordination and should therefore be the appropriate body to take further initiatives to facilitate and to enhance cooperation and operational efficiency.[132] At the same time the agencies have expressed the importance of their operational and legal autonomy.[133] COSI's role in the coordination of JHA agencies once again draws supposedly autonomous EU bodies back into the sphere of the Council.

[121] Council Document 11644/08, 9 July 2008.
[122] M Busuioc and D Curtin, above (n 95) 9.
[123] Art 27.
[124] Arts 29(2) and 30.
[125] Art 25.
[126] Art 38.
[127] Art 69. Council Decision 2011/292/EU, OJ 2011 L141/17.
[128] Council Document 8387/10, 14 April 2010.
[129] Council Document 18077/11, 5 December 2011.
[130] Council Document 5968/13, 1 February 2013.
[131] Common Approach, above (n 53).
[132] Council Document 6127/13, 7 February 2013.
[133] Council Document 5968/13, 1 February 2013.

For now it seems that the inter-agency cooperation has remained a very bottom-up approach, with the heads of JHA agencies reporting to COSI instead of COSI actively steering this process. If there is to be a more active role for COSI in the future, it is important that the limitation of COSI's remit to internal security does not exclude agencies such as the FRA and EASO, so as to ensure that the justice dimension of the AFSJ is also represented.

V. CONCLUSION: FAST FORWARD IN THE SHADOW OF AN INTERGOVERNMENTAL PAST

The overall picture that emerges from the developments discussed in this chapter is that of a policy field in full motion, growing steadily accustomed to its new legal framework, thereby resembling ever more traditional fields of EU competence. Obvious traces of the intergovernmental past do remain. These show most clearly in the executive implementation of this policy field. Sub-institutional actors, in particular agencies, continue to play a pivotal role in furthering integration in the AFSJ, increasingly forming a true JHA bureaucracy at EU level. The Council continues to play a prominent role in this coordination of these agencies through COSI. In general, this Committee allows the Council to retain important influence over priority-setting in the AFSJ, to the exclusion of the Commission and even more so the European Parliament.

Although there is a danger that the justice dimension of the AFSJ is too easily overlooked, especially in the field of internal security, there does seem to be a genuine desire to improve democratic scrutiny and ensure respect for fundamental rights. One may expect that former third pillar agencies such as Europol and Eurojust will soon come to fall under similar accountability mechanisms as their 'Community' counterparts. An agency such as Frontex is subject to ever closer scrutiny.

Yet, 'more of the same' seems too easy an answer to these concerns. By its very nature the AFSJ cannot be equated with more traditional EU policy fields. The multi-level nature of JHA cooperation, its inherent operational character and the fact that genuine executive – most importantly coercive – powers continue to lie in the hands of the Member States make it difficult to pin-point exactly who is to be held accountable and to whom. The shift in focus of the role of JHA agencies as information hubs for the collection, dissemination and facilitation of the exchange of information, rather than as genuine operational actors may show that the limits of operational cooperation under the current legal framework are in sight.

Despite its affirmation that Member States are ultimately responsible for internal security, the Lisbon Treaty seems to have left some room for a transfer of executive power to the exclusion of the Member States. The creation of a prosecutor and the gradual establishment of a European System of Border Guards could imply carrying over genuine enforcement powers to the EU level. Such steps would, however, have profound implications for the nature of the EU legal order and the relation between the EU, its Member States, and ultimately its citizens.

The Lisbon Treaty almost fully 'communitarised' the AFSJ, but the treaty drafters did not ask themselves whether this constitutional set up is actually suitable for deeper integration based not on substantive harmonisation but on joint operational activity. Future treaty reforms may need to better reflect the realities of JHA cooperation. More importantly, they will need to engage with the fundamental question of whether the Union is to remain a coordinator and facilitator or should rather become a decision-making actor in the AFSJ.

5

Fundamental Rights and Judicial Protection

THEODORE KONSTADINIDES AND NOREEN O'MEARA

I. INTRODUCTION

WHILE EU MEASURES related to criminal and security law have been adopted for the past 20 years, the legal framework of the Treaty of Lisbon and the political impetus behind the Stockholm Programme have given them a new direction. This chapter explores the basis of protection of fundamental rights enshrined in Title V, Chapter 4 of the TFEU entitled 'Judicial Cooperation in Criminal Matters and the Stockholm Programme'. This analysis is all the more important in the light of the new legal status attributed to the EU Charter of Fundamental Rights and the EU's prospective accession to the European Convention on Human Rights (ECHR). The chapter, therefore, also discusses whether these reforms will respond to allegations that fundamental rights and, in particular, the procedural constitutional right to judicial protection are taken for granted in the area of freedom, security and justice (AFSJ).[1] The Treaty of Lisbon has created a surfeit of rights protection by inserting a provision in the Treaty which aims to expand the scope of fundamental rights protection in EU law. As such, Article 6(1) TEU provides that the Charter has the same legal value as the treaties, raising it to primary law status, while Article 6(2) TEU not only provides for the possibility of EU accession to the ECHR, but expressly requires it.[2] In respect of the legal status of the Charter, references to it were increasing in frequency at the Court of Justice of the European Union (ECJ) even prior to the entry into force of the Treaty of Lisbon. Its 'primary importance' in ECJ case law has been recognised by the Presidents of both the ECJ and the European Court of Human Rights (ECtHR).[3] Notwithstanding the preparedness of the ECJ to invoke the ECHR when interpreting EU law, the

[1] E Guild et al, 'Challenges and Prospects for the EU's Area of Freedom, Security and Justice' (2009) CEPS Working Document No 313/April 2009, 2.

[2] Art 6(2) TEU provides that the EU 'shall accede' to the Convention. The respective entries into force of Protocol 14 ECHR, and Art 6 TEU, Lisbon Treaty provided the required bases for EU accession to the ECHR.

[3] Joint Communication from Presidents Costa and Skouris, 27 January 2011, available at: www.echr.coe.int.

eventual accession of the EU to the ECHR will raise questions concerning the relationships between the ECJ and ECtHR, and the extent and ease of convergence in the area of fundamental rights protection. Both the legally binding status of the Charter and the constitutional power of the EU to seek accession to the ECHR will have a qualitative and quantitave effect upon EU criminal law with reference to the rights of defendants and victims.

More specifically in criminal matters, the Treaty of Lisbon has abolished the former intergovernmental third pillar and brought its criminal justice aspects within the scope of EU law proper. Hence, with the Treaty of Lisbon coming into force, the third pillar's new home became the area of freedom, security and justice (AFSJ), a vast legal area consisting of immigration and asylum policies, as well as civil cooperation matters. Most significantly, the 'communitarisation' of the third pillar brought about by the Treaty of Lisbon encompasses a shift from unanimity to qualified majority voting and a changing of form of legal acts concerning criminal matters from conventions and framework decisions to the more robust directives. This is particularly important for the centralised enforcement of these provisions by the Commission, their invocability and decentralised enforcement by private individuals, and, ultimately, their justiciability before the ECJ whose jurisdiction extends to all EU law including the AFSJ.

With reference to the Stockholm Programme, it can be argued that if the Treaty of Lisbon altered the legal infrastructure in the field of criminal law and security law, the Stockholm Programme provided the necessary political stimulus for the realisation of the criminal justice objectives of the AFSJ based on a common foundation of democratic principles, respect for human rights, and fundamental freedoms. Building on the priorities of the earlier Tampere and Hague multi-annual programmes, the Stockholm Programme set out the European Union's priorities for the AFSJ for the period 2010–14.

This chapter focuses on whether the changes brought about by Lisbon and Stockholm indicate the strengthening or weakening of the protection of fundamental rights in this policy area. We place particular focus on effective judicial protection vis-à-vis common minimum standards of procedural rights in criminal proceedings. The chapter commences with an analysis of the implications of the Lisbon reforms, especially with reference to the binding status of the Charter and future accession of the EU to the ECHR. It then moves on to discuss Lisbon's fundamental rights protection and the legislative opportunities it provides with reference to individual judicial protection. Last but not least, it provides a review of the position accorded to fundamental rights and judicial protection within the Stockholm Programme.

II. IMPLICATIONS OF THE CHARTER'S BINDING STATUS AFTER LISBON

Before the entry into force of the Treaty of Lisbon, the non-binding character of the Charter did not prevent Advocates General (AG) and judges of the European

Courts from making occasional references to the Charter. After Lisbon, the impact of the Charter on ECJ case law was immediate, with the ECJ engaging with the Charter on an increasingly systematic and comprehensive basis.[4] Judicial recourse to the Charter soon moved beyond using it as an interpretative tool, to using the Charter as a basis for judicial review to annul secondary legislation.[5] Thus, whilst Presidents Costa and Skouris have jointly referred to the Charter's primary importance as the 'reference text and the starting point'[6] for the ECJ's assessment of fundamental rights, ECJ case law indicates real engagement with the Charter and a preparedness to exploit its legally binding nature to the fullest extent.

After Lisbon, given the overlap in fundamental rights protection offered by the Charter and the ECHR, a real test for adjudication is the degree of coherence achieved between Charter and Convention rights where such rights correspond. Article 52(3) of the Charter provides that, where rights protected by the Charter and Convention correspond, 'the meaning and scope of those rights shall be the same'.[7] The ECJ does appear to be engaging in the kind of 'parallel interpretation' of rights envisaged by the Charter in such cases, AG Opinions in particular placing detailed emphasis on systematic interpretation and cross-referencing between the guarantee of rights by the Charter and Convention. The Opinions of AG Cruz Villalón in *European Air Transport*[8] and AG Sharpston in *Volker* and *Eifert*[9] are early post-Lisbon examples that illustrate this engagement well, though references to the Convention were less detailed in the respective final ECJ judgments.

The impact of the Charter on the AFSJ in case law to date has been particularly striking in the *NS*[10] judgment (notwithstanding the argument that a similar result may well have been reached without recourse to the Charter). *NS* confirmed that EU law precludes the application of a conclusive presumption in relation to Member States' respect for fundamental rights, thus preventing the transfer of an asylum seeker to a Member State where he/she risks being subjected to inhuman or degrading treatment or punishment in violation of Article 4 of the Charter.[11] In clarifying the duties of Member States (including national courts) in respect of mutual recognition in the area of asylum, the ECJ was conscious that mutual

[4] See Joint Communication from Presidents Costa and Skouris, 27 January 2011, available at: www.echr.coe.int. The Joint Communication notes that the Charter was referred to in at least 30 judgments in the year following the Lisbon Treaty's entry into force.

[5] Joined Cases C-92/09 *Volker und Markus Schecke GbR* and C-93/09 *Hartmut Eifert v Land Essen* [2010] ECR I-0000.

[6] Joint Communication from Presidents Costa and Skouris, 27 January 2011, para 1, available at: www.echr.coe.int.

[7] Joint Communication, para 1.

[8] Case C-120/10 *European Air Transport SA v Collège d'Environnement de la Région de Bruxelles-Capitale*, Opinion of AG Cruz Villalón, 17 February 2011.

[9] Joined Cases C-92/09 *Volker und Markus Schecke GbR* and C-93/09 *Hartmut Eifert v Land Essen* [2010] ECR I-0000, Opinion of AG Sharpston, 17 June 2010.

[10] Joined cases C-411/10 and C-493/10 *NS v Secretary of State for the Home Department* and *ME et al v Refugee Applications Commission and Minister of Justice, Equality and Law Reform*, judgment of 21 December 2011.

[11] Note also *MSS v Belgium and Greece*, judgment of 21 January 2011 (ECtHR).

confidence is deeply rooted in the 'raison d'être' of the Union, the AFSJ and the Common European Asylum System. The Court's interpretation of Article 4 of the Charter demonstrates that the ECJ is mindful of the 'major operational problems' that can arise in a Member State, and of the overriding need to ensure asylum seekers' rights are not prejudiced by significant flaws in procedure or conditions, where there are substantial grounds to believe they exist.[12]

The 'spillover' effect of *NS* on the field of EU criminal justice is particularly evident in ECJ case law relating to the Framework Decision on the European Arrest Warrant (EAW).[13] A trend of recent cases on the execution of the EAW requests suggests that the approach of the ECJ is not as predictable as one might expect, and raises questions as to the interpretative approach where Convention and Charter rights correspond. The conceptual problems inherent in the Article 52(3) Charter's requirement to interpret corresponding Charter and Convention rights 'the same', noted by Beal and Hickman, may account for this apparent imbalance to some extent.[14] For example, in *Melloni*[15] both AG Bot and the Court's final judgment adopted a strict approach to refusals to execute (finding that an executing authority cannot make execution of an EAW conditional on the availability of judicial review of the issuing authority's decision) and to compatibility of the Framework Decision to the Charter (with scant references to the Convention). This contrasts with the Opinions in *Radu*[16] and, in a non-EAW context, *Fransson*[17] in which the level of protection on the facts appeared to be variously regarded by the ECJ as stronger in the Charter (*Radu*) and the Convention (*Fransson*). In a highly restrictive approach to fundamental rights, the recent judgment in *Radu*[18] illustrated a marked divergence from the Opinion of AG Sharpston, in ruling that a violation of fundamental rights in the issuing Member State (failure to hear the requested person) cannot per se justify non-execution of an EAW by a Member State under Articles 3 or 4 of the Framework Decision.[19] It is at least arguable that *Radu* may hint at a perhaps unwelcome 'sectoral' approach in fundamental rights protection in the AFSJ. In the context of the EAW, for example, *Radu* favours an unequivocal approach to mutual recognition, taking a strictly textual approach to the duty to execute at the expense of wider fundamental rights considerations that arguably underpin the Framework Decision itself.[20] By contrast, *NS* expressly indicated that

[12] *NS* (n 10) para 81.

[13] Framework Decision 2002/584/JHA on the European Arrest Warrant and the surrender procedures between Member States, OJ 2002 L190/1.

[14] K Beal and T Hickman, 'Beano No More: The EU Charter of Rights after Lisbon' (2011) *Judicial Review* 113, 117–19.

[15] Case C-399/11 *Melloni*, Opinion of AG Bot, 2 October 2012.

[16] Case C-396/11 *Radu*, Opinion of AG Sharpston, 18 October 2012.

[17] Case C-617/10 *Åkerberg Fransson*, Opinion of AG Cruz Villalón, 12 June 2012.

[18] Case C-396/11 *Radu*, judgment of 29 January 2013.

[19] Council Framework Decision 2002/584/JHA of 13 January 2002, as amended by Council Framework Decision 2009/299/JHA of 26 February 2009.

[20] See, eg detailed arguments advanced by AG Sharpston in *Radu* suggesting that a narrow approach excluding fundamental rights considerations from the decision on executing an EAW is not supported by either the wording of the Framework Decision on the EAW or relevant case law.

the presumption that Member States respect their fundamental rights obligations under the Charter and Convention in the field of asylum is not 'conclusive'.[21] While it is very early days for the case law in these areas, it is notable that in these early, landmark cases this fundamental presumption seems to be regarded differently by the ECJ across AFSJ fields.

This trend not only demonstrates the spillover effect of *NS* on criminal law cases – that is that 'mutual recognition' does not extend to Member States' compatibility with human rights guarantees. It also reveals the stark contrast in AG approaches when it comes to balancing the sources of fundamental rights at its disposal and to clarifying the Charter's impact, and – in the light of *Radu* – a diverging approach between AGs and the ECJ that may have sectoral consequences within the AFSJ. The ECJ has opportunities to address these imbalances and inject coherency in future cases. Its approach(es) may have an important impact on the interpretation of rights in the AFSJ context more generally.

III. EU ACCESSION TO THE ECHR AFTER LISBON

Further efforts to enhance the protection of fundamental rights will be realised with the EU's accession to the ECHR. Although the Draft Legal Instruments on the Accession of the European Union to the European Convention on Human Rights were tabled on 30 June 2011,[22] negotiations are continuing. Despite Article 6(2) TEU's requirement that the EU 'shall accede' to the Convention, the drafting process has raised complex questions which remain on the table for negotiators, and the scale of agreements needed could yet delay the process for some time. The Council of Europe Steering Committee for Human Rights (CDDH) has been in negotiations with the EU in the '*ad hoc* group' since June 2012 with a view to concluding a final Agreement.[23] Upon accession, the EU will become the 48th High Contracting Party to the Convention and the first non-state signatory.

Subjecting the EU to the external scrutiny of the ECtHR in respect of rights guaranteed under the Convention will place the EU on the same footing as the other High Contracting Parties in terms of external review of compliance with the ECHR. This exposure of the EU to external scrutiny is where accession will make its mark, rather than necessarily causing material changes in the level of fundamental rights protection at national or EU levels.[24] It is therefore the political and symbolic value of EU accession that tends to be welcomed, with views on

[21] *NS* (n 10) para 105.

[22] Draft Legal Instruments on the Accession of the European Union to the European Convention on Human Rights, 16 CDDH-UE (2011).

[23] Negotiations requested by the Committee of Ministers were scheduled for June 2012–January 2013; CM/Del/Dec (2011) 1126/4.1, COM(2011) 149, 13 June 2012.

[24] T Lock, 'End of an Epic? The Draft Agreement on the EU's Accession to the Convention' (2012) 31 *Yearbook of European Law* 162.

the substantive impact of accession rather more circumspect,[25] and some views expressed in European Parliament debates openly hostile.[26] It is clearly possible, however, that accession may impact on the detail with which the Convention is explicitly applied by the ECJ in relation to relevant Charter rights.

The Draft Accession Agreement envisages the creation of two main mechanisms to accommodate EU accession and the future closer engagement between the ECtHR and the ECJ.[27] First, the introduction of a co-respondent mechanism would govern how and to whom complaints will be addressed. Second, prior involvement of the ECJ would allow it to make a pronouncement on the compatibility of EU legal acts with ECHR rights, in the event that such an issue reaches the ECtHR before the ECJ has had an opportunity to adjudicate on the point in question. It has been mooted that the reform in Protocol 16 ECHR on extending the ECtHR's advisory jurisdiction to include 'advisory opinions' might be used or somehow adapted for the prior involvement mechanism. When the Draft Accession Agreement was tabled for adoption by the CDDH in October 2011[28] a number of delegations raised objections and/or reserved their views on aspects of the Draft Accession Agreement. While both mechanisms have been extensively critiqued in the literature, the draft provisions regulating to them may yet be subject to change.

The future contours of rights-based case law are often hard to predict, and speculating on developments or legal challenges arising as a result of EU accession remains premature without the final text of the Agreement. The value of accession in reinforcing the centrality of fundamental rights protection in the EU legal order, and on a practical level, subjecting the EU to external scrutiny should not be underestimated. The relationships between the ECtHR and ECJ may be tested, and emerging case law closely scrutinised in cases involving overlap between core Charter and Convention rights, with draft legislation coming under renewed scrutiny for compatibility with the Charter and ECHR. Commissioner Reding's

[25] FG Jacobs, 'The European Convention on Human Rights, the EU Charter of Fundamental Rights and the Court of Justice of the European Union – The Impact of European Union Accession to the European Convention on Human Rights' in I Pernice, J Kokott and C Saunders (eds), *The Future of the European Judicial System in a Comparative Perspective* (Baden-Baden, Nomos Verlag, 2006) 291. In contrast, note Leskinen's arguments in respect of the potential impact accession may have on the regulation of defences in competition proceedings: C Leskinen, 'An Evaluation of Rights of the Defense during Antitrust Inspections in the Light of the Case Law of the ECtHR: Would the Accession of the European Union to the ECHR bring about a Significant Change?' (2010) Working Paper IE Law School, No 10-04, 29 April 2010.

[26] Note, eg European Parliament – EU accession to the ECHR (debate), 19 April 2012.

[27] On the functioning of the proposed 'internal review' mechanism providing for the prior involvement of the ECJ in specific cases where the ECtHR exercises its power of 'external review', see further: S Douglas-Scott, 'The European Union and Human Rights after Lisbon' (2011) 11 *Human Rights Law Review* 645; J-P Jacqué, 'The Accession of the European Union to the European Convention of Human Rights and Fundamental Freedoms' (2011) 48 *CML Rev* 995; T Lock 'Walking on a Tightrope: The Draft Accession Agreement and the Autonomy of the EU Legal Order' (2011) 48 *CML Rev* 1025; N O'Meara, '"A More Secure Europe of Rights?" The European Court of Human Rights, the Court of Justice of the European Union and EU Accession to the ECHR' (2011) 12 *German Law Journal* 1813.

[28] Report to the Committee of Ministers on the elaboration of legal instruments for the accession of the European Union to the European Convention of Human Rights, CDDH (2011) 009.

statement that EU accession will increase the perception of the ECtHR as 'the European capital of fundamental rights protection'[29] does not diminish the duties of all courts to robustly adjudicate in defence of fundamental rights protection. The agreed legal instruments for EU accession have been long-anticipated; it is to be hoped that political will accelerates progress towards accession rather than create fresh obstacles or further delays.

IV. FUNDAMENTAL RIGHTS PROTECTION IN CRIMINAL MATTERS AFTER LISBON

Fundamental rights concerns with regard to judicial cooperation relate predominantly to adopted acts on mutual legal assistance, extradition, execution of sentences and the rights of the accused and the victim. In line with the principle of mutual recognition, the AFSJ presumption is that all Member States have a sufficient system of criminal procedure in place which contains a satisfactory level of fundamental rights protection. The idea is that the establishment of equal standards of fundamental rights protection across the EU will ultimately enhance mutual trust between Member States. The only explicit rule with reference to the protection of fundamental rights in AFSJ matters is the generic Article 6 EU which reinforces the centrality of fundamental rights protection in EU law. In this context reference is made to a three-layered fundamental rights shield: the Charter of Fundamental Rights (now legally binding), the ECHR (and the EU's prospective accession to it), and the constitutional traditions common to the Member States (now as relevant as ever in light of Article 4(2) TEU). The latter, together with the ECHR, constitute the general principles of EU law protected by the ECJ.[30] These enjoy primary law status.

Despite the thorough commitment expressed in the EU Treaty, fundamental rights protection with regard to EU criminal matters has traditionally enjoyed an ambivalent status, partly because penal law lay outside the scope of the former third pillar. Equally, before the Lisbon Treaty, individual judicial protection was never at the core of EU judicial cooperation in criminal matters. Three areas are worth highlighting with reference to the pre-Lisbon jurisdiction of the ECJ:

i) the preliminary reference procedure was subject to the former Article 35 TEU limitations where Member States had to make a declaration as to whether they accept the ECJ's jurisdiction;
ii) the third pillar instruments listed in former Article 34 TEU (framework decisions and conventions) had no direct effect; and

[29] Proceedings High Level Conference on the Future of the European Court of Human Rights, Council of Europe 2010, 26; see further M Kuijer, 'The Accession of the European Union to the ECHR: A Gift for the ECHR's 60th Anniversary or an Unwelcome Intruder at the Party?' (2011) 3 *Amsterdam Law Forum* 17, 31.

[30] For a detailed study of the general principles of EU law, see T Tridimas, *The General Principles of EU Law*, 2nd edn (Oxford, Oxford University Press, 2006).

iii) private individuals could not resort to an action for annulment to challenge effectively, for instance, the legality of a framework decision. This could only be done by the Commission or the Member States.[31]

The light-touch involvement of EU law in this area was due largely to the divergence of criminal justice systems in the Member States, especially in relation to rules of criminal procedure.

The above sentiment is partly manifest to this day. For instance, the UK Government recently stressed that it 'will approach forthcoming legislation in the area of criminal justice on a case-by-case basis, with a view to maximising our country's security, protecting Britain's civil liberties and preserving the integrity of our criminal justice systems'.[32] Indeed, crime definitions and the rights enjoyed by suspects and victims still vary considerably between Member States. As such, the establishment of a European 'area' of security and justice is a relatively slow process. Until the EU reaches a stage of convergence in criminal justice matters, individuals will continue to be subject to the varying requirements inherent in different penal regimes. Such requirements not only differ between Member States with regard to what type of conduct is criminal and punishable but also, and perhaps most significantly, with reference to substantive rights and procedural safeguards applicable in every case. For instance, there is a significant variation in the method and timing of the right of access to a lawyer in criminal proceedings across the EU. This is a single example, but perhaps sufficient to reveal the general fallacy of the AFSJ presumption of equivalence of criminal justice systems across the continent. The EU needs, therefore, a system of criminal law which is not merely based on a blind, or sometimes superficial, presumption of equivalence between Member States. The proliferation of EU criminal legislation and case law requires a system which is based on rigid checks, balances and periodic assessments. Only when due process, a principle rooted at the heart of all advanced legal systems, is guaranteed, will mutual recognition be capable of strengthening mutual trust among the judiciaries of the Member States.

The above argument demonstrates that the issue of fundamental rights protection in the AFSJ turns on the more complex question of how national differences in criminal law can be reconciled and ultimately resolved. Typical questions include, for instance, whether all Member States shall share an agreed list of cross-border crimes as well as establish a number of essential aspects of criminal procedure. Chapter 4 of the TFEU, entitled 'Judicial Cooperation in Criminal Matters', purports to answer this question in the positive. The Lisbon Treaty, therefore, presents a system based on mutual legal assistance which also leaves open the possibility for the EU to legislate on criminal and procedural law. Article 82(1) TFEU stresses that judicial cooperation in criminal matters shall be based on the principle of mutual recognition and shall include the approximation of national

[31] See Case C-303/05 *Advocaten voor de Wereld* [2007] ECR I-3633.

[32] *Hansard*, Written Ministerial Statements, The Lord Chancellor and Secretary of State for Justice (Kenneth Clarke), 5 September 2011, col 12WS.

laws. It further provides for institutional support through the adoption of measures which have as their objective the facilitation of jurisdictional conflicts and recognition of judgments in all cases.

Article 82(2) TFEU, on the other hand, elaborates further by providing for the enactment of minimum harmonisation directives in order to enable mutual recognition of judgments in criminal matters with a cross-border dimension. Such legislation, including procedural rights and the rights of victims, can be directly effective provided that it satisfies the relevant *Van Gend en Loos* criteria.[33] Still, however, one should not forget that paragraph 3 of both Article 82 TFEU (and to the same extent Article 83 TFEU) provides for an emergency brake which aims to make the idea of EU criminal law more palatable to Member States.[34]

V. JUDICIAL PROTECTION IN CRIMINAL MATTERS AFTER LISBON

With reference to effective judicial protection, it is by now well-established that the protection of the rights of the individual in criminal proceedings is a fundamental value of EU law and essential in order to maintain mutual recognition between Member States' practices and public confidence in the EU. It was not until the Lisbon Treaty that the preliminary reference procedure was expedited under Article 267 TFEU 'in a case pending before a court or tribunal of a Member State with regard to a person in custody'. Hence, it can be argued that the Lisbon Treaty assisted in the adaptation of the preliminary reference procedure to address the needs of the AFSJ. Of course, such adaptation of preliminary rulings is bound to be excluded under Article 276 TFEU from reviewing

> the validity or proportionality of operations carried out by the police or other law-enforcement services of a Member State or the exercise of the responsibilities incumbent upon Member States with regard to the maintenance of law and order and the safeguarding of internal security.

Since a person's rights in respect of a criminal charge, trial, and sentence are strictly confined within the national boundaries of Member States, the mutual recognition threshold has to depend on a high level of trust between judicial authorities. Furthermore, procedural rules need to respond to equivalent guarantees in relation to an individual's liberty. This is a rather thorny task, especially since the adoption and implementation of minimum standards of procedural rights across the Member States was never a precondition to the adoption of EU criminal legislation under the former third pillar. For instance, the Framework

[33] This is a lot more straightforward compared to the *Pupino* duty of consistent interpretation. See E Herlin Karnell, 'In the Wake of *Pupino*: *Advocaten voor de Wereld* and *Dell'Orto*' (2007) 8 *German Law Journal* 1147; Case 26/62 *Van Gend en Loos* [1963] ECR 1; Case C-105/03 *Pupino* [2005] ECR I-5285.

[34] See A Hinarejos, JR Spencer and S Peers, *Opting Out of EU Criminal Law: What is Actually Involved?* (CELS, September 2012). Note, however, the discussion in Peers' chapter in this volume about the likelihood or otherwise of use of that emergency brake. Available at: www.cels.law.cam.ac.uk/Media/working_papers/Optout%20text%20final.pdf.

Decision on the EAW does not foresee for Member States' refusal to surrender a suspect on grounds of concerns about human rights breaches.[35] There is a host of other issues in need of attention. These include suspects' entitlement to legal representation during surrender, pre-trial detention length and conditions, as well as proportionality checks regarding extradition requests for minor offences.[36]

To that end, the EU has aspired to establish common minimum standards of procedural rights in criminal proceedings, to ensure that the basic rights of suspects and accused persons are sufficiently protected. In 2004, the Commission proposed a draft framework decision on rights for criminal suspects that covered five basic rights. The proposal was met with dissent from six Member States (UK, Ireland, Malta, Cyprus, the Czech Republic and Slovakia). It was generally accepted that such a proposal contravened the principle of subsidiarity (also perhaps national identity under Article 4(2) TEU)[37] and compromised the rights already guaranteed by the ECHR.[38] It was not until 2009 that the Council agreed on a general approach to procedural rights of suspected or accused persons in criminal proceedings.[39] In this fashion, a proposal under Article 82(2) TFEU for a directive on the right of access to a lawyer in criminal proceedings and on the right to communicate upon arrest was put forward in order to set out minimum rules between the Member States. This proposal is in line with the rights guaranteed under the ECHR and the Charter.[40] Most importantly, the proposal emphasises that the rights provided for in this directive should also apply, mutatis mutandis, to proceedings for the execution of an EAW in the executing state and, in some cases, also in the issuing state. This is a welcome development and seems to remedy the current regime under which defence lawyers in either country cannot coordinate or jointly evaluate the evidence available throughout judicial proceedings. Yet, the UK decided to opt out (at least for the time being) because it was felt that certain provisions in the Commission's proposal go beyond the requirements of the ECHR and would, therefore, have an adverse impact on the UK's ability to investigate and prosecute offences.[41] Hence, the final wording of the Directive's Recital 33 will depend on the

[35] See further, Case C-396/11 *Radu*, judgment of 29 January 2013; discussed at s II, above.

[36] M Fichera, 'The European Arrest Warrant and the Sovereign State: A Marriage of Convenience?' (2009) 15 *European Law Journal* 70; J Komárek, 'European Constitutionalism and the European Arrest Warrant: In Search of the Limits of "Contrapunctual Principles"' (2007) 44 *CML Rev* 16; T Konstadinides, 'The Europeanization of Extradition: How Many Light Years away to Mutual Confidence?' in C Eckes and T Konstadinides (eds), *Crime within the Area of Freedom, Security and Justice: A European Public Order* (Cambridge, Cambridge University Press, 2011).

[37] See to that effect, T Konstadinides, 'Constitutional Identity as a Shield and as a Sword: The European Legal Order within the Framework of National Constitutional Settlement' (2011) 13 *Cambridge Yearbook of European Legal Studies* 195.

[38] See J Smyth, 'Irish lead resistance to draft EU law on suspects' rights', *The Irish Times*, 2007. Available at: www.ecba.org/extdocserv/projects/ps/Irish_lead_resistance_to_draft_EU_law_on_suspects.pdf.

[39] Council of the EU, 'Procedural Rights in Criminal Proceedings' 23 October 2009, 14828/09 (Presse 305).

[40] Arts 6 (right to a fair trial) and 8 (respect for private and family life) ECHR; and Arts 6 (right to liberty and security), 47 (effective remedy and fair trial), and 48 (presumption of innocence and the right of defence) of the EU Charter.

[41] HC Deb 11 October 2011, Written Ministerial Statements, 11 October 2011, col 17WS.

position of the UK and Ireland taken in accordance with the provisions of Protocol 21 of the TFEU.

Together with the strengthening of procedural rights of suspects or accused persons in criminal proceedings, there is also an urge to strengthen victims' rights with regard to information; access to victim support services; the right to be heard; and protection during criminal proceedings. The EU has already acted in the past on the rights of victims in criminal proceedings through Framework Decision 2001/220/JHA on the standing of victims in criminal proceedings and through Directive 2004/80/EC relating to compensation to crime victims. The recent proposal for a directive on establishing minimum standards on the rights, support and protection to victims of crime is indicative of the new approach under Article 82(2) TFEU to establishing common minimum rules. The objective is to build mutual trust through the approximation of national substantive rules on victims' rights as part of a range of EU policies relating to cross-border crime.[42] Hence, the proposal for a directive on victims' rights builds on existing legislation on human trafficking;[43] sexual abuse, exploitation of children and child pornography[44] and counter-terrorism.[45] The directive further complements the European Protection Order, endorsed by the European Parliament in December 2011, which provides protection of victims of violence when they move within the EU.[46]

VI. FUNDAMENTAL RIGHTS AND JUDICIAL PROTECTION IN CRIMINAL MATTERS AFTER STOCKHOLM

The Stockholm Programme builds on previous political agendas in outlining the EU's priorities for criminal justice measures and cooperation in a programme that expressly puts the citizen at its core.[47] Agreed simultaneously with the entry into force of the Lisbon Treaty, the Stockholm Programme could take advantage of the constitutional and institutional reforms provided by Lisbon; the 'communatarisation' of the former third pillar and its consequences (transfer to ordinary legislative procedure, relaxation of voting thresholds) increased the scope for a more vigorous pursuit of Stockholm's legislative agenda.[48] Moreover, an Action Plan implementing the Stockholm Programme contained a timetable for the adoption of all AFSJ measures up to 2014.[49]

[42] COM(2011) 275 final.

[43] Directive 2011/36/EU.

[44] Directive under negotiation to repeal Framework Decision 2004/68/JHA.

[45] Framework Decision 2008/919/JH.

[46] European Parliament, 'Parliament endorses European Protection Order for crime victims' 13 December 2011, available at: www.europarl.europa.eu/news.

[47] See further, S Coutts, 'Citizenship of the European Union' ch 6 in this volume.

[48] C Murphy, 'The European Evidence Warrant: Mutual Recognition and Mutual (Dis)trust?' in C Eckes and T Konstadinides (eds), *Crime within the Area of Freedom, Security and Justice: A European Public Order* (Cambridge, Cambridge University Press, 2011) 245–47.

[49] See Commission, 'Delivering an area of freedom, security and justice for Europe's citizens: Action Plan Implementing the Stockholm Programme' (Communication) COM(2010) 171 final, 20 April 2010, Annex.

These multiannual programmes shaping the development of the AFSJ face criticism on a number of fronts. For example, some past criticism has focused on the problem of a democratic deficit, with all priorities agreed in the European Council; though agreement of the Stockholm Programme was more transparent than the previous initiatives.[50] The security-oriented Hague Programme, agreed in the shadow of the 2001 New York and Washington DC attacks and the 2004 Madrid bombings, was strongly criticised for failing to strike the right balance between demands for security cooperation and underlying ethical and legal standards for fundamental rights protection. As Guild observes, the vocabulary relating to 'striking a balance' between security concerns and fundamental rights considerations, so prominent in the Hague Programme, is notably absent from the Stockholm Programme.[51] It will take concrete actions rather than a change of rhetoric to convince critics that this balance is struck in favour of fundamental rights protection – particularly as much of Stockholm clearly builds on pre-existing priorities and legislation, which, without exception, have implications for liberty and/or security considerations.

The Stockholm Programme sought to place the citizen at the heart of AFSJ initiatives, the language infusing the text emphasising citizenship and fundamental rights, with aims to overcome existing areas of fragmentation.[52] The Programme also has an external dimension, focusing on access to the Union and its role in a globalised world. The Programme's policy priorities are grouped under five main areas. The first of these, 'A Europe of Rights' focuses primarily on measures to protect the vulnerable (including children, victims of crime), criminal procedural rights, and rights relating to privacy and democratic participation). The second, 'A Europe of Law and Justice', focuses on the core AFSJ areas of mutual recognition in criminal and civil justice, and methods of developing and enhancing mutual trust. 'Europe's Security Strategy' is the focus of the third area, with priorities in relation to effectively exercising security priorities on the one hand, and a range of priorities against serious and organised crime on the other. A fourth area focuses on 'A Europe of Solidarity' in relation to asylum and migration, with a final category of priorities relating to external dimensions. Throughout, achieving the Stockholm priorities is envisaged with a combination of legislative proposals and dissemination of best practice.

Specifically in relation to judicial protection vis-à-vis procedural rights, the Stockholm Programme refers to the Roadmap for strengthening procedural rights of suspected accused persons in criminal proceedings, with a view to ultimately

[50] V Mitsilegas, 'General Report: The Area of Freedom, Security and Justice from Amsterdam to Lisbon. Challenges of Implementation, Constitutionality and Fundamental Rights' (FIDE, 2012) 77. Available at: www.fide2012.eu/index.php?doc_id=90.

[51] Guild et al, 'Challenges and Prospects for the EU's Area of Freedom, Security and Justice' (n 1) 4.

[52] The European Civil Liberties Network (ELCN) campaigned against the Stockholm Programme on the basis that it endangered 'the human rights situation in Europe and beyond'; 'Oppose the Stockholm Programme', Statement by the European Civil Liberties Network on the new five-year plan for Justice and Home Affairs, April 2009. Available at: www.ecln.org.

affording greater protection to the individual in the AFSJ.[53] The Roadmap may have sought to counter criticism that too much emphasis had been placed on prosecution-oriented procedure in the AFSJ due to its long-term overriding objective of driving forward mutual recognition, which some viewed as ultimately being at the expense of defence rights. On this front, the Hague Programme had failed to deliver on promised reforms.[54] In the light of the Charter's changing legal status and imminent EU accession to the ECHR, the time was ripe for the Stockholm agenda to deliver a re-balanced approach to procedural rights in criminal justice.

The Hague Programme's failure to deliver on the proposed Council Framework Decision on certain procedural rights in criminal proceedings,[55] or on watered-down versions of the proposals, has led to the Stockholm Programme taking an incremental approach to procedural rights.[56] This has been criticised in some quarters for the continued apparent lack of political commitment evident for setting minimum standards for fair trial rights and for failing to tackle the inherent structural shortcomings in relation to Article 6 ECHR; the results of which remained all too evident in the case law before the ECtHR.[57] Jimeno-Bulnes' suggestion that the continued block on the framework decision proposals by various Member States on the basis that Articles 5 and 6 ECHR sufficiently guarantee procedural rights, makes this criticism all the more ironic.[58]

The Roadmap's approach focuses on translation and interpretation; rights and information about charges; legal aid and provision of legal advice; the right to communication with relatives, employers and consular authorities; and safeguards for vulnerable suspects or accused persons; and pre-trial detention, with scope left by the Council to address other procedural rights. It is still too early to definitively conclude whether Stockholm will live up to expectations in providing concrete changes to secure defence rights. Yet at the mid-way stage, a range of legislative proposals, communications and Green Papers have been tabled.[59]

[53] Stockholm Programme, s 2.5. See, Presidency of the Council of the EU, Roadmap with a view to fostering protection of suspected and accused persons in criminal proceedings, Brussels, 1 July 2009, document No 11457/09; Resolution of the Council of 30 November 2009 on a Roadmap for strengthening procedural rights of suspected or accused persons in criminal proceedings, OJ 2009 C295/4, December 2009.

[54] 'Justice, Freedom and Security in Europe Since 2005: An Evaluation of the Hague Programme and Action Plan' COM(2009) 263 final, 10 June 2009, 14.

[55] COM(2004) 328 final, 28 April 2004.

[56] While the overall Roadmap has a sectoral approach, limited horizontal changes have been agreed, eg in the area of judgments *in absentia*: Council Framework Decision 2009/299/JHA of 12 February 2009 amending Framework Decisions 2002/584/JHA, 2005/214/JHA, 2006/783/JHA and 2008/947/JHA.

[57] D Spielmann J, 'Justice in the EU – From the Citizens' Perspective' (ECBA Conference 2009, 22 July 2009).

[58] M Jimeno-Bulnes, 'Towards Common Standards on Rights of Suspected and Accused Persons in Criminal Proceedings in the EU?' CEPS Policy Paper, February 2010, 4. Available at: aei.pitt.edu/15104/1/Jimeno-Bulnes_on_rights_of_suspects.pdf.

[59] Note, eg Commission, 'Proposal for a directive of the European Parliament and of the Council on the right to interpretation and translation in criminal proceedings' COM(2010) 82, 9 March 2010; 'Proposal for a directive of the European Parliament and Council on the right to information in criminal

Whether this incremental approach will have a greater chance of securing political agreement, and result in a genuinely coherent approach to securing procedural rights post-Stockholm remains to be seen.

VII. CONCLUSION

Both the Lisbon Treaty and the Stockholm Programme appear to be catalysts for change in respect of judicial cooperation in criminal matters. On the one hand, the Treaty of Lisbon has influenced the legal geography and legislative culture in this area, whilst on the other, the Stockholm Programme has reaffirmed the priority the EU attaches to the protection of citizens and the fight against serious crime. Indeed in the EU today, justice and security are both legally and politically in the epicentre of EU policy-making on cross-border policing and judicial cooperation in criminal matters. Yet, the AFSJ remains a diamond in the rough. Not only this area is characterised by numerous opt-outs[60] but also, according to the Treaty's Transitional Protocol, the criminal aspects of the AFSJ will only be fully effective in December 2014.[61] In respect of the UK's position in relation to the AFSJ, the clock is ticking for its decision on whether to exercise a mass opt-out from approximately 130 pre-Lisbon measures on police and criminal justice.[62] The options available to the Government in terms of opting out *en masse* by the 31 May 2014 deadline provided by Protocol 36 of the Lisbon Treaty, and opting back into certain measures are currently under consideration by the Government. Action taken to opt back into police and criminal justice measures would naturally be subject to future negotiations at EU level.

Although the reforms provided or promised through Lisbon and Stockholm have not yet been fully realised, we are witnessing a rebalancing of fundamental rights and judicial protection that individuals derive from EU law. These legal and policy priorities, and the means of attaining them, have changed. Although this appears to be a positive development, there is a risk that it may mask certain constitutional dangers vis-à-vis national competence to preserve the authenticity and integrity of national criminal justice systems, and the potential overlap of a 'Europeanised' inventory of procedural rights with the rights long guaranteed by

proceedings' COM(2010) 392, 20 July 2010; 'Strengthening victims rights in the EU' (Communication) COM(2011) 274/275/276, 18 May 2011; 'Proposal for a directive of the European Parliament and of the Council on the right of access to a lawyer in criminal proceedings and on the right to communicate upon arrest' COM(2011) 326, 8 June 2011; 'Strengthening mutual trust in the European Judicial Area – A Green Paper on the application of EU criminal justice legislation in the field of detention' (Green Paper) COM(2011) 327, 14 June 2011.

[60] See A Hinarejos, JR Spencer, S Peers, 'Opting Out of EU Criminal Law: What is Actually Involved?' (2012) University of Cambridge Faculty of Law Research Paper No 25/2012, 1 September 2012.

[61] See E Herlin-Karnell, 'What Principles Drive (or Should Drive) European Criminal Law?' (2010) 11 *German Law Journal* 1115.

[62] Protocol 36, Treaty of Lisbon. The House of Lords EU Select Committee, Sub-Committee E (Justice and Institutions) is currently managing an inquiry into the options available and the implications of a block opt-out in 2014.

the ECHR. In this regard, a significant risk relates to the challenge faced by the ECJ in consistently interpreting the different sources of rights now available under EU law and the contribution of these sources to the enhancement of judicial protection in criminal matters. The fact that most of the changes discussed in this chapter are either tentative or forthcoming may render some of the conclusions drawn speculative but nonetheless instrumental to the EU's rights' discourse.[63]

Notwithstanding the fact that many of these developments are in flux, it is clear that EU criminal policies in relation to the AFSJ are among those most affected by the Lisbon Treaty. Two main streams of EU law scholarship are emerging in this context. A first (and overriding) category of scholarship focuses on tracing the impacts of institutional, procedural and substantive changes that have already occured or are about to take place – scholarship which focuses on EU legislation which aims at producing a unified, simplified and therefore efficient common framework where more justice and security are guaranteed.[64] To a lesser extent, there are studies which emphasise the AFSJ's potential as a single area in which fundamental rights are respected and protected;[65] an emerging area in which fundamental rights adjudication is still relatively nascent (and arguably inconsistent), and in which the fundamental rights discourse has, as yet, made a limited impact. Although this chapter has claimed to do the latter, both streams of literature reflect the main concerns of the EU vis-à-vis the AFSJ: to become a credible justice and security actor while guaranteeing the effective protection and promotion of fundamental rights.

[63] See E Spaventa, 'Federalisation versus Centralisation: Tensions in Fundamental Rights Discourse in the EU' in M Dougan and S Currie, *50 Years of the European Treaties: Looking Back and Thinking Forward* (Oxford, Hart Publishing, 2009) 343–64.

[64] See C Eckes and T Konstadinides (eds), *Crime within the Area of Freedom Security and Justice: A European Public Order* (Cambridge, Cambridge University Press, 2011).

[65] S Douglas-Scott, 'The Rule of Law in the European Union – Putting the Security into the Area of Freedom, Security and Justice' (2004) 29 *EL Rev* 219.

6

Citizenship of the European Union

STEPHEN COUTTS

I. INTRODUCTION

THIS CHAPTER PRESENTS an overview of Union citizenship under the Stockholm Programme. It therefore analyses the links made between citizenship and the AFSJ in the Stockholm Programme and investigates the possible institutional motivations for such an association. It concentrates on broader institutional and historic themes rather than substantive legal developments. More specifically it has two goals: first, to describe the association between the AFSJ and citizenship, from their initial separation in the Treaty of Maastricht to their more recent association; and secondly, to offer some possible explanations as to why this relationship developed in this way and why it has recently been strengthened. It will argue that this recent convergence marks a point in the constitutional maturing of both the AFSJ and Union citizenship and, alongside the related association with fundamental rights, should be placed in the broader shift in integration moving beyond a purely economic Union towards, for want of a better term, a more political union.[1] Furthermore, it should be kept in mind that this evolution is by definition dynamic. Thus, while the chapter presents the association of citizenship with the AFSJ principally as a reflection or symbol of past changes, it is also constitutive of those changes and their nature. This association thus itself influences a transformation in the AFSJ and citizenship. The line between reflecting or symbolising change and constituting change is a blurred one and, while the below analysis is focused primarily on the former, the latter remains implicit.

Section II outlines the historic relationship between the two areas that may have been considered ideal candidates for a joint treatment but the actual coming together of which was delayed until relatively recently, primarily in the context of the Stockholm Programme. Section III offers some explanations for this shift from the perspective of the AFSJ. The rise of the citizen in the context of the AFSJ is

[1] The chapter does not situate the association of citizenship and the AFSJ in the construction of a more *democratic* Union and the development of a common space of political discourse. Political here is simply used to describe the construction of a community of normative non-economic values.

linked to the shift from an area of intergovernmental to supranational integration and an increasing focus on the individual. In light of these changes citizenship was seen as a source of legitimacy for the AFSJ. Section IV attempts to explain this evolution from the perspective of citizenship. As with the AFSJ it is suggested that this is the culmination of a process of constitutional maturing, this time of a status beyond the purely economic, towards a membership status (somewhat ambiguously) enriched with normative meaning and associated with fundamental rights.

A caveat is necessary at this point: this chapter is a discussion of citizenship policies as they are represented in the Stockholm Programme, a policy document with no direct legal effect, and this chapter does not analyse specific substantive legal developments. Rather the thoughts presented below arise from policy formulations of political actors and necessarily need to be placed in light of other developments. We would be wise not to draw too definitive conclusions. What this chapter simply aims to do is describe the association that has been made in the Stockholm Programme, to offer some thoughts as to why it occurred and its possible implications. However, nor should we dismiss out of hand the importance of either treaty changes, rhetorical though they may be, or policy documents, particularly those such as the Stockholm Programme. They are initially proposed by the Commission and are subsequently adopted by the European Council – the closest thing the EU may have to an ultimate political authority. Furthermore these documents are wide-ranging programmes offering detailed instructions that, if the examples of the Tampere Conclusions and the Hague Programme prove anything, genuinely determine and inform the legislative agenda over the medium term. In short, while conclusions drawn from the Stockholm Programme, in particular in relation to citizenship, must necessarily be placed alongside other developments and in particular the Court's non-AFSJ citizenship jurisprudence, they do form part of the citizenship practice of the Union. At the very least this chapter may provide useful indications of the institutional discourse and perception on citizenship and its future in the context of the AFSJ.

II. UNION CITIZENSHIP AND THE AFSJ

Union citizenship and the forerunner of the AFSJ, the third pillar of the EU, justice and home affairs (JHA), were simultaneously introduced as part of the new European Union at the Treaty of Maastricht. Their subject matter would suggest that the two areas should be related. Both areas are fundamentally concerned with the position of the individual in the political and legal community. Indeed 'within the scope of the AFSJ are matters that are crucial to and indeed almost at the heart of constitutional law, concerning the relationship between the individual and public authorities'.[2] It relates to the exercise of public power over the individual,

[2] S Douglas-Scott, 'The EU's Area of Freedom, Security and Justice: A Lack of Fundamental Rights, Mutual Trust and Democracy?' (2008–09) 11 *Cambridge Yearbook of European Legal Studies* 53, 55.

an exercise classically legitimised in the European constitutional tradition by the recasting of individual subjects as citizens with a status combining political participation and fundamental rights.[3]

The difficulties in articulating and conceptualising exactly what the AFSJ as a whole, rather than its component parts, actually entails have been pointed out.[4] Nonetheless it would seem that both the general connotations and the individual policy fields were somehow related to notions of fundamental rights, the rule of law and the constitutional state, notions with which citizenship is, as a matter of history and theory, clearly associated.

A separate argument, more specific to European integration, also points to some sort of institutional link between citizenship and the AFSJ: their common origin in the free movement of persons. The status of Union citizens was to a large extent based on the pre-Maastricht position of the individual in the internal market and in particular his or her rights of free movement. Much of the logic of JHA cooperation was focused on addressing the 'security deficit' supposedly created by this free movement. Rights contained in the internal market, later transformed and constitutionalised by the development of citizenship, constitute the source of free movement. However its fullest realisation, the collapsing of border controls, remained contingent on a whole host of 'flanking policies' both to achieve the abolition of internal frontier controls thereby removing legal barriers to free movement and to compensate for the perceived resulting 'security deficit' by the development of a common (and indeed heavily securitised) external border, a fact explicitly recognised by the Court of Justice in *Wijsenbeek*.[5] Thus the obligation to abolish internal border controls 'presupposes harmonisation of the laws of the Member States governing the crossing of the external borders of the Community, immigration, the grant of visas, asylum and the exchange of information on those questions'.[6] In one sense the link between citizenship and the AFSJ was relatively straightforward. If Union citizenship is primarily concerned with the right of free movement, then the JHA (and subsequently the AFSJ) and its collected policy areas and provisions could simply be understood as the means of facilitating such free movement.

Given what might be seen as clear theoretical and functional links between citizenship and justice and home affairs, their separation in the original design of the Maastricht Treaty may have struck some as incongruous and legally incoherent: detaching citizenship from perhaps a central part of its substantiation and JHA policies from what may have been a useful vehicle for their legitimation.

This rather peculiar positioning of citizenship in relation to JHA policies in the Treaty of Maastricht did not, however, occur by accident. Citizenship is a loaded

[3] J Monar, 'A Dual Citizenship: The Citizenship of the European Union' in M La Torre (ed), *European Citizenshp: An Institutional Challange* (The Hague, Kluwer, 1998).

[4] See Neil Walkers by now classic introductory essay exploring the 'coherence' of the AFSJ. N Walker, 'In Search of the Area of Freedom, Security and Justice: A Constitutional Odyssey' in N Walker (ed), *Europe's Area of Freedom, Security and Justice* (Oxford, Oxford University Press, 2004).

[5] Case C-378/97 *Criminal proceedings against Florus Ariel Wijsenbeek* [1999] ECR I-6207.

[6] ibid para 40.

concept and its use by any non-state entity carries with it strong connotations of political ambition. Presenting citizenship as 'merely' the continuation and codification of rights already acquired under the internal market, and denuding it of other potentially more politically charged implications was a conscious strategy pursued by negotiators in order to make it unthreatening to Member States. Citizenship was separated not only from justice and home affairs but also from fundamental rights in a deliberate attempt to render it uncontroversial and therefore acceptable. Anderson, den Boer and Miller point out that

> [t]here was an early consensus among the negotiators that a series of more sensitive issues, including border controls and internal security, should be deliberately excluded from [citizenship's] terms of reference and relegated to the separate pillar. It was undoubtedly this strategy of separation which made it possible for the British, among others, eventually to accept citizenship . . . another factor in making the subject of citizenship more palatable to the member states was the tacit agreement to avoid any notion of 'fundamental rights'. This had two different aspects. The first was the omission in the citizenship provisions of any reference to human rights . . . In the second place, the Treaty avoids any presentation of citizenship rights in a formal document like a charter addressed directly to the citizen.[7]

The Treaty of Maastricht therefore constructed a half-way house: providing the elements of a more political union, namely citizenship, justice and home affairs and some mention of fundamental rights, but not combining them in a meaningful way. By maintaining their separateness it diminished their impact and the possibility of constructing a meaningful, normatively inspired relationship between the individual and the European Union. It is suggested that the reasons for this are a matter of constitutional history. Union citizenship, when first introduced, was lamented as a mere fig leaf, a repackaging of economic rights without any meaningful political or rights-based content.[8] Justice and home affairs on the other hand, while incorporated within the EU itself, was separated out into a distinctly intergovernmental pillar. Finally, while fundamental rights were mentioned as part of the founding principles of the Union, there was no distinct policy for fundamental rights or a constitutive document such as a charter or bill of rights.[9] In short the core of integration remained economic rather than political. While certain elements were introduced, these were deliberately kept either presented as symbolic (in the case of citizenship and arguably fundamental rights)

[7] M Anderson, M den Boer and G Miller, 'European Citizenship and Cooperation in Justice and Home Affairs' in A Duff, J Pinder and R Pryce (eds), *Maastrict and Beyond: Building the European Union* (New York, Routledge, 1994) 108–09.

[8] In the words of Joseph Weiler, 'little more than a cynical exercise in public relations on the part of the High Contracting Parties' in J Weiler, 'Citizenship and Human Rights' in J Winter et al (eds), *Reforming the Treaty on European Union* (The Hague, Kluwer, 1996) as quoted by von Bogdandy et al in A von Bogdandy et al, 'Reverse Solange – Protecting the Essence of Fundamental Rights against EU Member States' (2012) 49 *CML Rev* 489, fn 78.

[9] Instead the EU's protection of fundamental rights relied on 'general principles' developed, it has been suspected, as a response to prompting by national judicial actors and more concerned with maintaining the primacy of European (economic) law.

or, if not presented as symbolic but rather technical, were cordoned off from the main site of supranational governance into a separate intergovernmental treaty (JHA cooperation). While the individual made an appearance in the Treaty of Maastricht as a distinct actor under Union law, the Treaty was careful not to accord him or her too central a place in the integration project. While certain actors made use of the language of citizenship through the development of first JHA and then AFSJ policies, the Hague Programme provided the first sign that the separation of the Maastricht Treaty may be undone and that citizenship would be more closely aligned with the AFSJ. Citizenship policies, including those aspects that would have previously been considered inherently related to the internal market, namely free movement, were incorporated *en masse* into the general policy-making process of the AFSJ and included under the rubric 'freedom' in the multi-annual programme signalling, at least from an institutional perspective, a shift from the internal market to the AFSJ.[10] This understated, but significant move, was completed in a more visible fashion with the Treaty of Lisbon and Stockholm Programme.

The Lisbon Treaty, replicating the provisions of the ill-fated Treaty Establishing a Constitution for Europe,[11] collapsed the pillar structure and thereby extended the application of Union citizenship law to all areas of Union law, including the former third pillar matters of justice and home affairs. Thus 'EU citizenship as a building block in the European integration process has been extended to the *whole* Area of Freedom, Security and Justice, including the – former – third pillar dimension'.[12] The relevant objective of the Union changes from an undertaking to 'maintain and develop the Union as an area of freedom, security and justice'[13] to ensuring that 'the Union shall offer its citizens an area of freedom, security and justice'.[14] However it is worth pointing out that complete consolidation as seemed to have been envisaged by Anderson, den Boer and Miller: the treatment of citizenship and the AFSJ under a single title or section of the Treaty has not come about in the context of the Treaty architecture.

A more complete unification has, however, come about from a policy perspective. The Commission has moved responsibility for citizenship and free movement policies from the internal market to DG Justice, one of the two JHA directorates.

[10] The Hague Programme: Strengthening Freedom, Security and Justice in the European Union, OJ 2005 C53/1.

[11] Treaty establishing a Constitution for Europe, OJ 2004 C310/01, using identical language in relation to the objectives of the Union and establishing the same arrangement with respect to organising the citizenship and the AFSJ within the Treaty.

[12] Pointed out at the time by the editors of the *Common Market Law Review*: 'The merging of the pillars, together with the close connection between the TEU and the TFEU brought about by the first Articles of the respective treaties has cleared up an existing anomaly, namely that *EU* citizenship was a matter of the First [sic] – *EC* – Pillar only. After the amendments, citizens of the Union shall "enjoy the rights and be subject to the duties imposed by the Treaties"', 'Editorial Comments: Two-Speed European Citizenship? Can the Lisbon Treaty Help Close the Gap?' (2008) 45 *CML Rev* 1, 7.

[13] Art 2 TEU (old), Consolidated Versions of the Treaty on European Union and of the Treaty Establishing the European Community, OJ 2006 C321, E/1, 11.

[14] Art 3(2) TEU, Consolidated Versions of the Treaty on European Union and the Treaty on the Functioning of the European Union, OJ 2012 C326/1, 17.

While in and of itself not legally determinative it does at least indicate a shift in the perspective of the main policy-making organ of the Union as to the appropriate location of citizenship and its relationship to other policies of the Union. Perhaps more importantly, recent multi-annual programmes for the AFSJ, the Hague Programme (adopted the year following the signing of the ill-fated Treaty Establishing a Constitution for Europe and drafted with its implementation in mind), and the Stockholm Programme, bring policies and legislative programmes associated with citizenship of the Union, including measures of free movement and political participation, within the ambit of the AFSJ. Most significantly the Stockholm Programme accords a central, indeed thematic place to citizenship intended as it is, in the words of the Commission 'to put the citizen at the heart of this project [the AFSJ].'[15]

Not only have citizenship policies been included within the AFSJ, they have undergone a transformation. For equally significant is what has now been collected under the title 'citizenship'. First, the free movement of citizens is explicitly linked to cooperation in the context of Schengen.[16] Secondly, in addition to the traditional 'core' of Union citizenship are found collected various policies relating to the rights of the child, information rights, rights of the individual in criminal procedure and victims' rights. But perhaps the most significant inclusion is that of the Union's fundamental rights policies, now explicitly linked with citizenship in the context of the AFSJ. The Stockholm Programme, in keeping with the higher profile generally accorded fundamental rights post-Lisbon, includes a significant section detailing steps to be taken in promoting fundamental rights including use of the EU Agency for Fundamental Rights, implementation of the Charter of Fundamental Rights and accession to the European Convention on Human Rights.[17] Not only has citizenship been incorporated into the AFSJ, but in doing so it would seem to have been subtly transformed and enriched.

Such changes in bureaucratic nomenclature and policy organisation alone do not amount to legal, let alone constitutional changes, and we should be careful not to overstate their significance. However, it does mark a shift in what has been termed the 'citizenship practice' of the polity.[18] Such multi-annual documents, issued by the European Council and laying out both the general principles are intended to guide the overall direction of the AFSJ, provide overall coherence and lay out a detailed legislative agenda. In the past their impact has been significant, and played a central role in both guiding policy and focusing commentary and discussion. Beginning tentatively with the Hague Programme, facilitated in the Treaty of Lisbon and completed by the Stockholm Programme, recent years have seen a shift in the context and practice of policy-making in relation to Union citizenship. Not only has it been

[15] Commission, 'An Area of Freedom, Security and Justice serving the citizen' (Communication) COM(2009) 262 final, 2.

[16] The Stockholm Programme – An Open and Secure Europe Serving and Protecting Citizens, OJ 2010 C115/1, 8.

[17] ibid.

[18] A Weiner, *European Citizenship Practice* (Boulder, Colorado, Westview Press, 1998).

incorporated within the AFSJ but it has been expanded to cover a far wider range of objectives including fundamental rights, which have, under citizenship, been brought within the AFSJ. The result is a nexus of fundamental rights, citizenship and the AFSJ pointing towards a symbiotic evolution of all three areas.

Thus citizenship and JHA/AFSJ policies from a certain point of view seem complementary but were originally separated in the Treaty of Maastricht. That was an exercise reflecting a then broader trend limiting the explicitly political elements of the new EU and in particular those elements that focused on the individual as a non-economic actor. Nonetheless more than a decade later they were brought together, primarily through clear and unambiguous policy developments and were associated with the growing EU fundamental rights policy. The development marks the constitutional maturing of both the AFSJ and citizenship and an overall trend towards a growing non-economic element to the European Union. The exact details of this constitutional maturing and their possible implications will be the subject of the rest of this chapter.

III. CITIZENSHIP AND THE CONSTITUTIONALISATION OF THE AFSJ

It is clear from a policy perspective, in particular in the Stockholm Programme, that the AFSJ and citizenship have become increasingly associated. The rest of this chapter is an effort to determine what this might mean both for the AFSJ and for citizenship. In general this association could be said to symbolise the ongoing constitutional maturing of both the AFSJ and Union citizenship, themselves indicative of the increasing importance of the individual as a political and legal figure, rather than simply economic, in the context of the EU. In the AFSJ the constitutional maturing that this association with citizenship represents is based on two related developments that appear as a recurring thread in this volume. First the move from an intergovernmental to a supranational institutional framework has meant that the individual, as well as the Member State, is the direct subject of AFSJ law. Secondly the increasing focus on individual and fundamental rights, what Peers has termed its 'liberalisation', has led it quite naturally to appropriate the language of citizenship as a means of both reflecting and furthering this development.[19] The prominence of the citizen and the language of citizenship, could be said to act as a symbol or even metaphor for the developments in the AFSJ. Furthermore, the use of the language of citizenship could be said to perform a legitimising function in this maturing. A final effect of an association with citizenship is the consolidation of the AFSJ as an area central to the EU as a political community.

[19] See ch 2 by Peers in this volume.

A. Supranationalism and the Individual as Subject

Under a classic intergovernmental arrangement the state is the principal actor. It is the entity that both creates and is bound by the relevant norm.[20] Obligations and rights created for individuals are done indirectly, and their interests are mediated and represented by the states of which they are members. This was reflected in the institutional framework of cooperation in (the extra-EU) Trevi and Schengen systems and to a large extent persisted in the third pillar under the original EU Treaty.[21] Unanimity remained the principal decision-making procedure, reflecting the principle of equality amongst states, instruments lacked binding direct effect and frequently required ratification. Enforcement was weak or non-existent. In contrast, under supranational governance, the individual is an actor of direct relevance in the legal order. In the law-making process he or she is represented both as a member of an individual state, through deliberations in Council, but also as a member of the wider supranational community, through the involvement of institutions such as the Commission and European Parliament. The interests of individuals as such are placed alongside, and not always easily, the interests of states.[22] At the same time individuals are directly implicated by the law in its legal effects and are directly involved in the enforcement of supranational law. The doctrines of supremacy or primacy and direct effect bypass requirements for mediation by national law and permit individuals to invoke such law in legal disputes. In a related fashion the application of the preliminary reference mechanism opens up a direct route for individuals to access the supranational judicial system, empowering them as agents in the supranational legal order but also reflecting their subjection to those norms. On one reading such a view lies at the heart of the Court's founding constitutional judgments with an explicit characterisation of the Community as a new legal order 'the subjects of which comprise not only the Member States *but also their nationals*' (emphasis added).[23]

As is well know, throughout its institutional history the AFSJ has developed, at times unevenly and often hesitantly, towards acquiring the features of a supranational legal order. This is not the place to explore in detail the history of this development but suffice to point out that in doing so it has also shifted from a system

[20] This is admittedly somewhat simplistic. This position has evolved considerably over the course of the 20th century and the position of the individual in international law is significantly more ambiguous. However, the fact remains that individuals, except in some specific fields, do not constitute subjects of international law in the same sense as states. See K Parlett, *The Individual in the International Legal System* (Cambridge, Cambridge University Press, 2011).

[21] Although it should of course be noted that the ECJ contributed somewhat to the 'constitutionalisation' of the third pillar. See in particular Case C-105/03 *Criminal proceedings against Maria Pupino* [2005] ECR I-5285.

[22] N Bolleyer and C Reh, 'EU Legitimacy Revisited: The Normative Foundations of a Multi-level Polity' (2012) 19 *Journal of European Publc Policy* 472.

[23] Case 26/62 *Van Gend en Loos v Netherlands Inland Revenue* [1963] ECR 3, 12. Similarly in *Costa v ENEL* the Court found that 'the Member States have limited their sovereign rights, albeit within limited fields and have thus created a body of law *which binds both their nationals and themselves*' (emphasis added), Case 6/64 *Costa v ENEL* [1964] ECR English Special Edition 585, 593.

that was *created by and bound states* to one in which *individuals* were implicated directly both in its law-making process and in its legal effects. The nature of the legal subject of the AFSJ as a body of law has shifted from being the state to being a mixture of states and individuals.

Citizenship is one form of institutionalising the relationship between the individual and the political community. Its use is not essential to such a development but as a discursive strategy it certainly reinforces the position of the individual. It recognises the fact that the individual forms an integral part of the constitutional system and as a person endowed with subjective public rights separate from that of the state. In other words it recasts the individual as an active agent with subjective interests that can moreover be opposed to those of the state. Characterising a legal order as being based on citizenship is in effect recognising an important, possibly central, role for the individual.

B. Citizenship and the Liberalisation of the AFSJ

Building on the shift in the institutional structure of the AFSJ, a second explanation for the belated association of citizenship with the AFSJ is the shift from an overbearing focus on security and state interests to the gradual strengthening of fundamental rights and the position of the individual.[24]

In earlier years the citizen, and language of citizenship, did figure occasionally in policy discourses surrounding the AFSJ but in a rather incongruous fashion. Documents stressed the need to provide citizens with 'security' and to construct the AFSJ as a secure space,[25] where in a neo-Hobbesian turn the primary relationship of the European lawmaker to the individual was to provide security, law and order. Freedom and justice were indeed defined in terms of security leading to a 'discursive chain of freedom, security and justice',[26] with security constituting the central link. The Hague Programme thus declared that:

> [T]he security of the European Union and its Member States has acquired a new urgency . . . The citizens of Europe rightly expect the European Union, while guaranteeing respect for fundamental freedoms and rights, to take a more effective, joint approach to cross-border problems such as illegal migration, trafficking in and smuggling of human beings, terrorism and organised crime as well as the prevention thereof.[27]

Not only was the language of citizenship rather incongruous in this context, it was also limited. While the Hague Programme was notable for including citizenship

[24] V Mitsilegas, 'The Limits of Mutual Trust in Europe's Area of Freedom, Security and Justice: From Automatic Inter-State Cooperation to the Slow Emergence of the Individual' (2012) 31 *Yearbook of European Law* 319.

[25] P Twomey, 'Construcuting a Secure Space: The Area of Freedom, Security and Justice' in D O'Keefe and P Twomey (eds), *Legal Issues of the Amsterdam Treaty* (Oxford, Hart Publishing, 1999).

[26] D Kostakopoulou, 'The Area of Freedom, Security and Justice and the European Union's Constitutional Dialogue' in C Barnard (ed), *The Fundamentals of EU Law Revisited* (Oxford, Oxford University Press, 2007)174.

[27] The Hague Programme (n 10) 1.

policies within the AFSJ, it was not particularly extensive in this regard. The figure of the citizen did not take centre stage until the Treaty of Lisbon and the adoption of the Stockholm Programme. At the same time there has been a noticeable change in the overall direction of the AFSJ. Roughly speaking a rebalancing in both the discourse and the practice of the AFSJ has been taking place, with a greater emphasis on 'freedom' and 'justice' rather than 'security'. This is reflected in concrete measures such as the Council Roadmap on procedural rights for suspects and accused persons[28] and an increased prominence of fundamental rights. Furthermore, changes have been noted in the case law of the Court of Justice.[29]

A change in the direction of the AFSJ towards a balancing of security with freedom and justice is reflected in a more extensive and appropriate use of the concept of citizenship. Thus in the Stockholm Programme:

> The European Council considers that the priority for the coming years will be to focus on the interests and needs of citizens. The challenge will be to ensure respect for fundamental rights and freedoms and integrity of the person while guaranteeing security in Europe. It is of paramount importance that law enforcement measures on the one hand, and measures to safeguard individual rights, the rule of law and international protection rules, on the other go hand in hand in the same direction and are mutually reinforced.[30]

Rhetoric and language are not only exercises in labelling. They reflect changes that have already taken place but also perform an important role in framing and shaping policy developments. Legal and institutional reality is to a large extent constructed through language.[31] The positioning of citizenship within the AFSJ may reinforce the general tendency to take fundamental rights more seriously in this context.

C. Citizenship, the AFSJ and Legitimacy

The recent association of the AFSJ with citizenship can be seen as a reflection of the ongoing development, and in particular what has been termed here the constitutional maturing, of the AFSJ represented by the growing importance of the individual. Underlying this is the fact that citizenship is a legitimising institution: mediating the relationship between the individual and the state. Contested a

[28] Resolution of the Council on a Roadmap for strengthening procedural rights of suspected or accused persons in criminal proceedings, OJ 2009 C295/1.

[29] See Joined Cases C-411/10 and C-493/10 *NS v Secretary of State for the Home Dept*, 21 December 2011, and the discussion by Konstadinidis and O'Meara in ch 5 in this volume. See, more generally, Mitsilegas, 'The Limits of Mutual Trust in Europe's Area of Freedom, Security and Justice: From Automatic Inter-State Cooperation to the Slow Emergence of the Individual' (n 24).

[30] The Stockholm Programme (n 16) 4. Begging of course the question of *which* direction. It is to be hoped that the overall tone of the passage, namely stressing the rule of law and fundamental rights, gives some indication.

[31] For an application of this constructivist approach to European citizenship, see D Kostakopoulou, 'Ideas, Norms and European Citizenship: Explaining Institutional Change' (2005) 68 *MLR* 233.

concept as it is, it almost invariably carries with it positive connotations. As Bosniak puts it, to 'characterise practices or institutions or experiences in the language of citizenship is to afford them substantial political recognition and social value . . . describing aspects of the world in the language of citizenship is a legitimising political act'.[32] Citizenship carries with it inherent legitimising connotations in situations where individuals are subject to direct legal authority. It directly relates the activity of the legal and political community to the individual and thereby (supposedly) generates reasons for the acceptance of its authority, a tendency that is intended to ultimately develop into a more diffuse legitimacy. In the European context, Union citizenship could be seen as a natural complement to national citizenship in performing this legitimating function.[33] The AFSJ, focusing as it does on the direct exercise of legal power on the individual at and across borders[34] is perhaps even more in need than other areas for a concept to reflect a proper institutionalised relationship between the individual and this now institutionalised area of supranational authority.[35] Citizenship provides such a concept.[36] The long-delayed association of citizenship with the AFSJ, artificially separated at Maastricht, therefore takes place at a time when the AFSJ has matured institutionally. It is suggested that this is not a coincidence but rather reflects the increasing centrality of the individual not simply as the object but also as the subject of what is now a supranational field of law complete with subjective public rights in the form of fundamental rights, a position that is best encapsulated and legitimised by the institution of citizenship.

On a final note not only does the association of citizenship with the AFSJ reflect the fact that it is now a fully-fledged area of supranational law with the Union acting as a site for the articulation of an autonomous interest of freedom, security and justice, but through its association with citizenship the centrality of the AFSJ to the European polity is underlined. The community as a collective entity is constituted by its individual members, which in a democratic context means citizens and all the implications that that status entails. As a corollary the status of citizen-

[32] L Bosniak, *The Citizen and the Alien: Dilemas of Contemporary Membership* (Princeton, New Jersey, Princeton University Press, 2006) 12.

[33] Monar, 'A Dual Citizenship: The Citizenship of the European Union' (n 3).

[34] Reviewing Walker's 2005 edited collection on the AFSJ (above n 4) Hans Lindahl pointed out 'three different but related aspects of a politics of borders: the spatial unity of the AFSJ, the organisation of power over its borders and the regulation and control of these borders'. See H Lindahl, 'Jus Includendi et Excludendi: Europe and the Borders of Freedom, Security and Justice' (2005) 16 *Kings College Law Journal* 235, 236.

[35] Thus 'the nature of all this [JHA] activity undermines the claim made by some theorists that the legitimacy of EU action should not be of primary concern because the EU lacks competences of a traditional state and its powers are mainly economic'. Douglas-Scott, 'The EU's Area of Freedom, Security and Justice: A Lack of Fundamental Rights, Mutual Trust and Democracy?' (n 2) 55.

[36] Even in relation to immigration law where it has been claimed that the legitimacy claimed for the Union in excluding (and including) others is related to its claim to represent the 'own place' of Union citizens. 'In effect, this constitutional passage [referring to the now Art 3(2) TEU stating that "the Union shall offer its citizens an area of freedom, security and justice"] claims that exclusion from (and inclusion in) AFSJ is justified because this area is the own place of European citizens' Lindahl, 'Jus Includendi et Excludendi: Europe and the Borders of Freedom, Security and Justice' (n 34) 242.

ship is a reflection of the broader constitutional community and its manifestation reflects the self-understanding of the community. As stated by Rosenfeld:

> The citizen is the core unit of the constitutional order and of constitutional identity . . . the citizen encapsulates the constitutional identity of his or her polity. Moreover, through his or her defining characteristics, the citizen projects in microcosmic perspective the core elements of the constitutional model prevalent in the polity to which her or she belongs.[37]

By establishing the AFSJ as a site for the future development of citizenship the AFSJ becomes increasingly central to the character of Union citizenship itself and accordingly may be seen as lying increasingly at the heart of the EU as a constitutional project. Of course in and of itself mere inclusion in the Stockholm Programme does not alone mark the AFSJ out as a central component of citizenship law, nor as a core element of the EU.[38] Nonetheless the association with citizenship certainly points in that direction and indicates the increasing importance of the AFSJ (now including fundamental rights, explored more fully below) to the constitution of the Union.[39]

IV. IMPLICATIONS FOR UNION CITIZENSHIP

This prominence of the citizen in the Stockholm Programme reflects the constitutionalisation and increasing importance of the AFSJ. However, this in fact only constitutes half of the story and the association likewise reflects a parallel development of Union citizenship, namely its evolution beyond a merely economic rationale. In this respect the effort to associate citizenship with the AFSJ could be seen as part of an effort to enrich it with non-economic values.

A. Beyond Market Citizenship

The first thing to note is that the positioning of citizenship policies within the AFSJ comes at a time when citizenship has clearly evolved beyond its economic character. Legal accounts[40] of European citizenship tend to stress its emergence

[37] M Rosenfeld, *The Identity of the Constitutional Subject: Selfhood, Culture and Community* (New York, Routledge, 2010) 211.

[38] Although there is certainly an argument to be made that the AFSJ does in fact now occupy a central place in the EU. See, eg the prominence it now occupies in the objectives as contained in Art 3 TEU of the Union post-Lisbon. Indeed 'it is not fortuitous that mention of the area of freedom, security and justice has "moved up" the list to become Article 3(2) of the TEU, thereby signifying its centrality to the EU polity'. P Craig, *The Lisbon Treaty: Law, Politics and Treaty Reform* (Oxford, Oxford University Press, 2010) 337.

[39] See, eg the rather dramatic statement of the ECJ in *NS* stating that 'at issue here is the raison d'être of the European Union and the creation of an area of freedom, security and justice', *NS* (n 29) para 83. It will not escape readers' notice that *NS* was primarily concerned with fundamental rights.

[40] As opposed to political accounts that tend to depict a more aspirational vision of citizenship highlighting its participatory elements and its identity-generating capacity.

from a unique legal system differing from older regimes of international law by the creation of a role for individuals as its legal subjects. This 'incipient European citizenship' focused on the individual in the context of the Treaty provisions on labour mobility.[41] Economically active individuals were empowered by directly effective rights located in the Treaty and later in legislation. This development of a rights-based approach to the free movement of workers was significantly strengthened by worker-friendly interpretations of the relevant provisions by the Court of Justice, thereby expanding the fundamental freedom's *ratio personae* and *ratio materiae*. With the introduction of the single market and the development of the free movement of services and consumer law this market citizenship came to encompass the more passive market participant and the 'citizen as consumer' became a primary role of the individual under Community law. This development was characterised by Everson as potentially leading to a selfish, individualised and instrumentalised figure.[42]

Regardless of the stance one might take regarding the merits or demerits of the market as a central organising constitutional or political principle,[43] or the manner in which this principle has been managed in the context of the European Union, the mechanics of the internal market, and in particular its powerful 'free movement/non-discrimination' logic of negative integration has had a profound effect on the legal structure of European citizenship. It has lead to a distinctly transnational status for citizens where the most important rights are those exercised not against the Union institutions themselves but rather against Member States;[44] national rights secured by supranational guarantees.[45] These historic ori-

[41] R Plender, 'An Incipient Form of European Citizenship' in F Jacobs (ed), *European Law and the Individual* (New York, North-Holland Publishing Co, 1976).

[42] M Everson, 'The Legacy of the Market Citizen' in J Shaw and G More (eds), *New Legal Dynamics of European Union* (Oxford, Claredon Press, 1995). More recently Nic Shuibhne has presented a more nuanced analysis of the merits and demerits of market citizenship as an organising principle for European citizenship, arguing that in a polity centred around a transnational economic constitution 'market citizenship' may in fact be not only an accurate description but a useful concept at the current stage of European integration. See N Shuibhne, 'The Resilience of EU Market Citizenship' (2010) 47 *CML Rev* 1597.

[43] For an early critical account, see Everson, 'The Legacy of the Market Citizen' ibid, for a more recent somewhat contrary opinion on the merits of 'market citizenship' in the specific context of the EU, see Shuibhne, 'The Resilience of EU Market Citizenship' ibid.

[44] See I Penot, 'The Transnational Character of Union Citizenship' in M Dougan, N Shuibhne and E Spaventa (eds), *The Empowerment and Disempowerment of the European Citizen* (Oxford, Hart Publishing, 2012).

[45] Characterised by Paul Magnette as representing an 'isopolity', see P Magnette, *La Citoyennéte Européenne* (Brussels, Editions de l'Université de Bruxelles, 1999) ch 2. The recent *Zambrano* line of case law may challenge, or at least complement, this dominant isopolity paradigm: see L Azoulai, 'A Comment on the Ruiz Zabrano Judgment: A Genuine European Integration' (2011) European Union Democracy Observatory on Citizenship, 29 March 2011, eudo-citizenship.eu/eu-citizenship#.UGsZHrv82H. While important symbolically the exact reach of this judgment may, at least for the time being be limited. See Case C-256/11 *Derici and ors v Bundesministerium fur Inneres*, 15 November 2011. For a critical account of the Court's jurisprudence, see N Shuibhne, '(Some of) The Kids are All Right – Case note on Case C-434/09 Shirely McCarthy v Secretary of State for the Home Department and Case C-256/11 Dereci and others v Bundesministerium fur Inneres' (2012) 49 *CML Rev* 349.

gins of citizenship in the free movement of workers also explain the more recent development of Union citizenship proper as a 'fifth fundamental freedom'[46] akin to the traditional four freedoms of the internal market.

However, while Union citizenship remains profoundly influenced in its legal structure by its internal market origins, in terms of its material scope it has evolved significantly. Although hesitant at first, the Court has put beyond doubt the fact that individuals need no longer exercise an economic activity in order to fall within the scope of the free movement provisions. Furthermore as the *ratio personae* of the citizenship provisions expanded so did their *ratio materiae* to encompass all matters that fell within 'the scope of the Treaty', an interpretation given extra weight by a generous reading of what constituted 'the scope of the Treaty'. The dual move of freeing the right of free movement from the exercise of an economic activity and the broad horizontal application of the non-discrimination provision lead to a considerable expansion in the integrative potential of Union citizenship. From a status allowing nationals of Member States access to the economy of other Member States[47] it evolved to encompass an altogether more wide-ranging autonomous notion of free movement and an increasingly social model of integration.[48] More recently in the context of the AFSJ, this integrative effect of citizenship has reached core aspects of the relationship of the state to the individual such as the gathering and storage of information for security purposes[49] and the residual 'nationality exemption' contained in the European Arrest Warrant.[50] European citizenship has moved significantly beyond 'mere' economic integration creating a transnational status for the individual that may touch on almost all facets of the relationship between the host state or society[51] and the individual. Notwithstanding the endurance of a transnational structure, citizenship has clearly outgrown its association with the market to constitute an altogether broader status. A different image of the individual, be it a *zoon politikon* or a *legalis homo* [52] or some other figure, appeared

[46] F Wollenschläger, 'A New Fundamental Freedom beyond Market Integration: Union Citizenship and its Dynamics for Shifting the Economic Paradigm of European Integration' (2011) *17 European Law Journal* 1. See also R White, 'Free Movement, Equal Treatment and Citizenship of the Union' (2005) 54 *ICLQ* 885.

[47] Although it should be noted that this status of 'market citizen' was never entirely divorced from a more human, social conception of the individual, particularly in the field of social rights and family reunification. For an early account, see AC Evans, 'European Citizenship' (1982) 45 *MLR* 497.

[48] See, in particular, a series of cases beginning with Case C-85/96 *Maria Martinez Sala and Freistaat Bayern* [1998] ECR I-2691 concerning rights to social benefits. See, generally, M Dougan, 'The Spatial Restructuring of National Welfare States within the European Union: The Contribution of Union Citizenship and the Relevance of the Treaty of Lisbon' in U Neergaard, R Nielson and L Rosebury (eds), *Integrating Welfare Function into EU Law: From Rome to Lisbon* (Copenhagen, DJOF Publishing, 2009).

[49] Case C-524/06 *Heinz Huber v Bundesrepublik Deutschland* [2008] ECR I-9705.

[50] Art 4(6) of Council Framework Decision on the European Arrest Warrant and the surrender procedures between Member States, OJ 2002 L190/1 and its interpretation in Case C-42/11 *Joao Pedro Lopes da Silva Jorge,* 5 September 2012.

[51] Also retaining in ties with the 'home' state, see I Penot, 'The Transnational Character of Union Citizenship' (n 44).

[52] For a discussion of these terms as representing two strands in the history of citizenship, see JGA Pocock, 'The Ideal of Citizenship Since Classical Times' in R Beiner (ed), *Theorizing Citizenship* (Albany, SUNY Press, 1995).

to be emerging from the 'market citizen'. What remains to be determined is what role the AFSJ can play in this regard.

B. Enriching Union Citizenship

The initial reasons for associating citizenship with JHA policies, outlined at the beginning of this chapter, no doubt play a part. There is a close relationship between the exercise and legitimation of public power and citizenship on the one hand and on the other hand the functional links between citizenship and the AFSJ through their common origins in free movement. Indeed the argument in favour of the latter as an explanation is particularly strong. In the relatively early case of *Wijsenbeck*, the Court, while denying the direct effect of the Treaty provision abolishing internal border controls, did make the link with free movement rights.[53] AG Cosmas, in particular, did not disguise the relationship between a status of citizenship and free movement within the territory of the political community.[54] This link appears to be made explicit in the Stockholm Treaty with the Schengen free travel area being firmly placed within the citizenship rights of free movement.[55]

However, in addition to strengthening the purely functional relationship one cannot help but suspect that the association with the AFSJ reflects a further desire on the part of institutions to enrich citizenship by placing it in a policy framework with strong political connotations. The poverty of Union citizenship, especially compared with its national counterparts, was bemoaned at its inception in 1992. One criticism was the distinct thinness of the Community to which it referred. It lacked any strong normative or political connotations and those that did exist were essentially economic and instrumental in nature.[56] If citizenship can be conceived as an empty container to be filled with rights and duties, at its inception some saw Union citizenship as distinctly half-empty.[57]

By contrast, associating citizenship with an area of freedom, security and justice offers, at least at the level of symbolism, more normative content. As pointed out by Twomey at the creation of the AFSJ '[a]rguably, on examination, the concepts . . . share a sense of being more significant for their connotation than their actual content'.[58] This 'triumvirate of values'[59] – 'freedom', 'security' and 'justice' – are heady stuff, rich in principled language, and when combined with the term area,

[53] *Wijsenbeek* (n 5) paras 41–43.

[54] 'Moreover, recognition of the possibility of moving (in principle) unchecked within the geographic area corresponding to a legal order is inherent in the status of citizen covered by that legal order' ibid, Opinion of AG Cosmos, para 101.

[55] The Stockholm Programme (n 16).

[56] Everson, 'The Legacy of the Market Citizen' (n 42).

[57] See Kostakopoulou, 'Ideas, Norms and European Citizenship: Explaining Institutional Change' (n 31) 234–35 labelling such a view as a 'minimalist conception' of European citizenship.

[58] Twomey, 'Construcuting a Secure Space: The Area of Freedom, Security and Justice' (n 25) 358.

[59] Walker, 'In Search of the Area of Freedom, Security and Justice: A Constitutional Odyssey' (n 4).

they suggest community, place and normative values central to the rule of law and a 'democratic society'. This rhetorical fact was grasped early on by the Commission:

> [T]he [AFSJ] enshrines at a European Union level the essence of what we derive from our democratic traditions and what we understand by the rule of law. The common values underlining the objective of an area of freedom, security and justice are indeed longstanding principles of the modern democracies of the European Union. The challenge set out by the Amsterdam Treaty is not to reinvent democracy and the rule of law but to allow citizens to enjoy their long-standing democracies in common . . . the three notions of freedom, security and justice are closely interlinked. Freedom loses much of its meaning if it cannot be enjoyed in a secure environment and with the full backing of a system of justice in which all Union citizens and residents can have confidence. These three inseparable concepts have one common denominator – *people* – one cannot be achieved in full without the other two. Maintaining the right balance between them must be the guiding thread for Union action.[60]

A further element, which has only been alluded to, is the inclusion of fundamental rights within the citizenship–AFSJ relationship contained in the Stockholm Programme. A frequent criticism of Union citizenship at its inception was the failure to make explicit a link with the status of citizenship and a body of fundamental rights. There are certainly dangers in too close and simplistic a link between citizenship and fundamental rights: treating them as synonymous risks importing the inherent exclusionary aspect of citizenship into what should properly be considered universal fundamental rights.[61] However, their association can be mutually beneficial. Framing the Union's fundamental rights policy in terms of citizenship provides a conceptual framework through which rights can be used to legitimise the Union and the use of public power.[62] Fundamental rights historically form an essential part of the citizenship package, fleshing it out and giving it more substantial and normatively desirable content.

Additionally, the cumulative effect of the newly entrenched positions of fundamental rights, citizenship and the AFSJ should not be ignored. Combined they indicate a shift in the focus of the Union onto the individual and moreover the individual as a legal and political rather than simply economic figure. The characterisation of something in terms of citizenship is both a legitimising act and one that asserts its importance to the polity. Similarly, the placing of fundamental rights in the context of the Stockholm Programme relates individual fundamental

[60] Commission, 'Towards an Area of Freedom, Security and Justice' (Communication) COM(1998) 459 final 1.

[61] For a discussion in the context of the EU, see S O'Leary, 'The Relationship between Community Citizenship and the Protection of Fundamental Rights in Community Law' (1995) 32 *CML Rev* 519, 540ff.

[62] As stated by Síofra O'Leary over a decade ago 'the construction of relationship between Community citizenship and fundamental rights could hold the key to the successful evolution of a status of citizenship peculiar to the European Union . . . Recognition of fundamental rights is an essential aspect of the foundational pact between government and the governed and the legal and political value of fundamental rights is also their potentially integrationary and legitimizing function in a given legal order', S O'Leary, *The Evolving Concept of Community Citizenship: From the Free Movement of Persons to Union Citizenship* (The Hague, Kluwer, 1996) 311.

rights to the communal political values of the AFSJ, thereby emphasising their importance not simply to singular individuals, but also in forming part of the civic fabric of the wider political community. The combination of these three concepts reinforces their growing importance to the EU as a project of integration. For now, post-Lisbon, we are told that 'the Union shall constitute an area of freedom, security and justice with respect for fundamental rights',[63] an area that moreover is 'offered' to its citizens.[64]

However, this development, while certainly offering opportunities for strengthening the position of citizenship, rebalancing the AFSJ and promoting fundamental rights, does carry with it some dangers. First the AFSJ should certainly not become the *sole* arena for the development of citizenship law. The social and the political in particular should not be neglected. While it is unlikely Union citizenship will ever constitute a thick political membership characterised by active and enthusiastic participation in a communal public space, it is to be hoped for the sake of the Union's future democratic legitimacy that a common space of political discourse can be fostered and a form of transnational and indeed supranational democracy advanced. Additionally, the potential weaknesses of the AFSJ as an environment for fostering citizenship should not be denied. Its ambiguity has already been alluded to and while at times this could be considered a strength it can also constitute a weakness. Such nebulous terms can mean much and also perhaps too little. The development of the EU into a space of values within which the citizen is located by the construction of an area of freedom, security and justice will have to be made concrete by particular measures and their implementation. This ambiguity also carries with it dangers. We have already seen how the language of citizenship was manipulated within the context of the Hague Programme to promote a heavily securitised agenda. The danger in such an approach is to reimport a securitised bias from the AFSJ back into our conception of citizenship thereby emphasising its own potential negative aspects, such as its exclusionary nature. While it is true that the pedigree of the citizenship concept and its generally progressive connotations may offer some resistance to this, such an outcome cannot be guaranteed. Finally, the fragmented nature of the AFSJ may pose a further problem.[65] If, as the Stockholm Programme seems to suggest, the AFSJ is to serve as an important reference point for citizenship, problems for the coherence of the Union legal order cannot be ruled out from the fragmented and less than wholehearted participation of some Member States. Will fragmentation in the AFSJ lead to the fragmentation of citizenship in its normative or identity generating functions? This outcome would, in many senses, be anathema to the concept of citizenship as equal membership in a single political community.

[63] Art 67(1) TFEU.

[64] 'The Union shall offer its citizens an area of freedom, security and justice' Art 3(2) TEU.

[65] I am indebted to Christina Eckes for highlighting this point (via a satellite or two) at the workshop at King's College London in November 2012.

V. CONCLUSION

The Stockholm Programme and its association of fundamental rights, citizenship and the area of freedom, security and justice is but a single policy document. Nonetheless, it reflects a broader process of constitutional change that has taken place over the past two decades. The Treaty of Maastricht introduced a status of citizenship to characterise the relationship between the Union and individuals, it assumed competence over justice and home affairs, later to be rechristened as an area of freedom, security and justice and cemented fundamental rights as a value of the Union. Nonetheless the transformation into a true 'political union' focused on the individual was incomplete. Citizenship was market focused with few substantive additions to the prior position of the economic agent. Justice and home affairs remained intergovernmental while the Union continued to lack a true human rights policy or even competence. Although the economic heart of the integration project has certainly not disappeared,[66] a more overtly political turn and more central role for the individual can be detected. Union citizenship, while remaining true to its transnational origins, has long out-grown its economic rationale. It is perhaps ready for more substantive normative content. The fundamental rights policy of the Union, though not constituting an independent competence per se, is increasingly important. The flurry of activity in this regard pre- and post-Lisbon is testimony to that importance. Finally, as this volume indicates, the AFSJ has become very much an area of supranational governance and a site of public interest for justice and home affairs independent of national arenas. Individuals, alongside Member States, are now represented within its governance and are its direct subjects. The association of citizenship with the AFSJ in the Stockholm Programme may, therefore, represent a moment in the constitutional maturing of the Union, reflecting the changes that have gone before and an increasingly central position for the individual. Taken individually these areas represent significant developments, however, it is perhaps together that they constitute the most far-reaching changes. They invite us to reimagine both citizenship and the AFSJ (and indeed fundamental rights) in the context of a symbiotic relationship, mutually reinforcing these various elements and ultimately the individual, at the heart of the European project.

[66] Indeed with recent moves towards greater integration in the context of EMU it may, if anything, be in the process of being reinforced to the point of constituting the hard core of a federal structure.

7

EU Criminal Law Competence after Lisbon: From Securitised to Functional Criminalisation

VALSAMIS MITSILEGAS

I. INTRODUCTION

THE EXTENT OF the competence of the European Union (EU) to criminalise – namely to define criminal offences and adopt criminal sanctions – has traditionally been contested and remains contested notwithstanding the abolition of the third pillar and the normalisation of EU criminal law after the entry into force of the Lisbon Treaty. Concerns with regard to the impact of Union action to criminalise on national sovereignty and the diversity and integrity of national legal systems have led to the evolution of EU criminalisation competence in a series of fraught, incremental steps reflecting a number of EU inter-institutional battles and necessitating the intervention of the Court of Justice. Informed by an overview of the evolution of EU competence in the field, this chapter will analyse the extent of the Union's power to define criminal offences and introduce criminal sanctions after Lisbon and the impact of such competence on the enforcement powers of the state. It will demonstrate that EU competence to criminalise can be justified in a twofold manner: upon the need for the Union to address security threats (securitised criminalisation); and upon the need for the Union to use criminal law in order to ensure the effectiveness of Union law (functional criminalisation). While the focus will be on an analysis of the Union's power to criminalise under Article 83 TFEU, the chapter will also test the wording of this article in relation to other Treaty legal bases and the practice of the institutions with regard to proposals on EU substantive criminal law after the entry into force of the Lisbon Treaty. These legal developments will also be evaluated in the light of the inter-institutional debate on EU criminalisation, as reflected in a series of policy documents published by the Commission, the Parliament, the Council and the European Council in the Stockholm Programme.

II. THE CONSTITUTIONAL POLITICS OF CRIMINALISATION BEFORE LISBON: THE INTERPLAY BETWEEN SECURITISED AND FUNCTIONAL CRIMINALISATION

Although the Treaty of Rome did not envisage express powers for the European Community in the field of criminal justice, European integration has demonstrated that it has been increasingly difficult to disassociate Community action in the main areas of Community competence (including free movement and the completion of the internal market) from criminal justice policy. Calls for Community action in criminal matters have emerged in order to protect perceived EU-wide interests (such as fraud against the Community budget) and ensure the effectiveness of Community law; and by calls for Community law to respond to serious forms of criminality perceived as global security threats including drug trafficking, organised crime, money laundering and terrorism.[1] These two justifications for Union action in substantive criminal law – the need to safeguard interests, policies and objectives of the Union and to achieve effectiveness on the one hand (functional criminalisation) and the need to respond to security threats posed by serious criminality on the other (securitised criminalisation) – have been recurring over time and, as will be seen below, are still highly relevant after the entry into force of the Lisbon Treaty.

As regards functional criminalisation, the Court further recognised in 1989 the principle of assimilation, placing national authorities under a duty to treat EU interests in an equivalent manner to domestic interests.[2] The absence of an express Community competence to define criminal offences and adopt criminal sanctions did not act as an obstacle to finding a legal basis in the Treaty of Rome to adopt Community anti-money laundering law.[3] In terms of constitutional politics, it is noteworthy that the Commission's initial proposal envisaged the express introduction of criminal offences and sanctions by a Community law instrument, arguing that such criminalisation is justified by the need to protect wider Community policies such as the stability of the financial system and thus the internal market. The directive that was eventually adopted did not contain an express requirement for Member States to adopt criminal sanctions (the directive called upon Member States to prohibit money laundering and to impose sanctions for non-compliance with the preventive duties set out therein). However, the directive represented a considerable alignment of Community law with global criminal law standards in the field[4] and resulted in the de facto criminalisation of

[1] For an overview see V Mitsilegas, *EU Criminal Law* (Oxford, Hart Publishing, 2009) ch 2.

[2] See, in particular, Case C-68/88 *Commission v Greece (Greek Maize)* [1989] ECR 2965.

[3] For an analysis, see V Mitsilegas, *Money Laundering Counter-Measures in the European Union: A New Paradigm of Security Governance versus Fundamental Legal Principles* (The Hague, Kluwer Law International, 2003).

[4] V Mitsilegas, 'The EU and the Rest of the World: Criminal Law and Policy Interconnections' in M Evans and P Koutrakos (eds), *Beyond the Established Orders. Policy Interconnections between the EU and the Rest of the World* (Oxford, Hart Publishing, 2011) 149–78.

money laundering in Member States when implementing the directive.[5] From the perspective of constitutional politics, the debate over the adoption of the first Anti-Money Laundering Directive reflects a recurring strategy on behalf of the European Commission to frame the adoption of substantive criminal law by the EU within the broader objective of ensuring the effectiveness of EU law in particular as regards the implementation of specific EU policies not necessarily related to criminal justice.

The third pillar under the Treaty of Maastricht introduced express legal bases enabling the adoption by the EU of concrete measures defining criminal offences and introducing criminal sanctions. An analysis of harmonisation of substantive criminal law today demonstrates that the Union *acquis* is a combination of instruments adopted post-Maastricht (eg the Fraud[6] and Corruption in the Public Sector Conventions),[7] post-Amsterdam (a series of framework decisions addressing security threats such as terrorism,[8] organised crime[9] and drug trafficking[10]) and post-Lisbon (see the recently adopted directives on human trafficking[11] and sexual exploitation[12]). On a number of occasions, such as in the case of human trafficking and sexual exploitation, continuity in EU law has meant that harmonisation measures have been evolving substantively and institutionally over time. Overall, the EU legislator has adopted an expansive approach to EU competence in substantive criminal law under the third pillar. Harmonisation has not been limited to the fields of crime expressly mentioned in the Treaty but has also been extended to harmonisation in the fields of, inter alia, irregular migration,[13] corruption[14] and cyber-crime.[15] The existence of express harmonisation legal bases in the third pillar and the expansive approach to harmonisation adopted by Member States has not stopped the Commission from arguing that the Community (and not only the Union under the third pillar) also had competence to legislate in the field. The funding by the European Commission of an academic project resulting in proposals for harmonised if not unified criminal law under the *corpus juris* was followed by a number of unsuccessful attempts by the Commission to introduce first pillar criminal law.[16] These attempts were based on the view that first pillar criminal law was necessary in order to achieve the effectiveness of Community law in relation to

[5] V Mitsilegas, *Money Laundering Counter-Measures* (n 3).

[6] OJ 1995 C316/49, 27 November 1995.

[7] OJ 1997 C195/2, 25 June 1997.

[8] See the 2002 Framework Decision on combating terrorism, OJ 2002 L164/3, 22 June 2002 as amended in 2008 (OJ 2008 L330/21).

[9] Framework Decision on organised crime, OJ 2008 L300/42.

[10] Framework Decision on drug trafficking, OJ 2004 L335/8, 11 November 2004.

[11] OJ 2011 L101/1, 15 April 2011.

[12] OJ 2011 L335/1, 17 December 2011.

[13] See the Framework Decision on the facilitation of unauthorised entry, transit and residence, OJ 2002 L328/1, 5 December 2002, and more recently the Directive on employers' sanctions, OJ 2009 L168/24, 30 June 2009.

[14] Framework Decision on corruption in the private sector, OJ 1998 L358/2, 31 December 1998.

[15] Framework Decision on attacks against information systems, OJ 2005 L69/67, 16 March 2005.

[16] In the areas of fraud and environmental crime. See Mitsilegas, *EU Criminal Law* (n 1) ch 2.

Community policies and objectives such as the protection of the Community financial interests or the protection of the environment. With these attempts being eventually unsuccessful in the Council, the Commission initiated legal basis litigation in Luxembourg. In two important rulings, the Court of Justice found in favour of the existence of the Community competence to define criminal offences and impose criminal sanctions.[17] Community competence was deemed necessary to ensure the effective protection of the environment, which was viewed as a key Community objective – with criminal law thus viewed not as a separate Union policy but rather as a means to an end towards achieving effectiveness of Community policies.[18] However, it was not clear from the Court's case law whether Community competence would extend beyond cases involving the protection of the environment, with the Commission adopting a maximalist approach and Member States disagreeing.[19] Moreover, following sustained opposition by Member States in the subsequent *Ship Source Pollution* litigation, the Court confirmed its *Environmental Crimes* ruling that the Community has competence to criminalise in the first pillar in order to achieve the effectiveness of Community law but at the same time limited Community competence in only defining criminal offences and imposing criminal sanctions *in abstracto*, with the concrete levels of sanctions to be established under the third pillar.[20] This case law has led to the adoption of pre-Lisbon first pillar criminal law, but with all three measures adopted introducing only very limited harmonisation as to penalty levels.[21]

The debate over the extent of EU competence to criminalise was also reflected in the work of the Convention on the Future of Europe entrusted with providing recommendations for the drafting of the Constitutional Treaty. The Final Report of Working Group X on 'Freedom, Security and Justice' produced a number of recommendations on the basis of the constitutional state of play of criminalisation under the third pillar and its members perceived needs for Union legislative intervention in the field.[22] The Report called for clearer identification of the scope of Union legislation in the field, recognising that Articles 30 and 31 TEU, which constituted the applicable legal bases for criminal law, were 'too vague in many respects, and too narrow in some other aspects'.[23] The Working Group made specific recommendations, a great number of which found their way into the text of

[17] Case C-176/03 *Commission v Council (Environmental Crime)* [2005] ECR I-7879, followed by Case C-440/05 *Commission v Council (Ship Source Pollution)* [2007] ECR I-9097.

[18] See V Mitsilegas, 'The Transformation of Criminal Law in the Area of Freedom, Security and Justice' (2007) 26 *Yearbook of European Law* 1.

[19] COM(2005) 583 final, Brussels, 24 November 2005; Council doc 6077/06 (Presse 38).

[20] Case C-440/05 *Commission v Council (Ship Source Pollution)* [2007] ECR I-9097, paras 70–71.

[21] See Directive 2008/99 on the Protection of the Environment through Criminal Law (OJ 2008 L328/28); Directive 2005/35 on Ship Source Pollution and the Introduction of Penalties for Infringements (OJ 2005 L 255/11); Directive 2009/52 providing for Minimum Standards on Sanctions and Measures against Employers of Illegally Staying Third-country Nationals (OJ 2009 L168/24). These three Directives contain general references to the introduction of 'effective, proportionate and dissuasive sanctions'.

[22] CONV 426/02, Brussels, 2 December 2002, WG X 14.

[23] ibid, 8.

the Lisbon Treaty. It recommended the inclusion of a legal basis in the new Treaty permitting the adoption of minimum rules on constituent elements of criminal acts and of penalties in certain fields of crime where the crime in question is both of a particularly serious nature and has a cross-border dimension and where the crime is directed against a shared European interest which is already itself the subject of a common policy of the Union (for example counterfeiting of the Euro, the protection of the Union financial interest).[24] The Working Group thus advocated the constitutional recognition of both securitised and functional criminalisation.[25] The majority of the Working Group supported enumeration of those types of crime considered to have a transnational dimension and advocated – if this enumeration were to be exhaustive – that the Council, acting by unanimity, and after the assent of the EP (or for a few members, consultation) may amend this list in case of need in order for the Union to respond adequately to changing patterns of crime. According to a widespread view in the Working Party, the Treaty could provide that approximation of substantive criminal laws although this should be carried out in the form of directives only. As will be seen below, both these recommendations have been incorporated in the Lisbon Treaty.

III. EU COMPETENCE TO CRIMINALISE AFTER LISBON: SECURITISED AND FUNCTIONAL CRIMINALISATION REVISITED

The dual securitised/functional criminalisation approach has been espoused by the drafters of the Lisbon Treaty, and in particular of Article 83 TFEU. The first paragraph of Article 83 confers upon the Union competence to establish, by means of directives, *minimum rules* concerning *the definition of criminal offences and sanctions* in the areas of *particularly serious crime with a cross-border dimension* resulting from the nature or impact of such offences or from a special need to combat them on a common basis. These areas of crime are enumerated exhaustively in Article 83(1). The list includes terrorism, trafficking in human beings and sexual exploitation of women and children, illicit drug trafficking, illicit arms trafficking, money laundering, corruption, counterfeiting of means of payment, computer crime and organised crime. As per the recommendation of the Convention Justice and Home Affairs Working Party, the list may be expanded 'on the basis of developments in crime' by the Council acting unanimously after obtaining the consent of the European Parliament. Article 83(1) thus affirms the acceptance of the added value of criminalisation at EU level in order to address

[24] ibid, 10. According to the Working Group, approximation of substantive criminal law should be part of the toolbox of measures for the pursuit of that policy whenever non-criminal rules do not suffice.

[25] The Working Group also called for further consideration to be given to the possible inclusion of a third criterion, which was proposed, namely 'when approximation is required to generate sufficient mutual confidence to enable the full application of mutual recognition of judicial decisions or to guarantee the effectiveness of common tools for police and judicial cooperation created by the Union' – however this criterion has not been explicitly included in the criminalisation legal basis of the Lisbon Treaty – ibid.

perceived serious security threats. The second paragraph of Article 83 constitutes an attempt to translate the Court's functionalist interpretation of the extent of Community (and now Union) criminal law competence in *Environmental Crimes* and *Ship Source Pollution*. Article 83(2) TFEU thus grants the Union competence to approximate national criminal laws and regulations if such approximation *proves essential* to ensure the effective implementation of a Union policy in an area which has been subject to harmonisation measures. For that purpose, directives may establish minimum rules with regard to the definition of criminal offences and sanctions in the area concerned.

A. Securitised Criminalisation – Article 83(1) TFEU

Article 83(1) TFEU reflects the securitised criminalisation approach in determining EU competence in substantive criminal law. EU competence to criminalise is justified as necessary to combat specified areas of criminality the majority of which have been elevated after the Cold War by the international community and the Union as global security threats.[26] The objective of Article 83(1) TFEU to address security threats is also confirmed by the requirement for harmonisation to apply only to areas of particularly serious crime. The securitised view of Article 83(1) TFEU has been recently confirmed by the Court of Justice, according to which the very enumeration of an area of criminality under Article 83(1) suffices for criminality to be considered serious enough to justify the limitation of citizenship rights and the expulsion of EU citizens on public security grounds, although arguably the offences themselves did not necessarily represent a threat to the wider public as such.[27] In this manner, Article 83(1) TFEU – whose purpose is to define the extent of EU competence in substantive criminal law – has been used for a very different purpose, namely to interpret exceptions to freedom of movement. By confirming the seriousness of the areas of crime enumerated in Article 83(1) *in abstracto*, the Court has transformed securitised criminal law into symbolic criminal law.

In an attempt to circumscribe EU competence in the field further, Article 83(1) TFEU contains an express enumeration of these areas of serious crimes and specifies that these areas must have a cross-border dimension resulting from the nature

[26] V Mitsilegas, 'Countering the Chameleon Threat of Dirty Money: "Hard" and "Soft" Law in the Emergence of a Global Regime against Money Laundering and Terrorist Finance' in A Edwards and P Gill (eds), *Transnational Organised Crime: Perspectives on Global Security* (London, Routledge, 2003).

[27] Case C-348/09 *PI v Oberbürgermeisterin der Stadt Remscheid* [2012] 3 *CMLR* 662. According to the Court, Art 28(3)(a) of the Citizens' Directive must be interpreted as meaning that it is open to the Member States to regard criminal offences such as those referred to in the second subparagraph of Article 83(1) TFEU as constituting a particularly serious threat to one of the fundamental interests of society, which might pose a direct threat to the calm and physical security of the population and thus be covered by the concept of 'imperative grounds of public security', capable of justifying an expulsion measure under Art 28(3), as long as the manner in which such offences were committed discloses particularly serious characteristics, which is a matter for the referring court to determine on the basis of an individual examination of the specific case before it.

or impact of such offences or from a special need to combat them on a common basis. This requirement has led commentators to argue that the justification for EU criminal law under Article 83(1) resides in its value-added function, drawing on a common capability to address the scale and nature of threats posed by transnational criminality.[28] While the wording of Article 83(1) can indeed be seen as an attempt to establish the added value of criminalisation at EU level, this added value is not limited to transnational criminality. The applicability of Article 83(1) to areas of serious crime with a cross-border dimension resulting from the nature or impact of such offences or from a special need to combat them on a common basis must be read as conferring on the Union competence to define criminal offences and adopt criminal sanctions in areas of crime which have a cross-border dimension but which do not involve cross-border or transnational criminality as such. Examples of areas of crime with a cross-border dimension resulting from their nature or impact or need to combat on a common basis – but which may involve criminality conducted purely at national level – include terrorism and corruption. In this way, the scope of Article 83(1) TFEU is broader than it appears at first sight.

This broad scope is confirmed by the fact that EU competence is defined on the basis of areas of crime, rather than on the basis of specific criminal offences. These areas of crime may actually correspond to a wide range of criminal offences or sanctions. A clear example of the potential to overstretch EU criminal law competence under Article 83(1) involves the use of the concept of organised crime. Not only is the definition of the concept vague and amorphous at EU level,[29] but it can also be used as a legal basis for harmonisation of a wide range of specific criminal offences and sanctions linked to the activities of a criminal organisation. Such a broad approach may serve to address some gaps in the Lisbon legal bases for criminal law, whose wording may be narrower than the third pillar legal bases and can thus be seen to exclude prima facie EU action in areas where the EU has legislated extensively under the third pillar. A prime example in this context constitutes the recent Commission proposal for a directive on confiscation,[30] where the Commission has used Article 83(1) TFEU as a broad legal basis to justify EU action on confiscation and enable confiscation of the proceeds to include all offences committed within the framework of organised crime. Limits to EU confiscation law appear to have been the side effects of EU efforts to clarify EU competence in criminal matters after Lisbon. If confiscation measures are to be considered measures of criminal procedure to facilitate mutual recognition, then their adoption is not possible under Article 82(2) TFEU as confiscation is not an area of criminal procedure expressly enumerated therein. If confiscation is to be

[28] C Harding and J B Banach-Gutierrez, 'The Emergent EU Criminal Policy: Identifying the Species' (2012) 37 *EL Rev* 758.

[29] V Mitsilegas, 'Defining Organised Crime in the European Union: The Limits of European Criminal Law in an Area of Freedom, Security and Justice' (2001) 26 *EL Rev* 565; V Mitsilegas, *EU Criminal Law* (n 1) ch 2.

[30] COM(2012) 85 final, 12 March 2012.

considered a sanction, it can no longer apply on a catch-all basis to all offences in the light of the limits placed on EU competence by Article 83(1) TFEU. The broad interpretation of Article 83(1) TFEU by the Commission seeks to address this lacuna, and constitutes the first example of a measure adopted under Article 83(1) TFEU focusing specifically and horizontally on sanctions and not on the definition of criminal offences. The use of Article 83(1) TFEU in this manner may constitute a precedent for the adoption of EU instruments introducing a general framework of sanctions for the areas of crime enumerated therein.

B. Functional Criminalisation – Article 83(2) TFEU

The introduction of Article 83(2) TFEU in the Treaty of Lisbon confirms a functionalist view of criminal law. Rather than assuming the status of a self-standing Union policy, criminal law is thus perceived as a means to an end, the end being the effective implementation of other Union policies.[31] Criminal law is thus used as a tool to achieve the effectiveness of Union law.[32] Article 83(2) TFEU flows naturally from the Court's interpretation of the Union's (then Community's) criminalisation competence under the first pillar in the *Environmental Crimes* and *Ship Source Pollution* rulings. The Lisbon Treaty attempts to address concerns with regard to the extensive use of Article 83(2) by introducing two central requirements for the use of EU competence in the field: the requirement that measures are essential to achieve effectiveness; and the requirement that measures are essential to ensure the effective implementation of a Union policy *in an area which has been subject to harmonisation measures*.[33] By using the term 'essential', the Treaty has adopted a high threshold for EU intervention in the area of functional criminalisation, but it is unclear what kind of action meets this threshold.[34] Demonstrating the essential character of EU intervention under Article 83(2) is prone to litigation in Luxembourg.[35] The interpretation of the second requirement of Article 83(2) TFEU, that measures are essential to ensure the effective

[31] V Mitsilegas, 'The Transformation of Criminal Law in the Area of Freedom, Security and Justice' (2007) 26 *Yearbook of European Law* 1.

[32] For a critical view, see M Kaiafa, 'The Importance of Core Principles of Substantive Criminal Law for a European Criminal Policy Respecting Fundamental Rights and the Rule of Law' (2011) 1 *European Criminal Law Review* 7, 19, arguing that the unique identity of criminal law cannot allow it to be reduced to a mere tool for the implementation of any policy.

[33] Emphasis added.

[34] It has, eg been put forward that the requirement of action under Art 83(2) is essential includes a strict proportionality requirement – J Öberg, 'Union Regulatory Criminal Law Competence after the Lisbon Treaty' (2011) 19 *European Journal of Crime, Criminal Law and Criminal Justice* 289, 290.

[35] Already the German Constitutional Court has adopted a narrow view of the Union's criminalisation competence under Art 83(2) TFEU. In its Lisbon ruling, the Court found that such competence exists 'only if it is demonstrably established that a serious deficit concerning enforcement actually exists and that it can only be remedied by the threat of a sanction, this exceptional constituent element exists and the annex competence for legislation in criminal law may be deemed conferred' para 362. See BVerfG, 2 BvE 2/08, *Gauweiler, Die Linke v Act of Approval of the Lisbon Treaty ('Lisbon')*, 30 June 30, 2009.

implementation of a Union policy in an area that has been subject to harmonisation measures, may also prove to be contested. On the one hand, it is noteworthy that effectiveness is related broadly to the implementation of Union policies and not of Union objectives.[36] On the other hand, the requirement that effectiveness must be in an area that has been subject to harmonisation measures may serve to limit the scope of EU competence under Article 83(2) TFEU. A lively academic discussion on the detail of this requirement (in particular on the temporal aspect of Article 83(2) and whether criminalisation can ensure in cases where no previous harmonisation has taken place, as well as on the level of detail of harmonisation to be required) has ensued.[37] In this context, Peers argues convincingly that while it could not be said that there is a Union policy that needs implementing effectively in the absence of harmonisation in specific areas of law, there is nothing in the current legal framework of the Treaty of Lisbon that requires full harmonisation as a pre-condition.[38] Indeed, in interpreting the scope of Article 83(2), the key focus must be whether EU action is essential to ensure effectiveness of Union law in a policy area that has been subject to a degree of harmonisation.

C. Extending the EU Competence to Criminalise elsewhere in the Treaty

The attempt by the drafters of the Lisbon Treaty to determine more clearly the extent of EU competence in substantive criminal law under Article 83 TFEU may be undermined not only by the inherent flexibility in the competence requirements of Article 83(1) and 83(2) TFEU, but also by the question of whether these provisions are the sole legal bases for EU action in the field. It is contested in particular whether Article 83(2) is the only legal basis for the adoption of functionalist EU criminal law or whether criminal law can be adopted by the EU by using a different, policy-specific legal basis elsewhere in the Treaty. Using a legal basis other than Article 83(1) and 83(2) TFEU has significant constitutional consequences: it may enable the adoption of EU substantive criminal law measures in the form of regulations; it deprives Member States from the option of using the emergency brake introduced under Article 83(3) TFEU; and it forces the participation of Denmark, Ireland and the UK in EU criminal law if the legal basis for EU criminalisation is located in a part of the Treaty to which these states have not negotiated an opt-out from. EU substantive criminal law rules adopted under a legal basis different to Article 83 TFEU may not necessarily be minimum rules. The adoption of regulations in the field of substantive criminal law challenges Treaty calls to respect national diversity as outlined in Title V of the TFEU on the

[36] P Craig, *The Lisbon Treaty. Law, Politics, and Treaty Reform* (Oxford, Oxford University Press, 2010) 365.

[37] For a narrow interpretation, see Öberg (n 34) 314–16. For broader interpretations, see P Asp, *The Substantive Criminal Law Competence of the EU* (Skrifter Utgivna av Juridiska Fakulteten vid Stockholms Universitet Nr 79, 2013), 134; and S Peers, *EU Justice and Home Affairs Law*, 3rd edn (Oxford, Oxford University Press, 2011) 775–76.

[38] ibid, 775.

area of freedom, security and justice.[39] It also – at least in theory – raises the prospect for EU measures defining criminal offences and imposing criminal sanctions to have direct effect, thus reversing the protective function of the principle in domestic legal orders. While the Court of Justice has excluded the direct effect of directives in this context,[40] direct effect is not excluded in the case of regulations that do not require further implementing measures by Member States.[41] However, it is difficult to see how in practice a regulation defining criminal offences and imposing criminal sanctions would be clear and unconditional enough not to be requiring a degree of implementation in order to secure an adjustment to the specificities of national criminal justice systems.

The first potential legal basis for substantive criminal law outside Article 83 TFEU is Article 325 TFEU on the fight against fraud affecting the Union's financial interests. Article 325(4) confers to the Union competence to adopt

> the necessary measures in the fields of the prevention of and fight against fraud affecting the financial interests of the Union with a view to affording effective and equivalent protection in the Member States and in all the Union's institutions, bodies, offices and agencies.

A comparative analysis of Article 325(4) TFEU with its pre-Lisbon version[42] reveals that the last sentence of Article 280(4) has been deleted in the Lisbon text. This sentence stated that measures to combat fraud (an area which is not expressly listed in Article 83(1) TFEU but may be included in 83(2)) will not concern the application of national criminal law and the national administration of justice.[43] The fact that the adoption of criminal law measures is not excluded by Article 325(4) TFEU, in addition to the general wording of the provision, can be seen to militate in favour of the conferral on the EU of competence to define criminal offences and impose criminal sanctions in the field not under Article 83(2) TFEU but solely under Article 325 TFEU. It has been noted that such competence is justified by the fact that Article 325(4) TFEU contains a stronger obligation to legislate in comparison with Article 83 (by the use of the verb 'shall' instead of 'may') as well as by the fact that Article 325(4) calls for the adoption of 'necessary measures', instead of the more minimalistic requirement of Article 83 TFEU for the EU to adopt 'minimum rules'.[44] It should also be added in this context that Article 325 TFEU is a legal basis for the adoption of measures in a specific criminal justice field (fraud). In terms of policy areas, Article 325(4) can thus be

[39] See Art 67 TFEU.

[40] Cases C-387/02, C-391/02 and C-403/02 *Berlusconi* [2005] ECR I-3565.

[41] For details, see V Mitsilegas, 'Article 49 (the Principles of Legality and Proportionality of Criminal Offences and Penalties)' in S Peers et al (eds), *The EU Charter of Fundamental Rights. A Commentary* (Oxford, Hart Publishing/Beck, 2014).

[42] Art 280(4) EC.

[43] A similar clause was deleted from Art 135 EC concerning customs cooperation (this is Art 33 in the TFEU).

[44] R Sicurella, 'Some Reflections on the Need for a General Theory of the Competence of the European Union in Criminal Law' in A Klip (ed), *Substantive Criminal Law of the European Union* (Antwerp, Maklu, 2011) 236–37.

considered as *lex specialis* in relation to Article 83(2). It is noteworthy, in this context, that the Commission has opted in favour of using exclusively Article 325 TFEU as a legal basis for its recent proposal for a directive on fraud.[45] The fate of the Article 325 legal basis in negotiations between the Council and the Parliament remains to be seen.

Attention should also been drawn to two further alternative legal bases for the adoption of EU substantive criminal law, one located within and the other outside the Treaty Title on the area of freedom, security and justice (Title V). Within Title V, the relevant provision is Article 86 TFEU, which enables the establishment of a European Public Prosecutor's Office. According to Article 86(2) TFEU, the European Public Prosecutor's Office will be responsible for investigating, prosecuting and bringing to judgment the perpetrators of, and accomplices in, offences against the Union's financial interests, as determined by the regulation establishing the Office provided for in Article 86(1). According to Article 86(4) TFEU, the powers of the European Public Prosecutor's Office may be subsequently extended by a decision of the European Council to include serious crime having a cross-border dimension amending accordingly Article 86(2) as regards the perpetrators of, and accomplices in, serious crimes affecting more than one Member State. The question thus arises whether legislation defining criminal offences and imposing criminal sanctions for the purposes of the operation of the European Public Prosecutor can be adopted not under Article 83, but under Article 86(2) and 86(4) TFEU – which would lead to the adoption of substantive criminal law under different legislative procedures, by different institutions (note the reference to the European Council in Article 86(4) and by different instruments). The wording of Article 86(2), which calls for fraud offences to be 'determined' by a regulation under Article 86(1), is open enough not to exclude the adoption of substantive EU criminal law on fraud. However, the function of any criminalisation based on Article 86(2) TFEU would be limited to the operation of a European Public Prosecutor's Office and would not exclude the adoption of parallel EU measures under Article 83(2) or Article 325(4) TFEU – with the risk of proliferation and fragmentation of the criminal law on fraud being visible. Article 86(4) TFEU on the other hand – which refers to the inclusion of further areas of crime – should be read as mandating not a criminalisation process, but merely the listing of offences already defined elsewhere.[46]

Another alternative criminalisation legal basis discussed by commentators is the catch-all provision of Article 352(1) TFEU, which confers competence to the EU if action by the Union should prove necessary, within the framework of the policies defined in the treaties, to attain one of the objectives set out in the treaties, and the treaties have not provided the necessary powers.[47] It has been pointed out

[45] COM(2012) 363 final, Brussels, 11 July 2012. Article 325(4) TFEU.

[46] But see here the analysis of Sicurella, who argues that Art 86(2) TFEU also implies a listing function.

[47] See E Herlin-Karnell, *The Constitutional Dimension of European Criminal Law* (Oxford, Hart Publishing, 2012) ch 4.

that Article 352(1) TFEU could lead to the adoption of EU substantive criminal law in cases where the requirement of Article 83(2) TFEU for harmonisation in the underlying policy area has not been met and it has been argued that Article 352 should not apply in the light of this requirement[48] and in the light of the existence of the specific provisions in Title V TFEU.[49] However, this analysis cannot mask the paradox inherent in the constitutionalisation of functional criminalisation in the Lisbon Treaty. If substantive criminal law is, under Article 83(2) TFEU, merely a means to the end of achieving effectiveness of EU law based on the specific EU policies outlined in the treaties, it is difficult to see in principle why the treaty legal bases related to these policies and located elsewhere in the treaties, in particular outside the Treaty Title on the area of freedom, security and justice, cannot be used as additional, or alternative, legal bases for the adoption of EU substantive criminal law. This is especially the case where the conditions of Article 83(2) TFEU are not met, in particular where an area has not been subject to harmonisation measures and there is an urgent need to address a social problem related to the implementation of an EU policy or objective.

D. Limiting Criminalisation: The Lisbon Treaty and Decriminalisation

Extending EU competence to criminalise is not a one-way street under the Lisbon Treaty. The Treaty on the Functioning of the European Union contains a number of possibilities to limit criminalisation. One way of achieving this is by placing limits to the EU competence to harmonise substantive criminal law, resulting largely from Member States' concerns regarding the impact of supranational criminal law on their sovereignty and the integrity of national criminal justice systems. These limits are in addition to the specific conditions for EU competence embedded expressly within Article 83(1) and 83(2) TFEU and which were subject to examination above. In this context, Article 67(3) TFEU calls for the approximation of criminal laws only if necessary – introducing thus in essence a proportionality test applicable to Article 83 TFEU as regards measures concerning the area of freedom, security and justice are concerned.[50] The respect for national legal diversity is further enshrined in Article 67(1) TFEU, according to which the Union shall constitute an area of freedom, security and justice with respect for fundamental rights and the different legal systems and traditions of the Member States. Respect for national diversity is also guaranteed by the emphasis of the Treaty on the respect of the principles of subsidiarity and proportionality, the use of directives to harmonise substantive criminal law under Article 83 TFEU, and

[48] Asp (n 37) 138.

[49] Herlin-Karnell (n 47) 87.

[50] But see the view of Satzger from a domestic criminal law perspective who argues that Art 67(3) TFEU correlates to the principles of subsidiarity and *ultima ratio*: H Satzger, *International and European Criminal Law* (Oxford, Beck/Hart/Nomos, 2012) 76.

the introduction of the emergency brake provision in Article 83(3) TFEU.[51] Criminalisation limits are also placed by the requirement for the Union to respect fully fundamental rights as enshrined in the ECHR (European Convention on Human Rights) and the Charter, in particular the principles of legality and proportionality in criminal offences and sanctions.[52]

On the other hand, the articulation of EU competence to define criminal offences and impose criminal sanctions in the Lisbon Treaty may result in actually limiting the criminalisation powers of Member States. The limited conferral on the EU of competence in substantive criminal law only via the adoption of minimum rules can be potentially decisive in limiting Member States' criminalisation competence. Hans Nilsson has set out the limits that the minimum rules requirement may pose for national sovereignty in substantive criminal law:

> One may argue that the term 'minimum rules' should be seen from the point of view of the Member State, so that the Member States may adopt the constituent elements of the offence as set out in the Framework Decision or Directive, but they are free to have less constituent elements, and thus criminalise more acts than the minimum ones. This is however hardly defendable, both for reasons of logic, legal certainty and respect for the principle of the unity of the common market (in this case the criminal law part of it), as well as for the uniform application of Community/Union law, as laid down in the AETR case law.
>
> It would therefore appear to me that the 'minimum rules' in all substantive criminal law Framework Decisions would not only be minimum, but also maximum rules and that they would in principle be not only 'harmonising' but also 'unifying' instruments in the real sense of the word.[53]

Notwithstanding the uncertainty as to what constitutes a 'minimum rule' under Article 83,[54] Nilsson is right in arguing that the requirement of the EU to legislate via minimum rules under Article 83 TFEU places barriers to Member States overcriminalising and adopting more extensive substantive criminal law provisions than those which have been selected by the European legislator. In this field of shared competence, Member States cannot jeopardise the effectiveness of

[51] V Mitsilegas, 'European Criminal Law and Resistance to Communautarisation Post-Lisbon' (2010) 1 *New Journal of European Criminal Law* 458.

[52] Mitsilegas (n 41) Art 49 commentary.

[53] H Nilsson, 'How to Combine Minimum Rules with Maximum Legal Certainty?' (2011) *Europaraettslig Tidskrift* 665. Nilsson refers to the analysis in the first edition of Klip's *European Criminal Law*, where the author argued that it is necessary to look at the spirit of the instrument when one examines the impact of minimum rules (154). In its second edition, Klip mentions Nilsson's argument but continues to argue that the starting point is the objective of the legal instrument in question (167). A Klip, *European Criminal Law*, 2ndnd ednition (Cambridge/Mortsel, Intersentia, 2012).

[54] There is also a debate on whether the minimum rules requirement allows the EU to adopt minimum maximum penalties as per the pre-Lisbon practice, or also minimum penalties as such: see Asp (n 37) 126. Asp argues that rules requiring a specific minimum penalty are not minimum rules as to require a certain minimum level would amount to full harmonisation as regards the minimum penalties. The Commission has inserted minimum penalty provisions in its recent 'Proposal for a directive on the protection of the Euro and other currencies against counterfeiting by criminal law, and replacing Council Framework Decision 2000/383/JHA' COM(2013) 42 final, 5 February 2013, Art 5(4).

Union legislation by making harsher criminalisation choices domestically.[55] This view is reinforced by the protective character of minimum harmonisation, which has been used traditionally in the context of the internal market as a means of addressing social concerns.[56] Similar concerns are addressed by the treatment of minimum harmonisation in the context of EU measures in the field of criminal procedure under Article 82(2) TFEU. The last indent of this Article states expressly that adoption of the minimum rules referred to in this paragraph (which involve the adoption of largely protective standards including measures on the rights of the defendant in criminal proceedings) will not prevent Member States from maintaining or introducing a higher level of protection for individuals. As Nilsson notes, Member States can go beyond minimum rules as expressly stated in Article 82(2) TFEU to protect individuals, but not so in Article 83 TFEU, as this is not expressly granted in the Treaty and would have the opposite effect.

Another avenue of decriminalisation at national level may arise from the interplay between criminal and administrative law after Lisbon in cases where EU measures are being put forward which envisage the adoption of both criminal and non-criminal (administrative) sanctions. This dual approach to sanctions has been adopted by the European Commission in its recent proposals for revised post-Lisbon legislation introducing sanctions for insider dealing and market manipulation.[57] Unlike the case of its recent proposal on criminal law on fraud, the European Commission here has used Article 83(2) TFEU for the adoption of criminal law provisions, with an internal market legal basis being used for the regulation. Two issues arise in this context in terms of criminalisation powers: the first, as mentioned above, is whether Member States are constrained by the adoption of criminal offences and sanctions under Article 83(2) TFEU in terms of their criminalisation choices at national level; the second, and related point, is whether Member States are similarly constrained by their choices of what to treat as an administrative infraction under the Regulation adopted under a separate legal basis. The requirement to ensure the effectiveness of Union law militates in favour of limiting national powers to criminalise in both cases. In the case of the interplay between EU administrative law and national criminal law, the choice by the EU legislator to address harmful behaviour (in this case market abuse) via merely administrative – and not criminal – sanctions would mean that the effectiveness of the EU policy and measure in question would be jeopardised if Member States adopted a harsher, criminal law approach. National criminalisation would also be

[55] Here the effectiveness of EU criminal law places a limit to domestic criminal law. The Court has already ruled that the need to ensure effectiveness of AFSJ instruments – and in particular the Returns Directive – places limits on national powers to criminalise: Case C-61/11 PPU *Hassen El Dridi, alias Karim Soufi* [2011] ECR I-3015. V Mitsilegas, 'The Changing Landscape of the Criminalisation of Migration in Europe. The Protective Function of European Union Law' in M Guia, M Van der Woude and J Van der Leun (eds), *Social Control and Justice. Crimmigration in an Age of Fear* (The Hague, Eleven International Publishing, 2012) 87–114.

[56] M Dougan, 'Minimum Harmonization and the Internal Market' (2000) 37 *CML Rev* 53.

[57] Commission, 'Draft directive on criminal sanctions for insider dealing and market manipulation' COM(2011), 654 final, 20 October 2011 accompanying a 'Proposal for a regulation under Art 114 TFEU' COM(2011) 651 final, 20 October 2011.

contrary to the principle of proportionality, as enshrined in Article 49(3) of the Charter. In this manner, the adoption of Union law may actually limit criminalisation and lead to decriminalisation at the national level.

IV. POLICY RESPONSES TO THE EU COMPETENCE TO CRIMINALISE AFTER LISBON

The redefinition of the Union's competence to criminalise by the Lisbon Treaty has led to an extensive inter-institutional policy debate over the extent and use of such competence. The European Council's intentions were revealed in the Stockholm Programme[58] that includes a special section on criminal law.[59] The Stockholm Programme confirms in this context that criminal behaviour in the areas of particularly serious crime with a cross-border dimension resulting from the nature or impact of such offences or from a special need to combat them on a common basis should become the object of common definitions of criminal offences and common minimum levels of maximum sanctions and that these are the serious criminal offences referred to in Article 83(1) TFEU. Priority should be given to terrorism, trafficking in human beings, illicit drug trafficking, sexual exploitation of women and children and child pornography and computer crime. The European Council invited the Commission in particular to examine whether the level of approximation is sufficient in relation to the adopted framework decisions and report on the need to establish common definitions and sanctions and to consider submitting new legislative proposals where further approximation is needed, adding that the relationship between approximation of criminal offences or their definition and the double criminality rule in the framework of mutual recognition should be further explored. Particular emphasis has been placed upon the justification and limits or conditions for the adoption of EU substantive criminal law. According to the Stockholm Programme, criminal law provisions should be introduced when they are considered essential in order for the interests to be protected and, as a rule, be used only as a last resort. Minimum rules with regard to the definition of criminal offences and sanctions may also be established when the approximation of criminal laws and regulations of the Member States proves essential to ensure the effective implementation of a Union policy which has been subject to harmonisation measures.

The Stockholm Programme was preceded by the adoption of Conclusions by the Council shortly before the entry into force of the Lisbon Treaty.[60] The Council's intervention can be seen as an attempt to set out a marker on what Member States

[58] The Stockholm Programme – An Open and Secure Europe Serving and Protecting Citizens, OJ 2010 C115/01.

[59] ibid, s 3.3.1.

[60] Draft Council conclusions on model provisions, guiding the Council's criminal law deliberations Council doc 16542/1/09 25 November 2009. See also Council doc 16798/09, 27 November 2009 – endorsed by the JHA Council of 30 November – 1 December 2009, doc 16883/1/09 REV 1 (Presse 355) 31.

consider the extent and limits of EU competence to criminalise after Lisbon. The Council predicted that the Lisbon Treaty is likely to have the effect that criminal law provisions will be discussed within the Council to an even greater extent than at present and that this may result in incoherent and inconsistent criminal provisions in EU legislation. In order to address this, the Council put forward a series of detailed guidelines for EU substantive criminal law. The Council emphasised in particular the requirement to assess the need for criminal provisions and stressed the application of principles including necessity and *ultima ratio* (namely that criminal law provisions should be introduced when they are considered essential in order for the interests to be protected and, as a rule, be used only as a last resort), proportionality and subsidiarity. The Guidelines also emphasised the need to address clearly defined and delimited conduct, which cannot be addressed effectively by less severe measures and added that when there seems to be a need to adopt new criminal provisions the following factors should be further considered: added value or effectiveness of criminal provisions compared to other measures; how serious and/or widespread and frequent the harmful conduct is both regionally and locally within the EU; and the possible impact of existing criminal provisions on EU law and on different legal systems. The Council Guidelines demonstrate a degree of ambiguity with regard to the impact of EU substantive criminal law on the domestic systems of penalties: it is stated that when it has been established that criminal penalties for natural persons should be included it may in some cases be sufficient to provide for effective, proportionate and dissuasive criminal penalties and to leave it to each Member State to determine the level of the penalties but that in other cases there may be a need for going further in the approximation of the levels of the penalties.

The European Commission reacted to the entry into force of the Lisbon Treaty by the publication of a Communication on European Criminal Policy.[61] The Commission focuses on what it considers to be the 'added value' of the harmonisation of substantive criminal law. This 'added value' is perceived to be fourfold: harmonisation of criminal law fosters the confidence of citizens in using their right to free movement and to buy goods or services from providers from other Member States through a more effective fight against crime; it prevents 'forum shopping' by criminals; it strengthens mutual trust among the judiciaries and law enforcement authorities of the Member States facilitating mutual recognition and judicial cooperation in criminal matters; and it helps to prevent and sanction serious offences against EU law in important policy areas, such as the protection of the environment or illegal employment. This is a rather mixed bag of assertions whose credibility is difficult to ascertain – this is the case in particular when the Commission emphasises the subjective elements of EU criminal law as enhancing the confidence of citizens in exercising their Union law rights and as leading to

[61] Commission to the European Parliament, the Council, the European Economic and Social Committee and the Committee of the Regions, 'Towards an EU Criminal Policy: ensuring the effective implementation of EU policies through criminal law' (Communication) COM(2011) final, 20 September 2011.

greater mutual trust among national authorities.[62] Aware that such a vague approach may lead to fears that the Commission would be unduly activistic in the field of substantive criminal law after Lisbon, the Commission proceeds to outline the principles that should guide EU criminal law.[63] These principles include subsidiarity and respect for fundamental rights. The Commission then calls for a two-step approach in criminal law legislation: step one concerns the decision on whether to adopt criminal law measures at all, where it is stated that necessity and proportionality must be respected and that criminal law is a means of last resort (*ultima ratio*); step two concerns the principles guiding the decision on what kind of criminal law measures to adopt: these include the adoption of minimum rules; necessity and proportionality; the existence of clear factual evidence about the nature and effects of the crime in question and about a diverging legal situation in all Member States which could jeopardise the effective enforcement of an EU policy subject to harmonisation; and tailoring the sanctions to the crime. These principles should not, however, be read as a sign of the Commission's limited ambition as regards the adoption of further substantive criminal law at EU level. The last part of the Communication reveals the primary purpose of the document, which is to set out the Commission's vision as to the areas where further EU standards on criminal offences and sanctions will be developed on the basis of Article 83(2) TFEU.[64] The list of such policies provided in the Communication is far-reaching. The Commission claims that it has been established that criminal law measures are necessary in order to protect the financial sector, to fight against fraud and to protect the Euro against counterfeiting and that it will further reflect on the use of criminal law to tackle the illegal economy and financial crime, and on the use of criminal law in areas as diverse as road transport, data protection, customs rules, environmental protection, fisheries policy and internal market policies. Rather than following the principles set out earlier in the Communication, this list confirms an expansive approach treating criminal law merely as a 'means to an end'.[65]

The European Parliament responded by the adoption of a resolution on an EU approach to criminal law.[66] The resolution focused on the principles that should govern EU action in the field of substantive criminal law. The European Parliament stressed the need for EU substantive criminal law to respect the principles of sub-

[62] V Mitsilegas, 'The Limits of Mutual Trust in Europe's Area of Freedom, Security and Justice. From Automatic Inter-state Cooperation to the Slow Emergence of the Individual' (2012) 31 *Yearbook of European Law* 319.

[63] Communication (n 61) 6–9.

[64] ibid, 9–11.

[65] This expansionist tendency is also reflected in the willingness of the Commission to maintain legal basis litigation concerning criminal law. The latest example is a case pending before the ECJ with the Commission requesting the annulment of a road traffic directive adopted under Art 87(2) TFEU (Directive 2011/82/EU facilitating the cross-border exchange of information on road safety related traffic offences, OJ 2011 L288/1, 5 November 2011), with the Commission arguing in favour of the more supranational legal basis of Art 91(1) TFEU (Case C-43/12). Although the case does not involve the adoption of substantive criminal law, it is a clear indication that the Commission will not hesitate to defend its choices or prerogatives in cases involving the use of Art 83(2) TFEU.

[66] Based on 'Report on an EU approach on criminal law' A7-0144/2012, 24 April 2012, rapporteur: Cornelis de Jong.

sidiarity and proportionality and fundamental rights. It was also noted that, in the adoption of EU substantive criminal law, it is not sufficient to refer to abstract notions or to symbolic effect, but that the necessity of new substantive criminal law provisions must be demonstrated by the necessary factual evidence making it clear that damage has occured; there are no less intrusive measures which can be adopted; that the crime in question is of particularly serious nature or is having a direct negative impact on the effective implementation of a Union policy which has been subject to harmonisation measures; there is a need to combat on a common basis; EU action is in conformity with Article 49(3) of the Charter and in particular the severity of the proposed sanctions is not disproportionate to the criminal offence. The European Parliament also recognised the importance of the other general principles governing criminal law (such as the principle of non-retroactivity of criminal sanctions) and welcomed the recognition by the Commission that the first step in criminal law legislation should always be to decide whether to adopt substantive criminal law measures at all.

The differences in the policy approaches of EU institutions towards substantive criminal law are noteworthy. The European Council has placed in the Stockholm Programme emphasis in the continuation of the adoption by the European Union of securitised criminal law. Member States in the Council aimed at pre-empting the supranationalisation brought forward by the entry into force of the Lisbon Treaty and emphasised conditions and limits to the exercise of Union competence under Article 83 post-Lisbon. The Commission has attempted to demonstrate the added value of criminalisation at EU level and focused primarily on functional criminalisation. The European Parliament emphasised the need for EU substantive criminal law to comply with fundamental rights. A common theme in these institutional approaches has been the call to respect either fundamental principles of domestic criminal law (such as *ultima ratio*) or constitutional principles of Union law, including effectiveness, subsidiarity and proportionality. Institutional practice after the entry into force of the Lisbon Treaty in terms of the production of secondary substantive criminal law has not yet revealed a major change to the pre-Lisbon practice as regards new initiatives proposed by the Commission, with a number of proposals on both securitised and functional criminal law tabled and in the pipeline. It is the Union law constitutional principles – and in particular the principles of legality and proportionality as enshrined in Article 49 of the Charter – that will prove influential in the development of EU substantive criminal law.

V. CONCLUSION

The debate over the extent of EU competence to criminalise and introduce criminal sanctions under the Lisbon Treaty is inextricably linked with the broader discussion of the substance of the EU criminalisation policy. In the pre-Lisbon third pillar world, the focus by EU institutions has been largely to determine the constitutional parameters of Union competence in the field, without considering the potential overcriminalisation impact this framing of the issue may have.[67] The entry into force of the Lisbon Treaty will not bring an end to the competence debate, but will serve to refocus the mind on the impact of the exercise of EU competence in substantive criminal law to the Union's criminalisation policy. A key question in this context is whether, irrespective of the existence of EU competence to legislate, criminal law is the most effective way to address security threats or achieve the effective implementation of Union policies. This question is central especially in the light of the constitutional affirmation by the Lisbon Treaty of the Union's functional criminalisation competence. The use of the Lisbon legal bases on substantive criminal law will test this assumption. The development of EU substantive criminal law in conformity with constitutional principles of Union law, and in full respect of the Charter, should lead to a more measured use of criminal law. In this context, it should not be forgotten that supranational criminal law after Lisbon and the limits that this places on Member States' competence to criminalise may lead in practice not to overcriminalisation, but to decriminalisation.

[67] V Mitsilegas, 'The Third Wave of Third Pillar Law: Which Direction for EU Criminal Justice?' (2009) 34 *EL Rev* 523.

8

EU Migration Law: The Opportunities and Challenges Ahead

DORA KOSTAKOPOULOU, DIEGO ACOSTA ARCARAZO AND TINE MUNK

I. INTRODUCTION

FOR MORE THAN four decades labour migration policy in Western Europe has gone without forward planning, coherence, or fairness. Being a by-product of top down decision-making, it has often been attuned to political expedience, shifting discourses about the usefulness or undesirability of migration and to fluctuating domestic economic needs.[1] Because governments tend to be more interested in their own 'office journeys' than in responding to increasing human mobility, migrant labour has been used to fill gaps in labour markets without attention to long-term horizons and the welfare of human beings.[2] Accordingly, there has been little interest in smart policy interventions and the fair regulation of migration since governments often assume that the future will resemble the present[3] and that what really matters are questions of 'who should enter' their territory and how popular anxieties about either growing numbers of migrants or the increasing diversity of the population or both could be appeased, rather than 'how' and 'what aspects' of human mobility should be regulated. In this respect, Western European labour migration policies have been situated in

[1] See generally: R Brubaker (ed), *Immigration and the Politics of Citizenship in Europe and North America* (Lanham, MD, University Press of America, 1989); S Castles and M Miller (eds), *The Age of Migration* (London, Macmillan, 1998); G Freeman, 'Modes of Immigration Politics in Liberal States' (1995) 29 *International Migration Review* 881; A Geddes, *The Politics of Migration and Immigration in Europe* (London, Sage, 2003).

[2] S Castles, 'How Nation-States Respond to Immigration and Ethnic Diversity' (1995) 21 *New Community* 293; D Kostakopoulou, *Citizenship, Identity and Immigration in the European Union: Between Past and Future* (Manchester, Manchester University Press, 2001); CU Schierup et al, *Migration Citizenship and the European Welfare State: A European Dilemma* (Oxford, Oxford University Press, 2006); C Dauvergne, *Making People Illegal: What Globalisation Means for Migration and Law* (Cambridge, Cambridge University Press, 2008).

[3] Interestingly, Dauvergne has observed that 'migration laws of prosperous Western states functioned primarily as sieves through which the shifting whims of national policy could be poured and made law in short order'. *Making People Illegal* (n 2) 9.

the borderlands of law, politics and ideology and one finds shifting paradigms, fluctuating policies and a great deal of unfairness.[4]

The gradual assumption by the EU of competence over migration policy had added several layers of complexity to this picture. This is not merely due to the unavoidable antagonism between competence centralism and 'home rule', but also due to the experimental nature of European integration and the willingness of the Member States to take risks. In this respect, the institutional journey from extra-communitarian agreements (Schengen) to the intergovernmental pillar of justice and home affairs in the context of the Union (the Treaty on European Union) and Title IV on the area of freedom, security and justice (AFSJ)[5] to the full communitarisation of AFSJ by the Lisbon Treaty[6] has shown that no system of temporary sensitive balances can conceal processes of continuous feedback loops of learning and trust-building as well as the desire for better and more efficient regulatory choices.

Accordingly, the Lisbon Treaty set the scene for a more open and accountable EU by infusing the AFSJ with effective parliamentary supervision and judicial scrutiny. Qualified majority voting in the Council and the ordinary legislative procedure have become the norm, thereby upgrading the Parliament to a co-legislative body in this domain. The Commission's exclusive right of initiative over labour migration policy is complemented by the involvement of the national parliaments in the evaluation of the implementation of EU policies in this area[7] and, most importantly, the increasing powers of the Court of Justice of the European Union (ECJ) to review and interpret EU migration law.[8] The ECJ has already delivered its first three rulings on the Long-term Residence Directive, which add to three other rulings on the Family Reunification Directive, in which it has clearly restricted Member State's discretion in light of the purpose of the directive and the principles of effectiveness and proportionality.[9] Finally, the fully binding EU Charter of Fundamental Rights will make migration policy more responsive to human rights protection across the EU. Indeed, the Court has used the Charter in its recent rulings on the Long-term Residence and Family Reunification Directives.[10]

[4] True, Western Europe is not unique in this respect; no national labour migration policy could be considered to be well-integrated and 'stainless'. For instance, in 1964 President Kennedy stated in connection with his proposed reform of US migration policy that 'immigration policy should be generous; it should be fair; it should be flexible. With such a policy we can turn to the world, and to our past, with clean hands and a clear conscience. Such a policy would be but a reaffirmation of old principles'. F Susan Martin, *A Nation of Immigrants* (New York, Cambridge University Press, 2010) 186.

[5] Amsterdam Treaty, in force 1999.

[6] In force 1 December 2009

[7] Art 70 TFEU.

[8] D Acosta and A Geddes, 'The Development, Application and Implications of an EU Rule of Law in the Area of Migration Policy' (2013) 51 *Journal of Common Market Studies* 179.

[9] Case C-508/10 *Commission v Netherlands*, 26 April 2012 nyr; Case C-571/10 *Kamberaj*, 24 April 2012 nyr; Case C-502/10 *Singh*, 18 October 2012 nyr. See on these cases S Peers, 'The Court of Justice Lays the Foundations for the Long-Term Residents Directive: Kamberaj, Commission v Netherlands, Mangat Singh' (2013) 50 *CML Rev* 529.

[10] Case C-571/10 *Kamberaj*; Cases C-356/11 and 357/11 *O, S, L*, 6 December 2012 nyr.

The Treaty of Lisbon has also introduced a new provision that deals expressly with labour migration policy[11] and refers to the

> development of a common immigration policy aimed at ensuring at all stages, the efficient management of migration flows, fair treatment of third country nationals (TCNs) residing legally in the Member States, and the prevention of, and enhanced measures to combat, illegal immigration and trafficking in human beings.[12]

It also contains explicit legal bases for EU action against unauthorised residence, in addition to irregular migration, including the removal and repatriation of persons residing without authorisation[13] and for EU supporting action in the field of integration of long-term resident TCNs.[14] Finally, the Member States' competence to 'determine volumes of admission of TCNs coming from third countries to their territory in order to seek work, whether employed or self-employed' has been explicitly affirmed.[15] This new institutional structure provides for avenues to have a more coherent EU migration law with a more liberal outcome and a stronger focus on the rights of the individual.[16]

The purpose of this chapter is to shed light onto the institutional openings that have appeared in post-Lisbon Europe and the new policy directions that are emerging. These move away from the logic of preventing, restricting and reducing extra-EU migration thereby opening the way for a different frame of labour migration which seeks to maximise migrants' contributions to economies and societies and to manage complex processes of change. Although it is difficult to predict what the future might hold, it is nevertheless the case that the Stockholm Programme and the strengthening of fundamental rights in the EU point towards the possibility of a labour migration policy that replaces national executives' monologues with conversations among multiple participants. The proposal, as yet unfulfilled to adopt an EU Immigration Code[17] could signal the creation of an EU labour migration policy[18] in ways that require refinement of our ethics and political morality while questioning vested interests and established ideology.

The subsequent discussion proceeds as follows. In section II, we examine the Stockholm and post-Stockholm dynamics and reflect on the institutional and analytical roadmap to the EU migration code. Sections III to VI critiques the EU's fragmented approach to labour migration and reflects on the three new directives on TCNs, two of which are under negotiation (the Seasonal Workers and Intra-corporate Transferees Directives). We argue that by seeking to add three new directives to the five existing migration directives, the EU has already laid the path

[11] Art 79 TFEU.

[12] Art 79(1) TFEU.

[13] Art 79(2) TFEU.

[14] Art 79(4) TFEU.

[15] Art 79(5) TFEU.

[16] See Peers, ch 2 in this book.

[17] S Peers, 'An EU Immigration Code: Towards a Common Immigration Policy' (2012) 14 *European Journal of Migration and Law* 33.

[18] C Bason, *Leading Public Sector Innovation: Co-creating for a Better Society* (Bristol, Policy Press, 2010).

for a comprehensive migration code. But more creative thinking, a human dignity-based approach, and a reappraisal of some of the underlying assumptions that underpin policy selection are also needed. The role of the ECJ and the legally binding Charter will also be essential in this regard. The concluding section comments on the changing dynamic and the challenges ahead.

II. IN ANTICIPATION OF THE EU MIGRATION CODE

The Stockholm Programme reflected the innovative processes established by the Lisbon Treaty and brought forward a more citizen-oriented perspective.[19] This appeared to balance the heavy emphasis on security displayed by its predecessor, the Hague Programme,[20] and, although the AFSJ's securitisation past was not disowned, more pragmatism, the 'reweighing' of freedom, human rights and citizens' rights featured quite prominently in it. The subtitle itself of the Stockholm Programme reflected this: 'An open and secure Europe serving and protecting the citizen'. Additionally, an explicit priority was 'the interests and needs of citizens'. Thus, 'the challenge will be to ensure respect for fundamental freedoms and integrity while guaranteeing security in Europe'.[21] The Commission had already laid the path for a more citizen-friendly institutional surrounding by outlining four key policy priorities for 'building a citizen's Europe' in its Communication on 'an area of freedom, security and justice serving the citizen' which was issued in June 2009.[22] Among these, the promotion of a 'Europe of rights' and 'promoting a more integrated society: a Europe that displays responsibility and solidarity in immigration and asylum matters' deserve special mention. This is because the Commission's perspective on the future common migration policy blended a global approach to migration with partnership with third countries and respect for fundamental rights and human dignity. Accordingly, the Communication contained explicit references to the need to promote a dynamic and fair immigration policy based on a comprehensive, innovative and coherent framework that takes into account increased mobility and the needs of national labour markets.[23] A key aspect of this institutional design was the articulation of an Immigration Code that would provide a uniform level of rights comparable to that pertaining to EU citizens thereby ending the present fragmented approach of adopting sectoral directives.[24] TCNs are of course beneficiaries of most rights in the Charter but

[19] C Kaunert and S Leonard, 'Internal Security Policies in the European Union – after the Stockholm Programme' special issue (2010) 19 *European Security.*

[20] A Baldaccini et al (eds), *Whose Freedom, Security and Justice? EU Immigration and Asylum Policy* (Oxford, Hart Publishing, 2007).

[21] Council, The Stockholm Programme – An Open and Secure Europe Serving and Protecting the Citizens, Brussels, 2 December 2009, 17024/09.

[22] D Kostakopoulou, 'An Open and Secure Europe? Fixity and Fissures in the Area of Freedom, Security and Justice after Lisbon and Stockholm' (2010) 19 *European Security* 151.

[23] Commission, 'An area of freedom, security and justice serving the citizen: wider freedom in a safer environment' Brussels, COM(2009) 262/4, 10 June 2009, 23–24.

[24] This is discussed in s III below.

an Immigration Code could provide more coherence with regard to the way they are treated in EU law under different migration directives. Unfortunately, irregular migration was omitted from the substantive framework of the code. This confirmed the maintenance of the present law enforcement and preventive approach to the regulation of undocumented migration.[25]

The key priorities of the Commission's Communication found expression in the Stockholm Programme: promoting citizenship and fundamental rights, on the one hand, and dealing with migration and asylum, on the other, were important policy priorities. However, it is noteworthy that national executives sought to close the conversation about the Immigration Code that the Commission had promoted. Thus, the notion of 'well-managed' migration replaced the Commission's reference to a 'fair immigration policy'. The Stockholm Programme also noted the need for a flexible labour migration policy that takes into account labour market requirements and the closer alignment of migration and development.[26] The Commission's Action Plan highlighted the importance of migration to the Europe 2020 strategy 'by providing an additional source of dynamic growth'[27] and resurrected the mandate of compiling an Immigration Code, which national executives had left out of the Stockholm Programme. The latter would provide a 'uniform level of rights and obligations for legal immigrants' and further contribute to the aim of designing a common migration and asylum policy 'within a long-term vision of respect for fundamental rights and human dignity'.[28] Accordingly, it comes as no surprise that a couple of months later the Council reacted by noting that 'some of the actions proposed by the Commission are not in line with the Stockholm Programme' and urged the Commission to 'take only those initiatives that are in full conformity with the Stockholm Programme'.[29]

Yet the design of a common legal framework would furnish a set of uniform conditions for the admission of the TCNs and a common set of rights and obligations – thereby offsetting a number of externalities in this area, including unfair competition. In the labour migration field, both TCNs and employers should benefit from the new common and more transparent consolidated European immigration framework. As highlighted in the Europe 2020 Strategy, and explicitly stated in the Commission's 2011 Communication on migration, the Member States should recognise that rational migration policies can bring economic dynamism, new ideas, and new jobs into the existing labour market. 'Migrant workers can fill gaps in the labour market, which the EU workers cannot, or do not wish to

[25] Kostakopoulou, 'An Open and Secure Europe?' (2010); E Guild and S Carrera, 'Towards the Next Phase of the EU's Area of Freedom, Security and Justice: The European Commission's Proposals for the Stockholm Programme' (2009) *CEPS Policy Brief*, No 196/20.

[26] Council of the EU 2009, 59.

[27] Commission, 'Delivering an area of freedom, security and justice for Europe's citizens – Action Plan implementing the Stockholm Programme' COM(2010) 171 final, 7.

[28] ibid, 7.

[29] Council, 'Council Conclusions on the Commission Communication "Delivering an area of freedom, security and justice for Europe's citizens – Action Plan implementing the Stockholm Programme"' COM(2010) 171 final, Luxembourg, 3 June 2010, 2.

fill'.[30] Moreover, labour migration can contribute to addressing the demographic challenge facing the EU in the future where it is estimated that the EU would need significant net migration in order to keep the ratio of working-age population to the total population of the 2008 level.[31] A more flexible and coherent labour migration policy would lead to increased competitiveness and economic vitality, and make the Member States more prepared for the future demand for labour.[32] Appreciating the positive impact of migration, however, would require the transcendence of existing policy orientations towards migration restriction and control in favour of an open, pluralistic and dynamic approach which puts more emphasis on human beings' actual contributions and cooperative practices than their state of origin.[33] As such, it would reflect Dewey's belief that:

> [D]emocracy is more than a form of government; it is primarily a mode of associated living, of conjoint communicated experience. The extension in space of the number of individuals who participate is an interest so that each has to refer his own action to that of others and to consider the action of others to give point and direction to his own, is equivalent to the breaking down of those barriers of class, race and national territory which kept men from perceiving the full import of their activity.[34]

True, threatening to remove the nationalist frame upon which contemporary political communities rest would give rise to social protectionist discourses about the strain that migration places upon social services such as education, health care, housing, job training and policing. Yet the argument that migration correlates negatively with both generous and high quality welfare services assumes incorrectly that migrants are just poor and recipients of welfare and that too many people would demand services at the same time. Both assumptions are simplifications and are contradicted by empirical data. Indeed, if one examines the economic contributions that migrant employees, self-employed persons, consumers and investors make and their impact on the economy's long-term or 'trend' rate of growth, any short-term difficulties are generally outweighed by overall welfare gains and long-term perspectives.[35] For this reason, changing perspectives must be linked with other processes including laws and changes in policy agendas. The drafting of an EU Immigration Code could reinforce changing perspectives on migration.

[30] Commission, 'Migration' (Communication) COM(2011) 248 final, 12.

[31] ibid.

[32] Compare Council of European Union, Note from the Presidency to the Council of Employment, Social Policy, Health and Consumer Affairs. Legal Immigration (Labour Immigration), Brussels, 1 December 2010, 16929/10. SOC 796, MIGR 132, 2.

[33] W Connolly, *The Ethos of Pluralisation* (Minneapolis, University of Minnesota Press, 1995); R Rubio-Marin, *Immigration as a Democratic Challenge: Citizenship and Inclusion in Germany and the United States* (Cambridge, Cambridge University Press, 2000); D Kostakopoulou, 'Towards a Theory of Constructive Citizenship in Europe' (1996) 4 *Journal of Political Philosophy* 337.

[34] J Dewey, *Democracy and Education* (New York, Macmillan, [1916] 1964).

[35] J Simon, *The Economic Consequences of Immigration* (Oxford, Blackwell, 1989); K Butcher and D Card, 'Immigration and Wages: Evidence from the 1980s' (1991) 81 *American Economic Review* 292. Compare also Commission, 'Immigration, integration and employment' (Communication) COM(2003) 336 final.

According to the 2010 Roadmap, the Immigration Code would not only codify the existing framework, but it would also make it more open, fair, flexible and coherent.[36] In its 2011 Communication,[37] the Commission notes that simplifying administrative procedures and reviewing the mobility restrictions for TCNs within the EU, and between the EU and third-counties, without the migrant workers losing their rights of residence and employment would help labour markets function better. The Communication was issued in response to the arrival of North African migrants and asylum seekers during the Arab Spring uprisings and to French and Italian calls for either a reconsideration or implementation of the Schengen Agreement. Nevertheless, it also included explicit references to the need for a coherent EU approach in this field that adopts a long-term perspective and a global approach. An important aspect of the latter constitute mobility partnerships between the EU and Southern Mediterranean countries (Morocco, Tunisia and Egypt) along the lines of those concluded between the EU and Moldova, Cape Verde and Georgia.[38] Such bilateral agreements are intended to facilitate the mobility of TCNs to the EU and the portability of social security rights in exchange for the state of origin's determination to ensure the effective management of border crossings and the prevention of irregular migration. This, in turn, is to foster Euro–Mediterranean cooperation 'in the framework of the renewed European Neighbourhood Policy'.[39] What is quite significant here is that despite the restrictive agendas pursued by the Member States towards migration in a recession-ridden Europe, the Commission 'has been continuously defending mobility as an important aspect of the cooperation with its neighbours'.[40] Having said this, it remains the case that mobility is embraced instrumentally as a means of filling European labour market shortages and eventually encouraging the return of migrant workers without a sustained attention to the rights of migrants, including their right to family reunification, as well as the broader EU strategy of securitising the southern Mediterranean border. Similarly, the securitisation paradigm that characterised the earlier phases of cooperation in migration matters has not disappeared. The Commission's Communication refers to ensuring 'a well managed mobility in a secure environment. Preventing irregular migration and maintaining public security is compatible with the objective of increased mobility'.[41]

Hopefully, the process of the articulation of the Immigration Code will bring more coherence in the propositions and policy orientations underpinning EU migration law as well as a reappraisal and possibly restructuring of the EU's policy

[36] See especially: Peers, 'An EU Immigration Code' (2012).

[37] Commission, 'Migration' (Communication) (2011) 12.

[38] On this, see Commission, 'Circular migration and mobility partnerships between the European Union and third countries' (Communication) COM(2007) 248 final; R Kunz, S Lavenex and M Panizzon (eds), Multilayered Migration Governance. The Promise of Partnership (Oxon, Routledge, 2011).

[39] Commission, 'Migration' (Communication) (2011) 13.

[40] M Martin, 'A Radically Changing Political Landscape in the Southern Mediterranean? The Dialogue for Migration, Mobility and Security with the Southern Mediterranean Counties' (2011) Statewatch Analysis, accessed at: www.statewatch.org/analyses/no-136-southern-med.pdf.

[41] ibid, 11.

towards irregular migration and the measures adopted in this domain thus far. After all, policies never remain still, environments are characterised by complexity and unpredictability and markets are in states of transition. In the next section we examine how the Immigration Code may tackle the current fragmentation in the existing (legal) migration regime. By adding three new directives, that is, the Single Permit, Seasonal Workers and the Intra-corporate Transferees Directives, to the five existing migration directives, the EU has already laid the path for a comprehensive Immigration Code which includes regulation of entry and residence into the EU, a set of uniform rights across the EU for TCNs, long-term residence status in the host Member States and mobility to a second Member State, the mobility of researchers and students, highly-skilled as well as low-skilled migrants, and the mobility of managerial and technical employees of branches and subsidiaries of multinational corporations. In the future a reappraisal of some of the underlying assumptions and value choices that underpin policy selection in the migration field may be required.[42]

III. THREE NEW DIRECTIVES ON THIRD-COUNTRY NATIONALS

It is anticipated that the Immigration Code would furnish a coherent and consolidated legal framework for the regulation of migration by building on, and further supplementing, the five existing directives in the fields of legal immigration; namely, Directive 2009/50/EC on the conditions of entry and residence of third-country nationals for the purpose of highly qualified employment (Blue Card); Directive 2005/71/EC on specific procedures for admitting third-country nationals for the purposes of scientific research; Directive 2004/114/EC on the admission of third-country nationals for the purposes of studies, pupil exchange, unremunerated training or voluntary service; Directive 2003/109/EC concerning the status of third-country nationals who are long-term residents and Directive 2003/86/EC on the right to family reunification. However, this process also presupposes the addition of new categories of workers,[43] given the fact that European labour markets face different types of labour skills shortages and the structural need for low-skilled and low-qualified workers is likely to intensify in the future.[44]

EU labour migration regulation has thus far been fragmented and incoherent. When the EU finally obtained a clear competence to deal with migration issues with the entry into force of the Treaty of Amsterdam in 1999, the Tampere Council Conclusions heralded a period in which the EU would adopt several provisions in the area. It was soon seen how dealing with economic migration was

[42] More than a decade ago, AGIT (Academic Group on Immigration – Tampere) sought to introduce such an interpretative turn by proposing a positive, humane and comprehensive approach to migration: 'Efficient, Effective and Encompassing Approaches to a European Immigration and Asylum Policy'. Final Draft, 9 June 1999. These proposals continue to be relevant.

[43] Roadmap, 'EU Immigration Code' No 2 10/2010, 1.

[44] Compare European Parliament, Procedure File. COD/2010/0210, 'Seasonal Employment: Conditions of Entry and Residence of Third-country Nationals' Summaries 13 July 2010, 2.

subject to controversy and disagreement between Member States. Indeed, the Commission proposed a directive in 2001 on the entry and residence of TCNs for the purpose of paid employment and self-employed economic activities that, despite being positively welcomed by the other institutions, was rejected by the Council.[45] This made the Commission change its strategy by re-launching the debate, following the Hague Programme, with a Green Paper issued in January 2005[46] and the subsequent adoption of a Policy Plan on legal migration in December of that year.[47] In this document, the Commission announced its intention to present several proposals consisting of a general framework directive and of four specific directives, thereby addressing the conditions of entry and residence of different categories of TCNs (highly skilled, seasonal workers, intra-corporate transferees and remunerated trainees). Accordingly, the by-product of the aborted attempt to adopt a horizontal directive designed to regulate the entry and residence conditions for all TCNs exercising paid and self-employed activities has been the adoption of a category by category worker regulative framework which accords different rights, standards and conditions of residence to different categories of third-country workers, as stated above. The Immigration Code would reverse the prevailing sectoral approach and establish a uniform set of rights for all TCNs legally residing in a Member State.

As of 1 June 2013, two of these directives had been adopted,[48] whereas two had already been proposed[49] and one was yet to be proposed.[50] Out of the two adopted directives, the EU Blue Card Directive facilitates the admission of highly-skilled migrants to the EU by establishing a common fast-track and flexible procedure for their admission with a view to advancing the EU's knowledge-based economy.[51] In December 2011 the EU finally adopted the Single Permit Directive.

Negotiations related to the Intra-corporate Transfer and Seasonal Workers Directives are still under way. The reports on these directives were approved by the Parliament in January 2012 and April 2012 respectively, by the Committee on Civil

[45] B Ryan, 'The European Union and Labour Migration: Regulating Admission or Treatment?' in A Baldaccini et al (eds), *Whose Freedom, Security and Justice?* (Oxford, Hart Publishing, 2007).

[46] Commission, 'An EU approach to managing economic migration' (Green Paper) COM(2004) 811 final.

[47] Commission, 'Policy Plan on Legal Migration' COM(2005) 669 final.

[48] Council Directive 2009/50/EC of 25 May 2009 on the conditions of entry and residence of third-country nationals for the purposes of highly qualified employment, OJ 2009 L155/17; Directive 2011/98/EU of the European Parliament and of the Council of 13 December 2011 on a single application procedure for a single permit for third-country nationals to reside and work in the territory of a Member State and on a common set of rights for third-country workers legally residing in a Member State, OJ 2011 L343/1.

[49] Commission, 'Proposal for a directive of the European Parliament and of the Council on conditions of entry and residence of third-country nationals in the framework of an intra-corporate transfer' COM(2010) 378 final, Brussels, 13 July 2010; 'Proposal for a directive of the European Parliament and of the Council on the conditions of entry and residence of third-country nationals for the purposes of seasonal employment' COM(2010) 379 final, Brussels, 13 July 2010.

[50] The Commission has yet to propose a directive on remunerated trainees.

[51] See, for a comprehensive analysis and critique of the Directive, S Peers, 'Legislative Update: EC Immigration and Asylum Law. Attracting and Deterring Labour Migration: The Blue Card and the Employer Sanctions Directive' (2009) 11 *European Journal of Migration and Law* 387.

Liberties, Justice and Home Affairs, which added amendments to the original proposals by the Commission. In turn, the Council reached a general agreement on inter-corporate transfers in June 2012[52] and on seasonal workers in December 2012.[53] As Peers has highlighted, it is noteworthy that the two EU presidencies (Denmark and Cyprus) in 2012 failed to reach agreements in this area.[54]

IV. THE SINGLE PERMIT DIRECTIVE

When the Commission proposed a directive on a single permit in 2007, it had in mind an instrument that would secure the legal status of third-country workers while at the same time providing for a simplified common procedure for the applicants. The main rationale behind the directive was that there existed a 'rights gap' between national workers, on the one hand, and third-country workers, on the other, and that addressing that gap would reduce the possibility of facing unfair competition for EU citizens, as well as the risk of exploitation for TCNs. It would also create a 'level playing field within the EU' for all those TCNs regularly working in the different Member States.[55] Whereas the establishment of a simplified common procedure did not prove that contentious during the negotiations, as shown by the fact that the final text is fairly similar to the proposal, the same cannot be said about the scope of the directive and the protection to be granted to third-country workers.[56] In fact, four years were necessary to reach agreement on a directive which from the very beginning had left issues aside which could have been much more controversial such as admission conditions or the grounds for the non-renewal of permits.[57] The Council was only able to reach an agreement after the shift with the Lisbon Treaty to qualified majority voting. In turn, the Parliament rejected the proposal when it first voted on it in December 2010.[58] There were two main bones of contention. First, some MEPs felt that the scope of the Directive was too limited since it did not include seasonal or posted workers

[52] Council of the European Union Permanent Representatives Committee, 'Proposal for a directive of the European Parliament and of the Council on conditions of entry and residence of third-country nationals in the framework of an intra-corporate transfer' (2012) Council doc 10618/12 available at: www.statewatch.org/news/2012/jul/eu-council-ict-10618-12.pdf.

[53] The Council of the European Union Permanent Representatives Committee, 'Proposal for a directive of the European Parliament and of the Council on the conditions of entry and residence of third-country nationals for the purposes of seasonal employment' (2012) Council doc 17100/12 available at: www.statewatch.org/news/2013/jan/eu-council-seasonal-workers-mandate-17100-12.pdf.

[54] S Peers, 'Analysis EU Immigration and Asylum Law in 2012: The Year of Living Ineffectually' (2012) available at: www.statewatch.org/analyses/no-210-immigration-asylum-12.pdf.

[55] Proposal Single Permit Directive, 2–3.

[56] See on the negotiations: G Brinkmann, 'Opinion of Germany on the Single Permit Proposal' (2012) 14 *European Journal of Migration and Law* 351.

[57] S Peers, 'Single Permits and Workers' Rights' in S Peers, E Guild, D Acosta Arcarazo, K Groenendijk and V Moreno-Lax (eds), *EU Immigration Law: Text and Commentary*, 2nd edn (Leiden, Martinus Nijhoff, 2012); Y Pascouau and S McLoughlin, 'EU Single Permit Directive: A Small Step Forward in EU Migration Policy' (2012) *European Policy Centre*, Policy Brief, 24 January 2012.

[58] Pascouau and McLoughlin (2012).

among others. Second, there were also some doubts regarding the many possible limitations on the right to equal treatment, especially with regards to the portability of pensions when a single permit holder decided to move to a third-country. Accordingly, the Civil Liberties, Justice and Home Affairs Committee and the Employment and Social Affairs Committee adopted opposing positions. It was only in March 2011 that the Parliament decided its position so that it could negotiate an agreement with the Council.[59] The exclusion from the scope of the directive of certain categories of third-country workers remained in the final text but the Parliament managed to secure the portability of pensions.

The Directive[60] aims at simplifying and harmonising procedural rules to obtain a single permit 'to reside for the purpose of work', so as to make the process easier for third-country workers as well as their employers. In line with the Tampere goal of ensuring fair treatment of TCNs, as re-stated in the Stockholm Programme, it also provides 'a common set of rights' for workers regularly residing in the EU, 'irrespective of the purposes for which they were initially admitted'.[61] Hence, the Directive is divided into Chapters II and III. Chapter II deals with the single application procedure and permit. The final version, although amended, does not largely depart from the spirit of the Commission's proposal. It establishes the procedure, rules related to the authority in charge of dealing with the procedure, remedies, access to information and fees. Chapter III enumerates a series of rights that third-country workers shall enjoy under equal conditions with nationals of the Member State where they reside. These include working conditions, freedom of association, education and vocational training, access to social security, tax benefits and access to goods and services including counselling services offered by national employment offices. Member States are, however, allowed to limit these equal treatment provisions in various ways.[62] This means that the level of protection enjoyed by long-term residents is much higher than that of third-country workers who would hold a single permit. In fact, the Commission's intention to address the 'rights gap' has not been successful in two crucial areas: access to labour markets and social assistance.[63] There are, however, other areas where the gap has been reduced such as unemployment and family benefits, portability of pensions and access to public services. This has left commentators with a 'sweet and sour' taste when discussing the Directive. Indeed, despite making a contribution towards ensuring equal treatment, the situation of single permit holders will remain somewhat precarious[64] even if certain provisions will improve their integration into the job market.[65] A complete evaluation is certainly difficult due to

[59] European Parliament. Procedure files: 2007/0229(COD). Text adopted: P7-TA(2011)0115. Single Application Procedure for Residence and Work, Brussels, 24 March 2011, 2.

[60] The UK, Ireland and Denmark are not bound by the Directive.

[61] Art 1.

[62] Art 12.

[63] Peers, 'Single Permits' (2012) 228.

[64] ibid; Pascouau and McLoughlin (2012).

[65] T Huddleston, 'EU Single Permit makes workplace "slightly favourable" for integration' (2011) MIPEX Blog.

the various 'may' provisions that will require an analysis of the transposition of the Directive in the different Member States. Importantly, the reference in the Preamble to the Tampere Conclusions, as well as the principle of effectiveness, will no doubt mean that the ECJ will have to consider its case law on EU citizens when interpreting this Directive. As argued earlier, the ECJ has drastically reduced Member State's margin of discretion when interpreting the provisions of the Long-term Residence Directive, even those with a reference to national law, so as not to deprive it of its effectiveness. These rulings will have an important effect on the way in which Member States implement this Directive as well. For example, Article 10 of the Directive provides that Member States may request applicants to pay fees which 'shall be proportionate and *may* be based on the services actually provided for the processing of the applications' (our emphasis). However, following *Commission v Netherlands*,[66] it is clear that this 'may' clause will need to be interpreted as a 'shall' one so as not to endanger the effectiveness of the Directive.[67] The Directive does not apply to several categories of third-country workers including those who have applied for admission or been admitted as seasonal workers or those who have applied for admission or been admitted as intra-corporate transferees, which are discussed below.

V. THE SEASONAL WORKERS DIRECTIVE

The Seasonal Workers Directive was proposed by the Commission in 2010[68] and its main rationale is to regulate the status of seasonal workers who are becoming less and less available from within the EU itself, but are needed for sectors such as agriculture, construction and tourism. Many third-country seasonal workers face exploitation and those economic sectors requiring seasonal workers are prone to employ migrants in an irregular situation. Hence, the Directive seeks to secure a legal status for seasonal workers and to furnish a fast-track procedure for the provision of a temporary permit while, at the same time, protecting EU citizens from unfair competition. Since the negotiations between the Council and the Parliament are still ongoing and there is not yet an agreed text, our discussion focuses on the most important provisions in the proposal which are proving contentious and on which the institutions' views diverge.[69]

[66] Case C-508/2010 *Commission v Netherlands*, 26 April 2012 nyr.

[67] Peers, 'An EU Immigration Code' (2012) 47.

[68] Commission, 'Proposal for a directive on the conditions of entry and residence of third-country nationals for the purposes of seasonal employment' COM(2010) 379.

[69] We will refer to the Council position by looking at the text that received the support of the majority of delegations at the meeting of the Permanent Representatives Committee on 5 December and that will thus serve as a mandate for the presidency to start discussions with the European Parliament: Council doc 17100/12. For the Parliament's stance we will use the LIBE Rapporteur's draft legislative resolution available at: www.europarl.europa.eu/document/activities/cont/201205/20120504ATT44532/20120504ATT44532EN.pdf. On 25 April 2012, the European Parliament's LIBE Committee held its orientation vote on the proposal. The result of the vote also incorporates the opinion of the EMPL Committee and serves as a mandate for the European Parliament for negotiations with the Council.

First, the proposal provides that the Directive would only apply to those TCNs residing outside the territory of the Member States and would not apply to those who arrive with the intention of staying for less than three months.[70] This provision is supported by the Council, but has been criticised by different NGOs that point to the presence of a large number of TCNs already residing and working in seasonal jobs with an irregular status.[71] Sharing these concerns, the European Parliament suggests that the Directive should apply to migrants in an irregular situation but only for a transitional period after the transposition of the Directive. This is, in our view, a fair acknowledgement of a reality on the ground with many irregular migrants working on seasonal employment.[72]

The meaning of seasonal work is another point of contention. According to the Commission,[73] it would refer to those sectors where there is a higher workforce requirement by virtue of an event or pattern including holiday periods in tourism or harvesting periods in agriculture. Again, NGOs have contested the vagueness of this provision as inadequate and the European Parliament would like to see this provision better defined and limited only to tourism, agriculture and the horticulture sector while at the same time allowing the Member States the option to extend it further provided that social partners agree to such an extension. By contrast, the Council would prefer to leave this definition fairly open.

Chapter II deals with the conditions of admission, grounds for refusal, withdrawal and non-renewal of the permit. While there are differences in the position of the three institutions, we prefer to focus on certain issues surrounding the procedure and the rights granted to seasonal workers that are, in our view, more important. With regard to the procedure, the possible length of the residence permit is a key element. The proposal provides for a maximum period of six months in any calendar year without any possibility to renew it beyond that period.[74] This is consistent with the idea provided in Recital 6 that there is the need to prevent any temporary stay from becoming permanent. The Council advocates for a period of between five to nine months whereas the Parliament, while agreeing with the Commission as regards the six-months limit, would like to introduce a new provision by which seasonal workers who may be entitled to stay in the Member State under a different permit or visa would not be required to return to their country of origin. Under any of the three possible scenarios seasonal workers would not be able to start counting their residence period towards the acquisition of a long-term residence status. This heightens the importance of clearly defining the jobs for which seasonal workers may be employed as opposed to those sectors where

[70] Art 2.

[71] Joint NGO Statement, 'EU Seasonal Migrant Workers' Directive: full respect of equal treatment necessary' 20 April 2011, available at: www.cire.be/ressources/EU-Seasonal-Migrant-Workers-Joint-NGO-Statement-20110420.pdf.

[72] T Maroukis et al, 'Irregular Migration and Informal Economy in Southern and Central-Eastern Europe: Breaking the Vicious Cycle?' (2011) 49 *International Migration* 129.

[73] Art 3.

[74] Art 11.

Member States would need to offer the TCN concerned a renewable temporary residence permit, which could eventually lead to obtaining long-term residence.

Another central issue concerns the rights of seasonal workers, addressed in Chapter IV, which tend to be more limited than those entailed by the Single Permit Directive. These include the right to enter and stay in the territory exercising the employment activity for which the permit has been granted, working conditions applicable to seasonal workers as established by the legislation or applicable collective agreements in the Member State concerned and equal treatment with nationals with regards to freedom of association, the branches of social security coming under Article 3 of Council Regulation 883/2004, payment of statutory pensions when they move to a third country and access to certain goods, with the exception of public housing and counselling services. Member States would also need to make sure that there is a mechanism to facilitate complaints and that the employers provide seasonal workers with adequate accommodation.

As expected, positions diverge on these issues with the European Parliament showing more concern for workers' rights and the Council aligning itself with the Commission or moving towards a more restrictive position. Yet this central element requires resolution particularly since avoiding the exploitation of migrants is a goal pursued by this legislation. Indeed, Peers argues that the proposal breaches Article 15(3) of the Charter of Fundamental Rights, which states that TCNs authorised to work in a Member State should enjoy working conditions equal to those pertaining to EU citizens.[75] These concerns seem to have been taken on board by the Council since its position provides for equal treatment with nationals with regard to 'working conditions including pay and dismissal as well as health and safety requirements at the workplace'.[76]

Finally, family reunification does not feature in the draft directive. So whereas the intra-corporate transferees' proposal, examined below, seeks to facilitate the admission of family members even when the sponsor TCN will reside for a short period of time, seasonal workers receive less protection. This gives rise to concerns that the EU privileges the economically stronger migrants while depriving of rights 'the equally needed but economically weaker' seasonal workers.

VI. THE INTRA-CORPORATE TRANSFEREES DIRECTIVE

The proposed Directive on Intra-corporate Transferees deals with the mobility of managerial and qualified employees belonging to the same undertaking or the same group of undertakings. The European Commission proposed this directive in July 2010[77] with a view to facilitating the movement of managers, specialist and graduate trainees in order to meet the needs of branches and subsidiaries of multinational corporations. In what follows we will refer to the proposal. The directive

[75] Peers, 'Single Permits' (2012) 181.
[76] Art 16 of the Council's Position, Council doc 17100/12.
[77] COM(2010) 378 final, Brussels, 13 July 2010.

provides for a transparent and simplified procedure for an intra-corporate transfer of key personnel thereby advancing the knowledge-based economy in Europe and promoting investment flows. Article 3(b) defines an intra-corporate transfer as

> the temporary secondment of a TCN from an undertaking established outside the territory of a Member State and to which the TCN is bound by a work contract, to an entity belonging to the undertaking or to the same group of undertakings which is established inside this territory.

In order to take advantage of this possibility, transferees must be managers, specialists and graduate trainees with a higher education qualification and must have been employed within the same group of undertakings for at least 12 months prior to the transfer. Member States have an obligation to provide all the necessary information on entry, residence and rights as well as the evidence that needs to accompany an application for an intra-corporate transfer. They are free to determine whether the application has to be made by the TCN or by the host entity,[78] but it can only be considered and examined if the transferee is outside the territory of the Member State to which admission is sought.[79] Member States have an obligation to grant successful applicants every facility to obtain the necessary visa, while there also exist provisions for simplified procedures for recognised groups of undertakings, including a fast-track admission procedure.[80]

If the conditions set out in the directive have been met, inter-corporate transferees will be issued with a specific residence permit, which would allow them to carry out their assignment in different units belonging to the same transnational corporation, including in entities located in another Member State. The permit shall have a minimum validity of one year, or of a shorter period if the duration of the transfer is shorter, and 'may be extended to a maximum of three years for managers and specialists and one year for graduate trainees'.[81] During its period of validity, transferees will have the rights to enter and stay, free access to the entire territory of the Member State issuing the permit, the right to carry out the economic activities they have been authorised to take up and to carry out their assignments at clients' sites.[82]

The permit would also give inter-corporate transferees favourable conditions for family reunification, including the absence of the obligation to comply with integration measures for family members and a brief waiting period of two months for obtaining residence permits for family members and equal treatment with nationals of the host Member State with respect to freedom of association and trade union membership, recognition of diplomas, certificates and other professional qualifications, provisions in national law regarding the branches of social security, the payment of statutory pensions and access to

[78] Art 10(1).
[79] Art 10(3).
[80] Arts 7 and 8.
[81] Art 11(2).
[82] Art 13.

goods and services except public housing and counselling services afforded by employment services.[83]

The Member States can always reject an application for an intra-corporate transfer if the conditions for admission are not met, the documents presented have been fraudulently acquired, falsified or tampered with, if the employer has been sanctioned for undeclared work and/or illegal employment, if they have concerns about the volumes of admission of TCNs and in case of several locations in several Member States, they can limit the geographical scope of the validity of the residence permit to the Member States where the conditions for intra-corporate transfer are met.[84] The specified grounds for the withdrawal or refusal to renew the intra-corporate transfer are fraud, residence for purposes other than those for which he/she was authorised to reside, if the conditions for the intra-corporate transfer are not met and reasons of public policy, public security or public health are.[85] The first two grounds bring about a mandatory withdrawal while the latter two fall within the discretion of the Member State concerned.

The amendments in the Civil Liberties Committee Report accommodate some of the issues discussed above. The key changes to the proposal improve the conditions of transferred workers between the EU Member States, and give their relatives the right to work in the host country. The amendments to the directive also provide for better definitions on host entity and the categories of workers covered by the directives and reduce the prior employment conditions.[86] As stated earlier, the Council achieved a Common Position in June 2012 when Member States finally reached a general agreement to begin negotiations with the Parliament.[87] One of the main disagreements between both institutions relates to the fact that the Council would like to give intra-corporate transferees similar rights to those enjoyed by posted workers whereas the Parliament would prefer to grant them rights equal to those enjoyed by EU citizens.

VII. THE CHANGING DYNAMIC AND THE CHALLENGES AHEAD

Notwithstanding the evolving legal framework in the field of legal migration, which was almost unthinkable 15 years ago, it nevertheless, remains the case that

[83] Art 14(2).

[84] Art 6.

[85] Art 7.

[86] On 14 February 2012, the European Parliament's LIBE Committee held its orientation vote on the proposal. The result of the vote also incorporates the opinion of the EMPL Committee and serves as a mandate for the European Parliament for negotiations with the Council. It is available at:www.europarl.europa.eu/document/activities/cont/201202/20120215ATT38244/20120215ATT38244EN.pdf. Rapporteur: Salvatore Iacolino. Twenty-five amendments are made to the original proposal. The Committee approved the report in 42 votes in favour, 5 against and 3 abstentions.

[87] The Council Position derives from the text which received the support of the majority of delegations at the meeting of the Permanent Representatives Committee on 30 May 2012 and which serves as a mandate for the presidency to pursue discussions with the Parliament. This is available at:www.statewatch.org/news/2012/jul/eu-council-ict-10618-12.pdf.

the drafting of an Immigration Code will lead the EU to navigate relatively uncharted waters. Minimalist and maximalist positions will undoubtedly collide and new dilemmas may arise. Yet, a Code would provide the opportunity to raise standards as well as giving more visibility to migrant rights and facilitating the cohesiveness and clarity of EU migration law.[88] Also, by bringing together rights in a single document a consolidation effect may take place since 'rights engender rights'.[89]At the same time concrete improvements have already taken place and the directives examined thus far show that there exists a changing dynamic and understanding of what is perceived to be a problem with TCNs mobility. Although the ongoing interplay between closing and opening dynamics is bound to continue, the legally binding Charter and the renewed role of the ECJ will prove essential in enhancing the rights of TCNs as is clear from its rulings on the Long-term Residence Directive and Family Reunification Directive in 2012.

True, like its preceding variegated institutional frameworks, this process will involve a leap of faith. Yet, it is also bound to give rise to new patterns of regulation of migration, display a great deal of emphasis on rights as well as respect for the fundamental rights of TCNs and the wearing out of the securitisation paradigm of migration owing to adjacent readings with the Citizenship Directive (2004/38) and the need to eliminate incoherence and unjustified distinctions among categories of migrants. As such, notwithstanding existing constraints in design and outcomes, it will capture the trend towards developing a long-term, integrated and simplified model of labour migration that is strong in mobility, genuine partnerships as well as rights protection. This will view migrants not just as vendors of labour power, but as participants in, and expected full contributors to, practices of socio-economic cooperation. The success of this approach will depend as much on the willingness of national executives to dispense with ideological narratives about migration restriction as on leadership and forward thinking.

[88] Peers, 'An EU Immigration Code' (2012) 61.

[89] E Guild, 'The Evolution of the Concept of Union Citizenship after the Lisbon Treaty' in S Morano-Foadi and M Malena (eds), *Integration for Third-Country Nationals in the European Union* (Cheltenham, Edward Elgar, 2012) 3–15, 5.

9

*Life After Lisbon: EU Asylum Policy as a Factor of Migration Control**

VIOLETA MORENO-LAX

I. INTRODUCTION

IN HIS CONTRIBUTION to this book, Peers asks the general question of whether the institutional changes introduced by the Lisbon Treaty have translated into a more liberal policy in the field of justice and home affairs.[1] In relation to asylum he reaches a mixed conclusion, establishing that liberalism in certain areas, such as qualification standards, may well be undercut by persistent conservatism in other respects, exemplified by very limited improvements in responsibility allocation and determination procedures.

This chapter investigates the structural reasons for this conclusion. After a review of the current regime and its evolution since Tampere, the chapter advances that, despite Lisbon providing the necessary legal tools for an improved supranational policy, the lack of political will to revise underlying principles inherited from previous eras has prevented the achievement of a Common European Asylum System (CEAS) in full compliance 'with the [1951] Geneva Convention . . . and other relevant treaties'.[2]

The main proposition is that asylum policy has been permeated by migration control preoccupations that have substantially transformed its object and scheme. Instead of a predominant focus on refugee protection, the CEAS combines humanitarian objectives with considerations of border management and the fight against unauthorised movement. This has happened through a process, whereby third-country nationals (including refugees) have been conceptualised as a threat to market integration requiring measures of exception and control.

* I thank Michael Dougan, Jean-François Durieux, Maria-Teresa Gil-Bazo, Helen Stalford, and Lilian Tsourdi for their invaluable comments on previous drafts.

[1] Treaty on EU (TEU) and Treaty on the Functioning of the EU (TFEU), OJ 2010 C83/13 and 47.

[2] Art 78(1) TFEU.

II. LISBON: AN OPPORTUNITY LOST?

In the aftermath of the Yugoslavian refugee crises, Tampere required the establishment of a regime 'based on the full and inclusive application of the Geneva Convention'.[3] The system was to be accomplished in two steps, adopting minimum standards in key areas as a first step and a 'common procedure' and 'uniform status' in the long term.[4]

The Amsterdam Treaty provided the legal bases for the adoption of the instruments of the first phase.[5] Three key directives introducing minimum qualification standards,[6] minimum criteria for determination procedures,[7] and minimum reception conditions were adopted,[8] in addition to a regulation establishing rules to apportion responsibility for asylum applications.[9]

Criticism has been voiced by multiple actors, including the UNHCR (United Nations High Commissioner for Refugees),[10] on the low quality of some of their provisions.[11] Although harmonisation may have had a positive impact on countries with little or no prior experience in refugee protection,[12] an overall picture of suboptimal standards emerges, especially as regards procedural norms.[13] This may be partly attributed to the need for consensus, with the Council acting by unanimous vote and the Parliament playing a marginal role through consultation. The fact that the Court of Justice did not have full jurisdiction at the time may have also had an impact.[14]

After the adoption of 'common rules and basic principles', asylum policy measures came to be decided through co-decision.[15] Second phase instruments have been agreed on this basis, after Lisbon entered into force, with the objective of ameliorating codified rules.[16] This has meant for the European Parliament the possibility to exert wider influence and help raise – albeit modestly – the quality of

[3] Tampere Conclusions, 15–16 October 1999, para 13, at: www.europarl.europa.eu/summits/tam_en.htm.

[4] ibid, paras 14–15.

[5] Art 63 EC, Amsterdam Treaty, OJ 1997 C340/1.

[6] Qualification Directive 2004/83, OJ 2004 L304/12.

[7] Procedures Directive 2005/85, OJ 2005 L326/13.

[8] Reception Conditions Directive 2003/09, OJ 2003 L31/18.

[9] Dublin II Regulation 343/2003, OJ 2003 L50/1, (DR II).

[10] For UNHCR analyses, see: www.unhcr.org/eu.

[11] See responses to Commission, 'The future of the CEAS' (Green Paper), COM(2007) 301 final, 6 June 2007, available at: ec.europa.eu/dgs/home-affairs/what-is-new/public-consultation/2007/consulting_0010_en.htm.

[12] N El-Enany and E Thielemann, 'The Impact of the EU on National Asylum Policies' in S Wolff et al (eds), *Freedom, Security and Justice after Lisbon and Stockholm* (The Hague, TMC Asser Press) 97.

[13] J Vedsted-Hansen speaks of 'below-minimum standards' in 'Common EU Standards on Asylum – Optional Harmonisation or Exclusive Procedures?' (2005) 7 *European Journal of Migration and Law* 369.

[14] Art 68 EC, Amsterdam Treaty.

[15] Art 67(5) EC, Amsterdam Treaty.

[16] Stockholm Programme, OJ 2010 C115/1, para 6.2.

some standards.[17] The recast Qualification Directive, the only instrument that has been formally adopted, has, indeed, better aligned recognition provisions with the Refugee Convention.[18] In turn, the revised Reception Conditions Directive has eliminated several optional clauses, improving access to education and employment and configuring a regime on detention with a number of procedural guarantees.[19] On the other hand, no substantial changes have been introduced either in the Recast Procedures Directive[20] or in the Dublin III Regulation.[21]

A radical reform of responsibility criteria or of current procedural norms would require the revision of the underlying philosophy of the entire system. In spite of the human rights abuses to which the application of Dublin transfers and 'safe third country' arrangements have led to,[22] no significant attempt has been made by the EU legislator to rethink the fundamentals of the first-phase regime. Although the Lisbon Treaty provides the legal tools necessary for such an overhaul, there appears to be no interest on the part of the Member States to bring it about. The recast instruments' objective is actually to 'achieve a higher level of approximation' on the basis of improved standards, but 'confirm[ing] the principles' underpinning the first phase.[23]

The overall logic these instruments share is that the CEAS 'is a constituent part of the European Union's objective of progressively establishing an area of freedom, security and justice'.[24] Whereas the provision of a common level of protection is designed as their 'main objective',[25] their Preambles also state that harmonisation 'should help to limit the secondary movements of applicants for international protection between Member States'.[26] In a Union in which 'Member States . . . are considered as safe countries for third-country nationals',[27] such movements are viewed as illegitimate. For their deterrence, CEAS instruments provide for the possibility of withdrawing reception conditions,[28] for the detention of applicants,[29] and for the reduction of procedural guarantees under certain circumstances.[30]

[17] For a summary of changes, see S Peers, *The Second Phase of the Common European Asylum System*, Statewatch Analysis, April 2013, available at: www.statewatch.org/analyses/no-220-ceas-second-phase.pdf.

[18] Recast Qualification Directive 2011/95/EU, OJ 2011 L337/9, (QD).

[19] Recast Reception Conditions Directive (agreed text), Council doc 14654/12, 14 December 2012, available at: register.consilium.europa.eu/pdf/en/12/st14/st14654.en12.pdf, (RCD).

[20] Recast Procedures Directive (agreed text), Council doc 7695/13, 22 March 2013, available at: www.statewatch.org/news/2013/mar/eu-council-procedures-7695-13.pdf, (PD).

[21] Dublin III Regulation (agreed text), Council doc 15605/12, 14 December 2012, available at: register.consilium.europa.eu/pdf/en/12/st15/st15605.en12.pdf, (DR III).

[22] Joined Cases C-411/10 and C-493/10 *NS and ME*, 21 December 2011.

[23] Recital 10 QD. See also Recitals 7 RCD and 9 DR III.

[24] Common Recital 2 QD, RCD, PD and DR III.

[25] Recitals 11, 31, 35 and Art 1 RCD; Recitals 11, 47 and Art 1 PD; and Recitals 12, 16 and Art 1 QD.

[26] Recital 13 QD; and common Recital 12 RCD and PD.

[27] Recital 3 DR III.

[28] Recital 25 and Art 20 RCD.

[29] Art 8 RCD.

[30] Arts 31 (prioritised procedures), 32 (unfounded applications), 33 (inadmissible applications), and 43 (border procedures) PD.

Moreover, the system should benefit only 'those who, forced by the circumstances, *legitimately* seek protection' (emphasis added).[31] Only persons 'genuinely in need' should have access to the CEAS.[32] Paradoxically, however, access to asylum has never been regulated. Notwithstanding assertions that the area of freedom, security and justice should remain 'open' to refugees,[33] these have been counteracted by the need 'for a consistent control of external borders to stop illegal immigration'.[34] So, although Stockholm posits that '[t]he strengthening of border controls should not prevent access to protection systems by those persons entitled to benefit from them',[35] no channels for such access have been created.

This contradictory rationale may be explained precisely by the fact that the CEAS does not concern itself exclusively with providing asylum, but intends to fulfil a series of conflicting objectives. Three other goals concur with its general humanitarian vocation.[36] The CEAS intends: to contribute to the creation of an area of freedom, security and justice; to control the movement of asylum seekers within and across Member States; and to prevent the abuse of domestic systems of international protection.[37] Second-phase instruments preserve this orientation.

It has been acknowledged that 'effective asylum adjudication systems [are those], which are capable of identifying refugees expeditiously and accurately thereby *balancing refugee protection with immigration control*' (emphasis added).[38] Along these lines, Stockholm reiterates that '[w]hile the CEAS should be based on high protection standards, due regard should also be given to fair and effective procedures capable of preventing abuse'.[39] The question hence arises as to why control and abuse have become part of the foundation of the European asylum regime.

III. THE 'FORTRESS' MENTALITY

The process of harmonisation of EU asylum policy did not start in 1999, as the Tampere Conclusions may lead us to assume. Discussions on the need to approximate domestic rules on refugees began already in the 1970s, in the context of negotiations on the removal of internal frontiers and the completion of the internal market. Asylum was an incident during the debate on the construction of a common border and migration management system. However, the emphasis at the time was not on international protection, but on the administration of refugee

[31] Common Recital 2 QD, RCD, PD and DR III.

[32] Recital 12 QD.

[33] Tampere Conclusions, para 4. See also common Recital 2 QD, RCD, PD, and DR III.

[34] ibid, para 3.

[35] Stockholm Programme, para 5.1.

[36] Art 78(1) TFEU. See also Joined Cases C-175/08, C-176/08, C-178/08 and C-179/08 *Abdulla* [2010] ECR I-1493, paras 51–54.

[37] Commission, '2000 Asylum Communication', COM(2000) 755 final, 22 November 2000, 6–7.

[38] Commission, '2000 Immigration Communication', COM(2000) 757 final, 22 November 2000, 14.

[39] Stockholm Programme, para 6.2.

flows and the prevention of abuse of the asylum regime as a way to avoid entry restrictions by other migrants. The seed of this original design has travelled through treaty reforms and underpinned the adoption of both first-phase and second-phase instruments of the CEAS.

Three principles have permeated the asylum discourse leading to a certain amalgamation of migration and refugee policies: *exclusion*, *compensation* and *illegitimation*. Exclusion and compensation relate to the process by which third-country nationals, including refugees, have been barred from free movement rights to become the object of 'compensatory' or 'flanking' measures designed to secure freedom, security and justice within the EU. Illegitimation refers, in turn, to the mechanism by which migration is construed as a threat to stability, and hence securitised. Consequently, controlling the movement of third-country nationals and preventing abuse of legal immigration routes has become the priority of EU migration policy.

A. Exclusion

For the completion of a common market, the Rome Treaty called for the abolition of 'obstacles' to freedom of movement of persons, services and capital.[40] Although the Treaty did not explicitly bar third-country nationals from free movement of persons,[41] both the European legislator and the Court of Justice prompted an indirect exclusion.[42] First, the term 'person' was assimilated to that of 'worker' to denote the economically active and 'worker', in turn, was given a restrictive interpretation as benefiting European nationals only.[43] Member States opposed any interpretation that would lead to a loss of control over immigration of third-country nationals and a tacit exclusion both from the scope of application of free movement rights and the European framework altogether took hold.[44]

The fortune of (recognised) refugees was no different. Despite pressures from the Economic and Social Committee and the Parliament to include them in legislation concerning workers,[45] the Council resisted the proposal. Instead, Member States 'declared' their intention to view with particular favour the entry of refugees settled in another Member State into their respective territories to take up employment,[46] but this never materialised in concrete terms.[47]

[40] Arts 2 and 3(c), Rome Treaty.

[41] 'EC' stands for 'European Community', as it then was.

[42] See Directive 64/221, OJ 1964 L56/850; Regulation 1612/68, OJ 1968 L257/2; Directive 68/360, OJ 1968 L257/13; and Regulation 1251/70, OJ 1970 L142/24.

[43] Case 48/75 *Royer* [1976] ECR 497; Case 118/75 *Watson* [1976] ECR 1185; Case 13/76 *Mantero* [1976] ECR 1333; and Case 238/83 *Meade* [1984] ECR 2631.

[44] E Guild, 'The Europeanisation of Europe's Asylum Policy' (2006) 18 *International Journal of Refugee Law* 630.

[45] TC Hartley, *EEC Immigration Law* (Amsterdam, North-Holland Publishing, 1978) 83.

[46] Déclaration 64/305 au sujet des réfugiés, OJ 1964 78/1225 (no English version).

[47] See, eg the dispute on Regulation 1408/71 in Case 95/99 *Khalil* [2001] ECR I-7413.

Things did not change after the Single European Act (SEA) was adopted.[48] Its Article 8a defined the single market as a frontier-free area, where free movement of persons would be ensured. That was supplemented by a series of provisions, arguably providing the Community with powers to regulate entry, movement and residence of nationals of third countries.[49] Nonetheless, a General Declaration on Articles 13 and 19 alongside a Political Declaration on Free Movement of Persons attached to the Treaty virtually withdrew competence from the Community. As a result, third-country nationals were made the object of separate initiatives decided by Member States alone.[50]

Controversies as to the need to abolish internal border controls on persons brought an elite of countries to start the Schengen cooperation with the understanding that free movement benefited only 'nationals of the Member States of the European Communities'.[51] However, because differentiating *prima facie* European nationals from third-country nationals was impossible in practice, if Member States were to refrain from discriminatory action, it was understood that controls had to be lifted for all.[52] This did not extend the right of free movement to third-country nationals. Aliens (in Schengen language) were solely granted a limited freedom to travel for up to three months under certain conditions.[53]

In parallel, intergovernmental cooperation, first within the European Political Cooperation, and then after the Maastricht Treaty within the Community,[54] took a much slower pace. The UK's opposition to subscribe to an interpretation of Article 8a SEA permitting crossings by third-country nationals without control blocked progress in the dismantling of internal frontiers. No agreement was reached in this period as to what an area without internal borders entailed and whom it should benefit. Nonetheless, immigration and asylum became 'matters of common interest' and certain measures were identified as 'desirable in their own right'.[55] At the same time, the introduction of EU citizenship reinforced the idea that treaty freedoms were reserved for Member State nationals.[56]

During negotiations for the reform of the Maastricht Treaty, the 1996 Reflection Group noted that the inadequacies of JHA cooperation were mainly caused by the 'lack of objectives'. The Group observed that

> [i]nstead of placing emphasis on the consolidation of an area of freedom and security in which there are no internal frontiers and where persons can move freely – the goal at

[48] Single European Act, OJ 1987 L169.

[49] See Arts 13, 18, 19, 100a and 100b SEA.

[50] MC Foblets, 'Europe and its Aliens after Maastricht' (1994) 42 *American Journal of Comparative Law* 783.

[51] Preamble, Schengen Agreement, OJ 2000 L239/13.

[52] Art 2(1), Convention Implementing the Schengen Agreement, OJ 2000 L239/19, (CISA).

[53] Arts 19(1), 6(2), 22, and 2 CISA.

[54] Maastricht Treaty, OJ 1992 C191/1.

[55] 'The Palma Document' para 3, in E Guild and J Niessen, *The Developing Immigration and Asylum Policies of the European Union* (The Hague, Kluwer, 1996) 443–48.

[56] HU Jessurum d'Oliveira, 'Nationality and the European Union after Amsterdam' in D O'Keeffe and P Twomey (eds), *Legal Issues of the Amsterdam Treaty* (Oxford, Hart Publishing, 1999) 396.

which all action should [have been] targeted – Article K merely [listed] areas of common interest.[57]

In truth, the lack of common objectives mirrored the absence of a common understanding of the legal framework.[58]

The Amsterdam Treaty remedied partly the situation by giving the 'matters of common interest', if not a common purpose, at least a common roof: the 'area of freedom, security and justice', to be accomplished through joined efforts in the EU's first and third pillars.[59] The incorporation of the Schengen *acquis* into the EU apparatus,[60] together with a remodelled Title VI EU for police and judicial cooperation and a new Title IV EC on borders, immigration and asylum came in assistance. The 10-year struggle over the correct interpretation of Article 7A EC was formally resolved through a series of opt-outs for the UK, Ireland and Denmark, allowing the remaining Members States to move ahead.[61]

The Treaty of Amsterdam not only consolidated the divide between EU citizens and third-country nationals, but also gave it supranational legitimisation. Although immigration and asylum were brought into the first pillar, the *Schengenisation* of the Union brought the logics of exclusion within the supranational framework.[62] As we shall see below, the notion of an area of freedom, security and justice 'flanking' the internal market confirmed the approach. Whereas free movement of persons was regulated in Title III EC, immigration and asylum, as policies *related* to it, pertained to Title IV EC,[63] within which the Council could define at expediency 'the rights and conditions under which nationals of third countries . . . legally resident in a Member State [could] reside in other Member States'.[64]

Reinforcing the split, the Asylum Protocol virtually eliminated any possibility for EU citizens to gain asylum in another Member State, reserving international protection to nationals of third countries.[65] Its foremost preoccupation was the prevention of abuse of the institution of asylum for purposes considered illegitimate.[66] The proposing government adduced two main reasons justifying the exception: the fact that 'the Member States of the European Union are all States which observe the rule of law, democracy and human rights' and that 'Member

[57] Report of the Reflection Group, SN 520/95, 5 December 1995, para 48.

[58] Art 7A EC (the successor of Art 8a SEA). See J Monar, 'European Union – Justice and Home Affairs: A Balance Sheet and an Agenda for Reform' in G Edwards and A Pijpers (eds), *The Politics of European Treaty Reform* (London, Pinter, 1997) 328.

[59] Art 2 TEU, Amsterdam Treaty.

[60] Protocol 2 integrating the Schengen *acquis* (1997), annexed to the Amsterdam Treaty; and Council Decisions of 20 May 1999, OJ 1999 L176/1 and 17.

[61] Protocols 3, 4 and 5 on the UK, Ireland and Denmark (1997), annexed to the Amsterdam Treaty.

[62] F Dehousse, 'The IGC Process and Results' in D O'Keeffe and P Twomey (eds), *Legal Issues of the Amsterdam Treaty* (Oxford, Hart Publishing, 1999) 97.

[63] S Peers, bearing this division in mind, has compared Title IV EC to a 'ghetto' in *EU Justice and Home Affairs Law* (London, Longman, 2000) 2.

[64] Art 63(4) EC, Amsterdam Treaty.

[65] Protocol 29 on asylum for nationals of Member States of the EU (1997).

[66] Asylum Memorandum, CONF 3826/1/97, 24 February 1997, 1.

States' nationals, *unlike third-country nationals*, . . . have the right to free movement . . . conferred by citizenship of the Union' (emphasis added).[67]

This formulation buttressed the dichotomy whereby free movement as a matter of legal entitlement pertained exclusively to EU nationals. Accordingly, the ambition since Tampere has been to 'ensure fair treatment of third-country nationals who reside legally on the territory of the Member States . . . granting them rights and obligations *comparable* to those of EU citizens', not to fully equate their position.[68] The acquisition of rights has been made incremental and related to the length and conditions of legal stay, so that there is no immediate access to free movement.[69] Refugees, in particular, acquire free movement rights after recognition and only if they become long-term residents.[70]

The Lisbon Treaty has inherited this philosophy, ensuring the continuity of the system. Third country nationals do not derive free movement rights directly from the Treaty. The TFEU regulates citizenship and free movement of persons separately from immigration and asylum, keeping the Asylum Protocol for EU nationals and furthering the Schengen line of measures in relation to border and migration control. The Charter of Fundamental Rights reflects this separation, distinguishing between EU citizens and migrants in the allocation of free movement rights. While 'every citizen of the Union *has the right* to move and reside freely within the territory of the Member States', for third-country nationals 'freedom of movement and residence *may be granted*' (emphasis added).[71]

B. Compensation

Not only have third-country nationals been excluded from free movement, but, most importantly, they have become the object of coercive measures adopted to compensate for the loss of control that the abolition of internal borders has been perceived to entail. In the construction of an 'area without internal borders',[72] controls over the movement of third-country nationals, far from being abolished, have been de-localised to the 'area of freedom, security and justice' that flanks the internal market.[73] Whereas the latter requires the abolition of borders for the

[67] ibid. This justification entered the Preamble to Protocol 22 annexed to the failed European Constitution, OJ 2004 C310/362.

[68] Tampere Conclusions, paras 18 and 21 (emphasis added).

[69] Free movement rights are granted to family members accompanying EU nationals; to employees of cross-border EU service providers; to third-country nationals covered by special Association Agreements; and to long-term residents. Outside these exceptions, the inexistence of free movement rights for third-country immigrants remains the rule. For commentry of the legislation concerned, see S Peers et al (eds), *EU Immigration and Asylum Law*, 2nd edn, Vol 2 (Leiden/Boston, Brill, 2012).

[70] Directive 2011/51 extending the scope of the Long-Term Residence Directive to beneficiaries of international protection, OJ 2011 L132/1. Note that rules on transfer of protection status have not been provided.

[71] EU Charter of Fundamental Rights (EUCFR), OJ 2010 C83/389. See Art 45(1) and (2).

[72] Art 26(2) TFEU.

[73] Art 3(2) TEU.

accomplishment of the free movement of persons that only EU citizens enjoy in full, the former is 'premised upon' the existence of borders for third-country nationals.[74] Two assumptions underlie this paradox: the myth of the loss of control and the supposed security deficit that comes with it.

Back in 1985, following the Fontainebleau Council's command to abolish 'all police and customs formalities for people crossing intra-Community frontiers',[75] the Adonnino Committee Reports identified the need to transfer the control of persons to the external borders of the EC. The transfer presupposed 'the gradual application of a common policy on third-country nationals' to regulate their entry, movement and expulsion.[76] In the eyes of the Commission it also entailed a loss of control over intra-Community borders that required 'alternative means of protection'.[77] Without further analysis, the Commission assumed that 'police checks at internal frontiers . . . [could] only be abolished as part of a . . . process whereby they [would be] transferred to the strengthened external frontiers of the Community'.[78] Thus, not only had the internal borders to be transferred to the external common frontiers of the EC, but they also needed to be reinforced in order to compensate for a perceived loss of control over third-country nationals crossing them.

The principle has become common knowledge and underpinned all subsequent action in relation to immigration and border policy.[79] However, it remains open to question whether the absence of internal controls necessitates a reinforcement of the external frontiers that necessarily translates into restricted criteria of access for third-country nationals. There is no connection of structural necessity. What has been portrayed as a technical constraint involves, in reality, a political choice.[80]

The loss of control has also been perceived as involving a security deficit. The European Council emphasised in 1985 that 'the achievement of the objective of abolishing frontier formalities must remain compatible with the need to combat terrorism and drug-trafficking'.[81] The Commission added immigration to the list of 'relevant problems' with which it was necessary to deal before removing physical barriers to free movement.[82] Thereafter, the link combining immigration and asylum with public order and security concerns has inspired the Schengen

[74] J Crowley, 'Differential Free Movement and the Sociology of the "Internal Border"' in E Guild and C Harlow (eds), *Implementing Amsterdam* (Oxford, Hart Publishing, 2001) 16.

[75] Fontainebleau Conclusions, 25–26 June 1984, 8, available at: www.european-council.europa.eu/media/849292/1984_june_-_fontainebleau__eng_.pdf.

[76] 'A People's Europe', *EC Bull Suppl* 7/85, paras 5 and 7.2.

[77] Commission, 'Completing the Single Market' COM(85) 310 final, 14 June 1985, para 29.

[78] ibid, para 53 (emphasis added).

[79] Perceiving compensatory measures as 'inevitable', see K-P Nanz, 'The Harmonisation of Asylum and Immigration Legislation within the Third Pillar of the Union Treaty' in J Monar and R Morgan (eds), *The Third Pillar of the European Union* (Brussels, EIP, 1994) 124.

[80] J Huysmans, 'The EU and the Securitization of Migration' (2000) 38 *Journal of Common Market Studies* 751.

[81] Brussels Conclusions, 29–30 March 1985, SN 1381/2/85, 9.

[82] Commission, 'Completing the Single Market', para 11.

provisions,[83] the Maastricht 'matters of common interest', and their successive development under the Treaties of Amsterdam and Lisbon.[84]

Connecting the internal borders of the Member States with the external frontiers of the EU has produced a spill-over effect. Because a border-free market could potentially facilitate the movement of law-abiding agents as well as criminals and irregular immigrants, border controls have been reframed into a security question, whereby uncontrolled migration is pictured as challenging public order as much as terrorism, drug trafficking or money laundering.[85] It is the institutionalisation of this perceived side-effect of market integration that has led to the establishment of a transversal security continuum, where the connotations of cross-border crime have been imported into the immigration and asylum discourse.[86] Under this view, the foreigner is not only perceived as alien to the free movement project, but is also reified as a potential danger to it.[87]

In order to keep the danger under control, the need has been felt for compensatory measures 'to safeguard internal security and prevent illegal immigration'.[88] In this way, immigration and asylum policies have become, together with police and judicial cooperation and border control, the means to prevent and combat public order threats. They have become the measures flanking the transfer of border controls to the external frontiers of the Union.

The Schengen Convention constitutes the first comprehensive catalogue of flanking measures. In relation to third-country nationals, it assembled the 'prohibitions and restrictions on which [internal border] checks [were] based', which, together with 'complementary measures to safeguard internal security and prevent illegal immigration', would allow intra-EC free movement.[89] Crucially, it included a system to allocate responsibility for asylum applications.[90] The objective was 'to ensure the protection of the entire territory of the [Contracting] States against . . . activities which could jeopardize security',[91] guaranteeing 'freedom from' the threat they could pose to the completion of the internal market.

In parallel, the first characterisation of the EU as an area of freedom, security and justice (AFSJ) took place during the 1996 Intergovernmental Conference.[92] The Irish Presidency, drafting the general outline for the revision of the treaties, deemed that the concept flowed directly from the establishment of the internal market. It considered that 'issues such as immigration, asylum, visas and external

[83] Art 9 Schengen Agreement.

[84] Commission, '2000 Immigration Communication', 19.

[85] Art 7 Schengen Agreement.

[86] D Bigo, *Police en réseaux: L'expérience européenne* (Paris, Presses de Sciences Po, 1996).

[87] JPH Donner, 'Comments on the Article by R Fernhout' in JA Winter et al (eds), *Reforming the Treaty on European Union* (The Hague, Kluwer, 1996) 402, stating that: 'Re-enforcing the rights of immigrants and criminals will not result in an ever closer Union, but rather in the opposite'.

[88] Art 17 Schengen Agreement.

[89] ibid and Preamble to the CISA.

[90] Ch VII CISA.

[91] Art 7 Schengen Agreement.

[92] P Twomey, 'Constructing a Secure Space: The Area of Freedom, Security and Justice' in D O'Keeffe and P Twomey (eds), *Legal Issues of the Amsterdam Treaty* (Oxford, Hart Publishing, 1999) 354.

borders . . . [were to be] handled collectively if free movement in the Union [was] to be achieved without jeopardizing the security of citizens'.[93] How exactly the AFSJ would complement the single market was left obscure.[94] The advantage of the term laid, ultimately, in its vagueness, as it was flexible enough to accommodate the disparate positions of the UK, Ireland, Denmark and the Schengen associates. As a result, the EU became a two-pronged project including a core border-free market and a 'flanking' AFSJ that would facilitate cross-border movement while providing citizens with a high level of safety.[95]

Furthering this line, the 1998 Vienna Action Plan acknowledged that freedom, security and justice were 'three inseparable concepts', asserting that 'one cannot be achieved in full without the other two'.[96] Yet, by also avowing that '[f]reedom [would] lose much of its meaning if it cannot be enjoyed in a secure environment and with the full backing of a system of justice', it established a hierarchy among them.[97] The concept of security was made preponderant, absorbing the notions of freedom – depicted as the right to live in safety – and justice – construed as redress in case of abuse of freedom.[98] In this setup, the function of migration policy was to produce an 'as high as possible level of security for the public'.[99]

The construction of migration and security policy as a means to guarantee freedom has been subsequently confirmed.[100] After the September 11 2001 attacks, the Hague Programme deemed the security of the EU to have acquired 'a new urgency'.[101] While the principles of freedom and justice remained untouched, security was decomposed into 'control at the external borders, internal security, and the prevention of terrorism'.[102] Alongside terrorism, irregular immigration and organised crime were, once again, pictured together as equivalent 'cross-border problems' threatening the EU.[103] To confront them and achieve 'an optimal level of protection', the plan was to strengthen the management of migration flows by establishing 'a continuum of security measures', linking visas to entry and exit procedures at the external borders.[104] Without detailing why and how, such measures were viewed also of importance for the prevention and control of crime, 'in particular terrorism'.[105]

[93] 'The EU today and tomorrow', CONF 2500/96, 5 December 1996, 11.

[94] For a critique, see D Kostakopoulou, 'The "Protective Union": Change and Continuity in Migration Law and Policy in Post-Amsterdam Europe' (2000) 38 *Journal of Common Market Studies* 497.

[95] In its current configuration, the AFSJ is presented both as an aim in itself and as a tool to facilitate free movement. See Art 3(2) TEU and Arts 26 and 67 TFEU.

[96] Vienna Action Plan, OJ 1999 C19/1, para 5.

[97] ibid. See also para 9.

[98] ibid, para 6. For a critique, see C Harlow, 'Endpiece' in E Guild and C Harlow (eds), *Implementing Amsterdam* (Oxford, Hart Publishing, 2001) 310.

[99] Vienna Action Plan, paras 25 and 32.

[100] Tampere Conclusions, paras 5, 2 and 9.

[101] The Hague Programme, 14292/1/04 REV 1 Annex I, 8 December 2004, 12.

[102] ibid, 13.

[103] ibid, 12.

[104] ibid, 13.

[105] ibid, 25.

The belief that migration management provides a means fit to address issues 'linked to the security of our societies' has grown deep roots in EU imagery.[106] Stockholm confirms this tendency, establishing that '[t]he Union must continue to facilitate legal access to the territory of its Member States while in parallel taking measures to counteract illegal immigration and cross-border crime and maintaining a high level of security'.[107] As the next section details, the apprehension of immigrants as a potential danger – without any distinction as regards refugees – and the conceptualisation of migration and border policy as instruments to combat (perceived) security threats have crystallised in EU law. Controlling the movement of third-country nationals at 'all stages', in particular through 'enhanced measures to combat illegal immigration', constitutes a priority of Lisbon codified in Article 79(1) TFEU.

C. Illegitimation

Post-war openness to work-related immigration in Europe soon came to an end. Faced with high unemployment rates and increasing immigration pressure through the 1980s and 1990s, politicians started calls for 'zero immigration'.[108] In keeping with the security imperative and the framing of (uncontrolled) migration as a threat to stability, Member States found in the termination of guest worker schemes a possible solution. The wish to accomplish the internal market as a border-free space added to their domestic preoccupations; the abolition of internal frontiers had the potential to render immigration control impossible.[109]

Against this background – and without any particular basis, 'the principle gradually became established that integration of immigrants could only be achieved by controlling migration flows'.[110] It was believed that 'an effective integration policy [should] not [be] constantly undermined by the addition of further groups of third-country nationals'.[111] Also without evident cause, the control of the common borders – joined to that on people – was considered an instrument facilitating the integration of those already settled.[112] This way, immigration management and border surveillance became constituent parts of actions aimed at the integration of third-country nationals.[113]

[106] 'A Common Immigration Policy for Europe' COM(2008) 359 final, 17 June 2008, 3. See the overall proposed design composed of three strands: prosperity, solidarity and *security*, 4ff.

[107] Stockholm Programme, para 5.1. See also 'European Pact on Immigration and Asylum', Council doc 13440/08, 24 September 2008.

[108] See, eg former Interior Minister announcing that 'France has been a country of immigration but no longer wants to be one' and setting the target of 'zero immigration' in (1993) 39 *Keesing's Record of World Events* 39527.

[109] '1991 Immigration Communication', SEC(91) 1855 final, 23 October 1991, 8.

[110] ibid, 9.

[111] 1991 Work Programme, SN 4038/91, 3 December 1991, in E Guild and J Niessen (n 55) 449–91, 473.

[112] Braun Report, SEC (90) 1813 final, 28 September 1990, para 46: 'Member States borders have to be controlled effectively if their integration policies are to succeed'.

[113] For a critique, see M Ugur, 'Freedom of Movement vs Exclusion: A Reinterpretation of the "Insider" – "Outsider" Divide in the European Union' (1995) 29 *International Migration Review* 964.

This principle of 'exclusion for integration'[114] transpired the initiatives taken during the intergovernmental period.[115] In the *communautarised* era, acknowledging a change in the economic and demographic reality, the Commission has argued that the zero immigration paradigm that had 'dominated . . . over the past 30 years [is] no longer appropriate'.[116] It has pleaded instead for a mitigated version that translates in 'the controlled admission of economic migrants to the EU' coupled with an intensified fight against irregular immigration.[117]

'Managing' new admissions for the sake of integration and stability has remained the target. But, because integration may only be achieved in the long run, immigration control has become its short-term prerequisite.[118] Already in the 1970s and 1980s, uncoordinated action at domestic level quickly converged towards restrictive policies and practices.[119] On the other hand, such disharmony was perceived to provoke undesired secondary movements, so the need for a harmonised approach was considered necessary for the lifting of internal frontiers.[120] Harmonisation, in turn, had to be restrictive for Member States to 'take account of their economic and social situation' and 'enable [resident] immigrants . . . to be satisfactorily integrated'.[121]

Despite changes and the evolution of European integration, priorities have by and large remained unchanged.[122] In 1998, a strategic paper established that '[i]n view of current challenges . . . [c]urbing illegal immigration and facilitator networks must . . . be the main task'.[123] Reflecting this urgency, the Amsterdam Treaty introduced a five-year period for the adoption of common border controls and measures to combat irregular immigration, leaving legal immigration and integration policy without a deadline.[124]

With these priorities in mind, it was soon realised that unilateral action by the EU would not suffice. In addition to the internal dimension of migration and border policy, there was an external – and multilateral – facet that required attention. The Adonnino Committee recognised in 1985 that 'agreements with third countries on expanded cooperation in frontier passage' would facilitate border and migration administration.[125] The Commission developed then the idea of 'a joint response', combining internal measures on integration of residents and management of flows

[114] D Kostakopoulou has formulated this as 'fewer immigrants, better race relations' in 'Is there an Alternative to "Schengenland"?' (1998) 46 *Political Studies* 886, 891.

[115] Commission, '1994 Immigration and Asylum Communication', COM (94) 23 final, 23 February 1994, 11.

[116] '2000 Immigration Communication', 6.

[117] ibid, 21, 16 and 22. See also 'European Pact on Immigration and Asylum', 3.

[118] '1991 Immigration Communication', 9: 'Better control of migration flows, the prerequisite for any harmonious integration'.

[119] H Vetter reports a 'closed border policy' in *Report on the Right of Asylum*, A2-227/86/A, 23 February 1987, paras 17–25.

[120] 'The Palma Document', 446–47.

[121] ibid, 469–70 (emphasis added).

[122] Council Resolution laying down the priorities for JHA cooperation, OJ 1996 C319/1.

[123] Strategic Paper on Immigration and Asylum, Council doc 9809/98, 1 July 1998, para 1, retrieved from: www.proasyl.de/texte/europe/eu-a-o.htm, paras 42 and 64.

[124] Arts 61(a), 62, 63(3), and 63(4) EC, Amsterdam Treaty.

[125] 'A People's Europe', para 7.2.

with external action to counter migration pressure and improve control.[126] The 1991 Work Programme built on these propositions. However, as 'no short term reduction of migratory pressure could be expected . . . specific agreements could be made with [third] countries in order to combat illegal immigration'.[127]

To this limited approach to international cooperation, serving mostly European interests, there joined a conviction, on the basis of experience gathered during the humanitarian crises in Yugoslavia, that the management of migration, especially of refugee flows, should be internationalised and that [c]ountries of origin and transit should take their share of responsibility.[128]

When the Treaty of Maastricht entered into force, the 1994 Communication on immigration and asylum brought all these elements together under a 'comprehensive approach'.[129] Then, the Austrian Presidency put forward a model focused on the expansion of the control side of that approach, promoting an 'overall concept of control of legal entry, at all stages of the movements of persons'.[130] The Tampere Conclusions echoed the concept, calling for a 'more efficient management of migration flows at all their stages . . . in close cooperation with countries of origin and transit',[131] while the Hague Programme reinstated that 'a comprehensive approach, involving all stages of migration . . . [was] needed'.[132] The Lisbon Treaty has eventually codified the notion of 'a common immigration policy aimed at ensuring, at all stages, the efficient management of migration flows'.[133]

As a result, the idea of 'integrated border management', that emerged under the Amsterdam Treaty[134] and was constitutionalised in the Lisbon Treaty,[135] comprises a system of measures extending 'from the time [the migrant] begins his journey to the time he reaches his destination',[136] including visas,[137] carrier sanctions,[138] maritime patrols coordinated by Frontex,[139] and 'thorough checks' at the external borders.[140] If an application for asylum is lodged on arrival, the Dublin Regulation establishes criteria for determining the state responsible for its examination – although such responsibility may be diverted towards 'safe third countries'.[141] Eventually, those who do not meet entry conditions or whose asylum claims are rejected are removed from the EU.[142]

126 '1991 Immigration Communication', 1991, 19–20.
127 1991 Work Programme, 468 and 467.
128 Declaration on Principles Governing External Aspects of Migration Policy, SN 456/92, para xvi.
129 '1994 Immigration and Asylum Communication', 11.
130 Strategic Paper, para 41.
131 Tampere Conclusions, paras 11–12 and 22–27.
132 The Hague Programme, 16.
133 Art 79(1) TFEU.
134 Presidency Conclusions, 4-5 December 2006, Press 15801/06, 27.
135 As noted above, the notion has been codified in Art 77(1)(c) TFEU.
136 Strategic Paper, para 85.
137 Visa Regulation 539/2001, OJ 2001 L81/1; and Community Code on Visas, OJ 2009 L243/1.
138 Carrier Sanctions Directive 2001/51, OJ 2001 L187/45.
139 Frontex Regulation 1168/2011, OJ 2011 L304/1.
140 Art 7(3), Schengen Borders Code (replacing most of CISA), OJ 2006 L105/1, (SBC).
141 Art 3(3) DR III.
142 Return Directive 2008/115, OJ 2008 L348/98.

As a complement to 'integrated border management', the 'external dimension of migration policy' has developed since the Hague Programme.[143] The resulting 'Global Approach to Migration'[144] purports precisely to engage in 'actions to build capacity in third countries and supporting a more secure global, rules-based environment'.[145] The emphasis, though, has been 'on joint management of migration flows and on compulsory readmission in the event of illegal immigration'[146] – asylum has been incorporated in 2011 as a way to provide for a more balanced system,[147] but results have been limited due to scepticism from third countries and the lack of a rights-based approach to international displacement.[148]

'Integrated border management' and the Global Approach to Migration, combining territorial and extraterritorial measures, constitute the main strategies through which the inflow of third-country nationals (including refugees) is being administered. There are, however, two problems in this respect. Whereas most controls are implemented abroad, there has been very limited recognition that the fundamental rights of refugees and migrants may equally have extraterritorial applicability.[149] Similarly, Member States have also failed to recognise the special character of refugees within mixed flows, without differentiating between voluntary and forcibly displaced and disregarding entitlements to international protection when implementing offshore controls. Despite formal recognition in policy documents and legislative instruments that pre-border mechanisms must respect fundamental rights and the prohibition of *refoulement*,[150] there has been no meaningful engagement with these principles in practice.[151]

IV. THE ABUSE OBSESSION

The enlarged scope of application of migration measures has not been accompanied by a similar development in the asylum field. On the contrary, Member States have embraced a territorial conception of their protection obligations that they have transposed to the EU.[152] Moreover, the security focus dominating the

[143] The Hague Programme, 20–23.

[144] Global Approach to Migration, Council doc 157744/05, 13 December 2005.

[145] A Strategy for the External Dimension of JHA, Council doc 14366/3/05, 30 November 2005, para 8.

[146] Seville Conclusions, Council doc 13463/02, 24 October 2002, para 33. In light of the shortsightedness of this approach, the Commission asked for 'other policy areas . . . such as legal migration and integration' to be included, because 'experiences have demonstrated that to broker a deal the EU needs to offer something in return'. See 'Global approach one year on', COM(2006) 735 final, 30 November 2006, 2 and 9.

[147] 'The Global Approach to Migration and Mobility', COM(2011) 743 final, 18 November 2011, 5–7.

[148] Summary of discussions on Migration and Asylum, Council doc 5663/13, 22 February 2013.

[149] *Cf Hirsi v Italy* (27765/09), 23 February 2012 (ECtHR). See also M Milanovic, *Extraterritorial Application of Human Rights Treaties* (Oxford, Oxford University Press, 2011).

[150] See, eg Recital 20 and Art 3 SBC.

[151] For a detailed account, see V Moreno-Lax, 'Must EU Borders have Doors for Refugees?' (2008) 10 *European Journal of Migration and Law* 315, and 'Seeking Asylum in the Mediterranean' (2011) 23 *International Journal of Refugee Law* 174.

[152] See territorial clauses in common Art 3(1) DR III, RCD, and PD.

migration discourse has permeated the asylum regime. The policy is being used not only as a means to provide sanctuary to a particular category of persons, but also as a tool to prevent abuse and administer refugee flows.

The refugee regime of the 1951 Convention was designed in the aftermath of World War II, premised in the refusal of persecution and marked by the political supremacy of the Allies and their rejection of the communist ideology. Against this background, during the Cold War period, the system developed a somewhat liberal trend that culminated in the 1967 Protocol, removing the temporal and geographical limitations to the application of the Convention.[153] The trend prevailed until the mid-1970s, with the oil crisis marking the beginning of a new era in the understanding of refugee protection in Western countries.[154]

The negative perception of migration influenced the perception of asylum policy. At the same time, through the 1970s and 1980s there was a change in the pattern of refugee flows that consolidated after the Iron Curtain fell. Traditionally regarded as a factor in East–West relations, there was increasingly a South–North dimension that started gaining ground, followed by a dramatic increase in the number of arrivals.[155] The shift was due to wars related to decolonisation processes. By the mid-1970s, the new flows began to be larger and their motives more complex than in the past, blurring the lines between refugees and other migrants.[156] After the collapse of the USSR, conflicts around the world fed mass displacement and asylum applications peaked on a global scale.[157]

However, throughout the 1980s and 1990s, Western countries, including the EU Member States, focused on restricting admissions. They started interpreting the Geneva Convention restrictively,[158] and adopting policies of *non-entrée*.[159] The fortress mentality[160] helped tie the rise in asylum applications to a perceived generalised misuse of the asylum procedure. With little effort to understand their needs and realities, the 'new refugees'[161] were portrayed as a threat to the integrity of the asylum system and disqualified as economic migrants in disguise.[162] There was a widespread conviction that, since the ending of guest worker schemes, the

[153] *Protocol Relating to the Status of Refugees*, 606 *UN Treaty Series* 267.

[154] D Joly, 'A New Asylum Regime in Europe' in F Nicholson and P Twomey (eds), *Refugee Rights and Realities* (Cambridge, Cambridge University Press, 1999) 336.

[155] *Report on the Right of Asylum*, Pt B: Explanatory Statement, A 2-227/86/B, 23 February 1987, para 5.

[156] J Sztucki, 'Who is a Refugee?' in F Nicholson and P Twomey (eds), *Refugee Rights and Realities* (Cambridge, Cambridge University Press, 1999) 69.

[157] L Barnett, 'Global Governance and the Evolution of the International Refugee Regime' (2002) 14 *International Journal of Refugee Law* 238.

[158] GS Goodwin-Gill, 'The Individual Refugee, the 1951 Convention and the Treaty of Amsterdam' in E Guild and C Harlow (eds), *Implementing Amsterdam* (Oxford, Hart Publishing, 2001) 141.

[159] T Gammeltoft-Hansen, *Access to Asylum* (Cambridge, Cambridge University Press, 2011).

[160] A Geddes, *Immigration and European Integration: Towards Fortress Europe?* (Manchester, Manchester University Press, 2000).

[161] D Joly and R Cohen, 'Introduction: The "New Refugees" of Europe' in D Joly and R Cohen (eds), *Reluctant Hosts* (Aldershot, Avebury, 1989) 5.

[162] For the variant of 'illegal refugees', see Action Plan on the influx of migrants from Iraq, Council doc 5573/98, 26 January 1998.

asylum route was being used to circumvent immigration restrictions.[163] As a result, '[t]he need to combat . . . [the] abuse of the right of asylum' became the centre of Member States' interests.[164]

Simultaneously, the growing influx of asylum seekers was deemed in itself to pose serious problems to social and economic stability. The completion of the internal market constituted an additional source of disquiet, as it entailed the removal of internal borders.[165] Marked by the 'zero immigration' paradigm prevailing before the Amsterdam Treaty, attention turned 'more and more from the refugee drama itself towards means of controlling the influx of asylum-seekers'.[166] The 1991 Work Programme called for 'common answers', concluding that harmonisation could be used to 'influence the flow of asylum-seekers'.[167]

With the objective of controlling numbers and reducing abuse, Member States negotiated a system to allocate responsibility for asylum applications lodged in the EU. Until the Tampere Conclusions, the only legal measure in the asylum field was the Dublin Convention – superseding Chapter VII CISA within the EC.[168] The instrument was thought to have 'stimulated the process of harmonising asylum policies',[169] resting on the assumption that Member States afforded similar levels of protection and that the choice by applicants of destination country motivated by differences in reception conditions, recognition rates or procedural standards was unjustified. The Dublin Regulation – in both versions – has embraced these principles,[170] ensuring their 'continuity' in the post-Amsterdam era and marking the way in which the CEAS will be accomplished under Lisbon.[171] Its main objective remains, accordingly, to allocate responsibility for each asylum application lodged in the EU to a single Member State following specific apportioning criteria.[172] This serves not only to preclude unauthorised movement across the Union, but tends also to diminish the volume of asylum seeker flows, as opportunities for status recognition are reduced to one only.[173] The criteria, save for some humanitarian exceptions, are strongly grounded in the so-called 'authorisation principle', according to which the state responsible for examining the claim is the one that allowed the refugee's presence in the EU – usually due to negligence in the control of its borders.[174]

[163] '1991 Asylum Communication', SEC(91) 1857 final, 11 October 1991, Annexed Discussion Paper, para 2.

[164] ibid, para 8.

[165] 1991 Work Programme, 457.

[166] '1991 Asylum Communication', 1991, Annexed Discussion Paper, para 6.

[167] 1991 Work Programme, 450.

[168] Dublin Convention, OJ 1997 C254/1.

[169] Recital 5 DR II.

[170] Recitals 5 and 10 DR II and 9 and 29 DR III.

[171] See Stockholm Programme, para 6.2.1, establishing that the Dublin system constitutes 'a cornerstone' of the CEAS. See also Recital 7 DR III.

[172] Art 3(1) DR II and III.

[173] ECRE, 'Sharing Responsibility for Refugee Protection in Europe', March 2008, retrievable from: www.ecre.org/component/downloads/downloads/104.html; UNHCR, 'The Dublin II Regulation', April 2006, available at: www.unhcr.org/refworld/pdfid/4445fe344.pdf.

[174] Recital 25 DR III.

Moreover, as protection should benefit only *genuine* refugees,[175] mechanisms have been introduced to distinguish them from the rest. Beside harmonised qualification criteria, the notion of 'asylum seeker' or 'asylum applicant' plays a crucial role in this regard. Despite formal acceptance that status determination is a declaratory act and that a person is a refugee as soon as he meets the Geneva Convention definition,[176] the term was coined to denote the third-country national who had lodged an application for recognition as a refugee, but who would only be considered to be one after a final decision on the merits. Both the Schengen Convention and CEAS instruments have adopted this definition,[177] making status determination indispensable in practice.[178] Most importantly, this re-conceptualisation of refugees has permitted their assimilation to the general category of third-country nationals for border control and migration management purposes. As access to asylum has not been regulated, reaching the CEAS – as other asylum systems in Western countries – depends 'not on the refugee's need for protection, but on his or her own ability to enter clandestinely the territory of [a Member State]'.[179]

Although no official statistics exist, it has been estimated that up to 90 per cent of those eventually recognised as beneficiaries of international protection entered the EU irregularly.[180] The reconceptualisation of refugees into asylum seekers, combined with the notion that protection obligations are territorially bound, and added to the absence of channels for legal admission, leaves refugees with no option but to use the services of traffickers and smugglers to flee oppression.[181] The fact that they are not distinguished from other immigrants at the pre-entry stage, and they face interdiction like any other third-country national when attempting to reach the Union, has rendered the CEAS virtually inaccessible.

The 'safe third country' concept also plays a role. Conceived of as a procedural device to rationalise determination proceedings, its effect is to push responsibility for asylum claims away from the EU upon arrival. The first codification of the notion was in Chapter VII CISA, where the obligation to process them was considered 'not [to] bind a Contracting Party to authorising all asylum seekers to enter or remain within its territory'. Each Contracting Party was supposed to 'retain the right to refuse entry or to expel asylum seekers to a third State on the basis of its national provisions'.[182] The principle has been retained in CEAS instruments of

[175] Common Recital 2 QD, RCD, PD and DR III.

[176] UNHCR, *Handbook*, HRC/1P/4/Eng/REV 2, Geneva, 1979, para 28. See also Recital 21 QD.

[177] Art 1 CISA; common Art 2(c) DR III and PD; and Art 2(b) RCD.

[178] Warning against this practice, see JC Hathaway, 'What's in a Label?' (2003) 5 *European Journal of Migration and Law* 1.

[179] Mutatis mutandis, UNHCR, 'Brief as amicus curiae', 21 December 1992, *McNary v Haitian Centers Council Inc*, US Supreme Court Case No 92-344, para 18.

[180] ECRE, 'Broken Promises – Forgotten Principles', June 2004, 17, available at: www.ecre.org/topics/areas-of-work/access-to-europe/97-broken-promises-forgotten-principles-ecre-evaluation-of-the-development-of-eu-minimum-standards-for-refugee-protection.html.

[181] J Morrison and B Crosland, 'Trafficking and Smuggling of Refugees: The End Game in European Asylum Policy' (2001) *New Issues in Refugee Research*, Working Paper No 39, Geneva, UNHCR.

[182] Art 29(2) CISA.

both phases,[183] where the preference is that Member States contemplate whether 'safe third country' removals are possible 'before considering whether or not to transfer responsibility . . . to another Member State'.[184]

The Procedures Directive distinguishes several options: 'first country of asylum', 'safe third country', and 'European safe third country'.[185] Although each of them possesses different characteristics, they produce similar outcomes. Their application implies that Member States are dispensed from assessing whether the applicant qualifies as a refugee,[186] either because 'it can be reasonably assumed that another country would do the examination or provide sufficient protection' or 'due to a connection to a third country as defined in national law, [the applicant] can reasonably be expected to seek protection [there]'.[187] In such circumstances the application may be considered both inadmissible and unfounded and processed through accelerated procedures.[188]

This is the context in which the Hague Programme started 'the external dimension of asylum'. The idea was to promote access to international protection 'at the earliest possible stage'.[189] But rather than being conceived as a way of granting admission to the CEAS, the initiative has focused on facilitating access to protection *elsewhere*. The underlying rationale seems to be that regions of origin and transit should assume the responsibility of hosting 'their' refugees.[190] Several actions have thus been proposed or are being implemented, including Regional Protection Programmes (RPPs),[191] a (voluntary) resettlement scheme,[192] and offshore processing strategies.

However, the EU resettlement programme is still in its early stages,[193] while the 'new approaches concerning access to asylum procedures targeting main countries of transit' that the Stockholm Programme called for remain to be explored.[194] Only RPPs have been pursued so far, seeking to create the conditions for 'durable solutions' to thrive in recipient countries, enhancing their capacity to provide 'effective protection'.[195] On the other hand, it is also expected that the programmes

[183] Art 3(3) DR II and III.

[184] Resolution on Host Third Countries, 30 November – 1 December 1992, para 3(a), available at: www.unhcr.org/refworld/publisher,COUNCIL,,,3f86c3094,0.html.

[185] Arts 35, 38 and 39 PD (formerly Arts 26, 27 and 36).

[186] Art 33 PD (formerly Art 25).

[187] Recitals 34 and 35 PD (formerly Recitals 22 and 23).

[188] Arts 33, 32 and 31(5) PD (formerly Arts 25, 28 and 23(3)).

[189] The Hague Programme, para 1.6.1. For analysis, see P De Bruycker et al, *Setting Up a Common European Asylum System* (2010) Study PE 425.622, Brussels, European Parliament, 476ff.

[190] Declaration on Principles Governing External Aspects of Migration Policy (n 128).

[191] Regional Protection Programmes, COM(2005) 388 final, 1 September 2005.

[192] EU Resettlement Programme, COM(2009) 447 final, 2 September 2009.

[193] ERF Decision 281/2012, OJ 2012 L92/1, allocating funds and determining resettlement priorities for 2013. During the Arab Spring, only 700 resettlement places were offered EU-wide. See 'Results of the Ministerial Pledging Conference', MEMO 11/295, 13 May 2011.

[194] Stockholm Programme, para 6.2.3.

[195] For an evaluation, see 'First annual report on immigration and asylum', COM(2010) 214 final, 6 May 2010, 6.

will 'enable those countries better to manage migration',[196] linking RPP activities with the overall vision of the Global Approach to Migration.

All these mechanisms combined translate the control rationale underlying the border and migration policy of the Union to the realm of asylum. Their end result is an inaccessible CEAS, which is meeting more of a control task than a protective function. The main problem relates to the reconceptualisation of refugees into third-country nationals through the medium of the 'asylum seeker' concept. This mechanism denies extraterritorial rights and makes the supposed recipients of international protection also the object of the 'fight against illegal immigration'. Through this strategy, Member States are, in fact, combatting the same people they are called on to protect.[197] While it is true that not all irregular immigrants are refugees, it is however certain that, due to the lack of legal channels to protection, most refugees need to take irregular routes to reach the EU.

V. CONCLUSION

The links between asylum and immigration policy are not superfluous and have determined the way in which refugee systems have evolved in the Member States. From dedicated regimes of international protection, they have gradually transformed into factors of migration control. An overall principle has emerged that considers '[a] comprehensive and integrated CEAS' to be one that 'ensure[s] coherence with other policies that have an impact on international protection', including 'border control, the fight against illegal immigration, and return policies'.[198] Having defined the prevention of unauthorised arrivals as their overall rationale, it appears that 'immigration control and asylum policies are gradually merging'.[199]

This chapter has explored the different layers and assumptions underpinning this merger. The basis is a conception of third-country nationals as foreign to the free movement project and framed as a threat to security and stability that needs to be neutralised. As a second step, migrants and refugees have been made the object of a reinforcement of controls. Following apparently contradictory dynamics to the ones governing market integration and the removal of internal frontiers, both asylum and immigration policies have been construed (together with border surveillance) as measures integrating the area of freedom, security and justice 'flanking' the internal market. The third stage relates to differences in treatment and entitlement that, boosted by cycles of economic recession and humanitarian crises since the 1970s, have served to justify a restrictive entry policy. Although

[196] RPPs, 3.

[197] See Implementation of the EU Action Plan on the influx of migrants from Iraq, Council doc 6518/99, 12 March 1999, para 5: 'as a result of the Action Plan, the number of asylum-seekers and illegal migrants from this region had stabilized'.

[198] 'Policy Plan on Asylum', COM(2008) 360 final, 17 June 2008, 3.

[199] G Noll and J Vedsted-Hansen, 'Non-Communitarians: Refugee and Asylum Policies' in P Alston (ed), *The European Union and Human Rights* (Oxford, Oxford University Press, 1999) 359, 368.

calls for 'zero immigration' have transformed today into calls for 'controlled admission', the 'fight against illegal immigration' remains the main priority of the EU migration policy. The 'external dimension' and 'the Global Approach to Migration' provide a means for 'combating illegal immigration with an integrated approach',[200] reaching beyond Member States' boundaries. The last step of the reasoning consists of expanding the scope of controls, without recognising a parallel extension to fundamental rights. As the last section has emphasised, the scope of application of international protection has not benefited from an analogous enlargement. Quite the opposite, protection obligations have been given a strict territorial understanding. And without solid statistical or other evidence, asylum has been apprehended as a secondary route to immigration. As a result, refugees have been characterised as potentially bogus and the abuse of international protection systems as a scourge to eradicate.

The abuse paradigm rests, nonetheless, on the unverified assumption that the majority of asylum seekers, because they are denied refugee status, constitute evidence of misuse of the system. However, '"failure" is commonly just a matter of degree, dependent upon complex and varying assessments of the individual elements in the refugee definition'.[201] Moreover, what is considered unfounded in one Member State may result in status recognition in another.[202] The 'myth of invasion' – to use the words of De Haas – is also unwarranted.[203] According to the UNHCR, 'the available statistical evidence confirms that most refugees flee to neighbouring countries and that they, thus remain within their region of origin'. In fact, 'the major refugee-generating regions host on average between 83 and 90 per cent of "their" refugees'.[204] In addition, the number of asylum applications lodged in the EU has progressively decreased to reach historical lows in recent years[205] – partly, precisely, because of policies of *non-entrée*.[206]

Nevertheless, it does not seem asylum and immigration control will dissociate in future. The second phase of the CEAS ensures the continuity of the system, perpetuating its original rationale. The regime will thus remain focused on fighting abuse and unauthorised movement. This would not be such a concern, if protection and control had been accorded a similar territorial range. This way, 'genuine' refugees would also be 'legal' immigrants. But this is not what has happened. Access to international protection has been regulated neither by the first nor by the second phase of the CEAS, bringing about a situation of absence of legal channels for entry to seek asylum. In fact, Member States are building a system of protection that its address-

200 'Measures to prevent and combat illegal immigration', Council doc 10017/02, 14 June 2002, 3.

201 GS Goodwin-Gill, 'Asylum 2001 – A Convention and a Purpose' (2001) 13 *International Journal of Refugee Law* 1, 9.

202 'Report on the application of the Qualification Directive', COM(2010) 314 final, 16 June 2010.

203 H de Haas, 'The Myth of Invasion' (2008) 29 *Third World Quarterly* 1305.

204 UNHCR, '2007 Global Trends', 7, at: www.unhcr.org/statistics/STATISTICS/4852366f2.pdf.

205 'Policy Plan on Asylum', 3.

206 ECRE, 'Defending Refugees' Access to Protection in Europe', December 2007, available at: www.ecre.org/topics/areas-of-work/access-to-europe/95-defending-refugees-access-to-protection-in-europe.html.

ees cannot legally reach, denaturalising in the process the essence of their human rights obligations. The conclusion, therefore, is that the Lisbon Treaty's opportunity to construct a liberal regime 'in accordance with the Geneva Convention . . . and other relevant treaties' has yet to be seized.[207] Meanwhile, it will fall on the Court of Justice of the European Union and European Court of Human Rights to correct the situation on a case-by-case basis.[208]

207 Art 78(1) TFEU.

208 See, in this respect, the discussion of the *NS v Secretary of State for the Home Department* and *MSS v Greece and Belgium* judgments of the Court of Justice of the European Union and the European Court of Human Rights, respectively, throughout this volume.

10

Counter-Terrorism Law and Policy: Operationalisation and Normalisation of Exceptional Law after the 'War on Terror'

CIAN C MURPHY

I. INTRODUCTION: THE 'WAR ON TERROR' IN EUROPE

EU COUNTER-TERRORISM LAW has its genesis in the need to respond to the Al-Qaeda attacks in New York and Washington DC on September 11, 2001 – it is a policy field given birth to by the events of that day. The response exhibits characteristics of both risk-based government and moral panic.[1] Thus, scholars in disciplines close to law have written of a '*dispositif* of risk' in the 'war on terror' and EU counter-terrorism action may be understood as a 'pre-emptive *dispositif*'.[2] This is because modern governance considers terrorism to be 'catastrophic': a 'risk beyond risk' that must be subject to prevention, even pre-emption, rather than management.[3] A *dispositif* can be understood as 'a thoroughly heterogeneous ensemble consisting of discourses, institutions, architectural forms, regulatory decisions, laws, administrative measures, scientific statements, philosophical, moral and philanthropic propositions – in short, the said as much as the unsaid'.[4] It has 'as its major function at a given historical moment that of responding to an urgent need'.[5] This is an apt characterisation of EU counter-terrorism law and policy after September 11, 2001. The *dispositif* is the exercise of power for counter-terrorism action through all available means. The different elements of EU counter-terrorism efforts present a disparate collection of governmental actions. There are examples of engagement with discourse (solidarity

[1] On government of risk, see CR Sunstein, *Worst Case Scenarios* (Cambridge, MA, Harvard University Press, 2009). The classic work 'moral panics' is in S Cohen, *Folk Devils and Moral Panics: The Creation of the Mods and Rockers*, Routledge Classics edn (London, Routledge, 2011).

[2] See: C Aradau and R van Munster, 'Taming the Future: The *dispositif* of Risk in the "War on Terror"' in L Amoore and M deGoede (eds), *Risk and the War on Terror* (Oxford, Routledge, 2008).

[3] ibid, 29.

[4] M Foucault, 'Confessions of the Flesh' in C Gordon, *Power/Knowledge: Selected Interviews and Other Writings 1972–77* (Harlow, Longman, 1980) 194.

[5] ibid, 195.

declaration), institutions (Europol, Eurojust), architectural forms (border controls), laws (Framework Decision on combating terrorism) and philosophical propositions (one version of the Council Action Plan includes the goal of 'ensuring the voices of mainstream opinion prevail').[6] Power is therefore used against the population and particular individuals within it. Some tools, such as the 'restrictive measures' formerly known as targeted asset-freezing sanctions, blur the lines between legal categories of criminal, civil and administrative law. In contrast with the narrative of the empowerment of EU citizens, the population of Europe has been an object of control in the 'war on terror'.[7]

The rise of EU counter-terrorism law and policy as the central driver of European criminal justice cooperation has been the tale of the past decade.[8] The effect of the September 11 attacks was obvious both from the new legislation that came into effect soon afterwards and from its impact on the Hague Programme in 2004. This effect was one of 'catalysis and shift'.[9] The attacks had a catalytic effect because they led to an increase in criminal justice cooperation in the EU. The attacks also saw a shift in the EU towards the development of a criminal justice that is pre-emptive in nature. This approach to criminal justice, and to security in general, treats the population as a whole as a potential suspect and makes them subject to surveillance and systems of control. It aims to use specific interventions to incapacitate those who are thought to be a particular threat – for example using restrictive measures. In the face of concerted action by the Member State governments, acting as the Council, both the European Parliament and the Court of Justice of the European Union (ECJ) have had difficulty in their efforts to uphold constitutional values such as the rule of law. Thus, while the European Parliament has spent over half a decade seeking to improve data protection in EU–US Passenger Name Record Agreements, it has had little success.[10] In respect of restrictive measures, although the Court of Justice, and later the General Court, found in favour of Yassin Abdullah Kadi in 2008 and 2010 it was ultimately his removal from the UN Al-Qaeda Sanctions List that prompted his removal from the equivalent EU list.[11] There is, of course, a link between the legal process before the ECJ and Kadi's ultimate delisting by the UN. However, the operation of EU counter-terrorism law and policy is less reflective of the rule of law and more characteristic of rule by executive power that finds its expression through law (and other means).

[6] European Council, 'EU Action Plan on combating terrorism', Brussels, 15 November 2010.

[7] See the discussion in ch 6 by Coutts in this book. In many respects those subject to EU counter-terrorism law bear greater resemblance to those that are the object of EU migration control – as Moreno-Lax explores in ch 9 in this book.

[8] CC Murphy, *EU Counter-Terrorism Law: Pre-emption and the Rule of Law* (Oxford, Hart Publishing, 2012).

[9] ibid, 219.

[10] CC Murphy, 'Transatlantic Perspectives on Counter-Terrorism Surveillance: Technology, Borders and the Culture of Legality' in N McGarrity, F Davis and G Williams (eds), *Surveillance, Counter-Terrorism and Comparative Constitutionalism* (London, Routledge, 2013).

[11] See Commission Implementing Regulation 933/2012/EU of 11 October 2012 amending for the 80th time Council Regulation 881/2002/EC imposing certain specific restrictive measures directed against certain persons and entities associated with the Al-Qaeda network, OJ 2012 L278/11.

Despite ongoing problems with much counter-terrorism law around the world it is possible to conclude that today we are in a post-'war on terror' world. There are two traits of government in this world. The first is that governments have made commitments to change their approach since the events of September 11, 2001 – often as a result of a change in leadership. There has been widespread recognition that the response to the attacks was over-zealous and in many respects counter-productive. This acknowledgement was made most eloquently in the inauguration address of US President Barack Obama. The new President made the claim that 'we reject as false the choice between our safety and our ideals'.[12] The choice of 'ideals' would prove a prescient turn of phrase. Although the President sought to close the controversial Guantanamo Bay detention facility within one year of taking office this deadline was soon proven to be too idealistic. The Obama administration may claim that it is Congress that is preventing it from trying detainees such as Khalid Sheik Mohammed in a Manhattan courtroom.[13] The reality is that the dynamics of counter-terrorism policy processes make extraordinary measures very difficult to reverse. To put it in blunt terms – no police officer, intelligence official, or politician wants to be responsible for releasing a suspect who may subsequently commit an offence or for repealing a measure that might prevent an attack. The institutional demands on those who are part of the state security apparatus are such that there is little, if any, incentive to restrict counter-terrorism powers. There remains, however, strong pressure on the Obama administration in the US to close Guantanamo Bay. At the time of writing a hunger strike was increasing focus on the detention facility and the President was renewing his promises to close the base.[14] This, then, is the second trait of government in the post-'war on terror' world – the *realpolitik* of ratcheting down extraordinary security measures is such that significant reform may be very difficult, if not impossible to achieve.

The preventive detention of individuals who are called 'enemy combatants' is one problem EU counter-terrorism law and policy has not had to address.[15] However, the EU has seen a range of illiberal legislative measures brought into force, such as the Framework Decision on Combating Terrorism, the systems of restrictive measures, and surveillance laws such as the Data Retention Directive and the Third Anti-Money Laundering Directive. The list of laws attributable to post-September 11 counter-terrorism action also includes the most well-known of EU criminal justice measures, the European Arrest Warrant (EAW), and its lesser-known sibling, the European Evidence Warrant. The danger for Europe is that these measures were brought into being at a time when the shift towards

[12] President Barack Obama, 'Inauguration Address', Washington DC, 20 January 2009.

[13] F de Londras, 'Closing Guantanamo Bay: The Triumph of Politics over Law?' (2012) *Public Law*, Spring 18–26.

[14] 'Amid hunger strike, Obama renews push to close Cuba prison' *New York Times*, 30 April 2013.

[15] Though note the problematic role of European countries in the rendering of detainees across Europe. See European Centre for Constitutional and Human Rights, *CIA 'Extraordinary Rendition' Flights, Torture and Accountability – A European Approach*, 2nd edn (Berlin, ECCHR, 2009).

securitisation of criminal law and criminal justice, as Mitsilegas puts it in this book, was at its most extreme.[16] The development of a new system of security and criminal justice cooperation in the middle of a 'war' is not ideal. The resulting EU law infringes upon a wide range of human rights and suffers from deficiencies in safeguards for those subject to the law.

The persistent danger is that given the diffuse nature of power at European level, and the absence of a European public sphere, these illiberal developments might not attract sufficient public scrutiny to trigger the sort of resistance that is occurring in relation to Guantanamo Bay in the US. Thus, the EU runs the risk of enshrining a pre-emptive approach to counter-terrorism in its criminal justice system and its broader security architecture. The problems of the European public sphere aside, the near-simultaneous coming into effect of the Lisbon Treaty and the Stockholm Programme has given the EU an opportunity to re-examine its approach to counter-terrorism action. Furthermore, although there may be little by way of pan-European public discourse there are strong civil society efforts within the Member States that, along with the efforts of the European Parliament, may force law reform in certain fields. The principal example in this respect is the opposition to the Data Retention Directive across the EU and in particular in Germany.[17] The legislation is currently under review by the European Commission and, although its central tenets are unlikely to change, its operation may be subject to revision.[18] Thus, this chapter will consider counter-terrorism law and policy after examining the 'constitutional moments' of Lisbon and Stockholm to determine if there is cause to expect a more liberal approach in the future. The chapter is in some respects different from those that surround it. Those chapters tend to address distinct fields of law. Although in some jurisdictions, such as the United Kingdom, counter-terrorism law has long been understood as a discrete field of law the same cannot be said for the EU.[19] Indeed, perhaps the most surprising development in EU counter-terrorism law is the ontological one – who would have thought, as one correspondent put it to the author – that such a field could even be possible? The field is part constitutional law, part criminal law, and increasingly, part administrative law.[20] As it is not a distinct field of law several of the measures under examination in this chapter as counter-terrorism law also feature in other parts of this book. This leaves counter-terrorism law and policy in the EU as a pre-emptive *dispositif* that is struggling for coherence and as a result is difficult to characterise.

[16] See ch 7 by Mitsilegas in this volume.

[17] See the analysis in Murphy (n 8) ch 6.

[18] See the European Commission's evaluation of the Directive's operation: European Commission, 'Evaluation Report on the Data Retention Directive (Directive 2006/24/EC)' COM(2011) 225 final, Brussels, 18 April 2011. Note too the litigation before the ECJ on reference from the Irish High Court wherein a civil society group, Digital Rights Ireland, is challenging the lawfulness of mass surveillance through data retention (C-293/12). The case has been joined with a reference from the Austrian Constitutional Court (C-594/12).

[19] On UK counter-terrorism law see the encyclopedic C Walker, *Terrorism and the Law* (Oxford, Oxford University Press, 2011).

[20] CC Murphy, 'The Constitution of EU Counter-Terrorism Law' *EJIL: Talk!* 16 July 2012.

The remainder of the chapter has three parts. It first provides a critical assessment of the constitutional changes brought about by the Lisbon Treaty in the field of counter-terrorism. This assessment is not exhaustive. For example, the development of the legal basis for criminal law and justice in Article 83 TFEU is the subject of examination elsewhere in this book.[21] The consideration of it in this chapter is therefore brief. However, there are aspects of the Treaty that are attributable, at least in part, to EU counter-terrorism policy. These are the further development of the common security and defence policy, new competences for criminal law and justice, new competences for restrictive measures, the restatement of Europol's role in combating terrorism, and the introduction of a solidarity clause. After a critique of these developments the chapter turns to the Stockholm Programme to examine the extent to which it may reflect a change in counter-terrorism policy. The influence of the September 11 attacks (and other attacks around the world) was plain to see in relation to the Hague Programme. However, the Stockholm Programme offers a more complex subject of study. Its focus on the citizen and fundamental rights suggests a rhetorical, if not a substantive, shift. The chapter concludes with a brief consideration of the constitution of EU counter-terrorism law and policy today. It asks whether the pre-emptive *dispositif* of the 'war on terror' is subject to true reform after the Lisbon Treaty and the Stockholm Programme or whether we remain the objects of control of a power that is seemingly everywhere and nowhere at the same time.[22]

II. COUNTER-TERRORISM IN THE TREATIES AFTER LISBON

The term 'terrorism' appears twice in the Treaty on European Union (both in the same Article) and three times in the Treaty on the Functioning of the European Union.[23] The four Articles across the two Treaties merit consideration. However, it is necessary to bear in mind that such a crude, textual analysis may mislead us into thinking that the constitutional impact of EU counter-terrorism law and policy has been rather minimal. The true impact of EU counter-terrorism law may well be much broader and more difficult to perceive – a point to which the analysis must also return.

[21] See the work by Peers in ch 2 in this volume.

[22] The criticism that Foucault's work left us the victims of a power that is pervasive and yet somewhat ethereal has force. However, today, with an increasing focus on governance through surveillance, Foucault's work appears more and more prescient. For the criticism see: J O'Neill, 'The Disciplinary Society: From Weber to Foucault' (1986) 37 *British Journal of Sociology* 42.

[23] Before the Lisbon Treaty amendments the two references to terrorism in the treaties were in Articles 29 and 31 TEU in relation to criminal justice cooperation.

A. Common Security and Defence Policy

The references to 'terrorism' in the EU Treaty occur in relation to the Common Security and Defence Policy (CSDP).[24] Article 42 TEU refers to the Common Security and Defence Policy as part of the Common Foreign and Security Policy. The Article states that the CSDP shall 'provide the Union with an operational capacity drawing on civilian and military assets'. It makes reference to missions that the EU may carry out 'outside the Union for peace-keeping, conflict prevention and strengthening international security'. These 'tasks' are to be fulfilled using 'capabilities provided by the Member States'. The Treaty describes the tasks as including 'joint disarmament operations, humanitarian and rescue tasks, military advice and assistance tasks, conflict prevention and peace-keeping tasks, tasks of combat forces in crisis management, including peace-making and post-conflict stabilisation'.[25] All of these tasks, the Treaty claims, 'may contribute to the fight against terrorism' including 'by supporting third countries in combating terrorism'.[26] The Treaty places the Member States under an obligation to 'progressively improve their military capabilities'. It also affords a strong position to the European Defence Agency to promote the development of capabilities in this field. The Agency describes itself as 'the place to go for defence co-operation'.[27] All EU Member States – except Denmark – are members of the Agency and it has as its head Baroness Catherine Aston, the High Representative of the Union for Foreign Affairs and Security Policy.[28]

There is much in these few Articles. The rise of the CSDP is something of a success in a rather crowded policy field. Its predecessor, the European Security and Defence Policy, had to contend with the obligations Member States had under the (now defunct) Western European Union, under the North Atlantic Treaty Alliance, as well as to their own sovereignty. The ending of the Western European Union and the renaming of the EU field to CSDP may mark a greater effort to 'Unionise' defence cooperation. The field has been the subject of an increasing, if somewhat fragmented, scholarly literature in recent years.[29] Although some describe the CSDP as 'the exercise of executive power based on legal intergovernmentalism',[30] a

[24] For a discussion of early EU security and defence cooperation, see M Trybus, *European Union Law and Defence Integration* (Oxford, Hart Publishing, 2005). See also M Trybys, 'With or Without the EU Constitutional Treaty: Towards a Common Security and Defence Policy?' (2006) 31 *EL Rev* 145.

[25] Art 42(1) TEU and Art 43(1) TEU.

[26] Art 43(1) TEU.

[27] See the Agency's website: www.eda.europa.eu/Aboutus, last accessed 15 June 2013. See also Art 45 TEU.

[28] For a discussion of the constitutional relationship between the Common Foreign and Security Policy and the CSDP, and the role of the High Representative in relation to both, see D Thym, 'The Intergovernmental Constitution of the EU's Foreign, Security and Defence Executive' (2011) 7 *European Constitutional Law Review* 453.

[29] CJ Bickerton, B Irondelle and A Menon, 'Security Cooperation beyond the Nation State: The EU's Common Security and Defence Policy' (2011) 49 *Journal of Common Market Studies*, Special Issue 17. Note also the other contributions to the special issue.

[30] Thym (n 28) 453.

persuasive critique is that too great a focus on the legal structures 'ignores the reality of foreign policy-making and overestimates the significance of legal rules and procedures' in this field.[31]

A common, if somewhat simplistic, assessment of the post-September 11 transatlantic divide was to identify the United States as taking a military approach to counter-terrorism with the EU taking a criminal justice approach (the United Kingdom can be said to have done both).[32] The inclusion of combating terrorism as a goal that may be furthered by the tasks of the CDSP indicates the potential for a militaristic EU counter-terrorism policy. This is not yet being borne out in practice – perhaps because of a lack of political will. It is noteworthy that the tasks set out in the treaties do not include the sort of strategic operations the US conducts in Afghanistan, Pakistan and Yemen.[33] Indeed, the emphasis in the tasks is on the peace-making rather than the war-making side of defence policy. The idea that these tasks have a role to play in combating terrorism reflects a belief that security in other parts of the world will have a positive effect on security in Europe. The Stockholm Programme also acknowledges the point.[34] However, to date, there is little evidence of the CSDP playing a significant operational role in EU counter-terrorism policy. The difficulties in agreeing an EU position to address violence in Mali is but one example of how politics often prevents common action.[35] For now, security and defence remains a field where proclamations regarding integration find their greatest expression not in operational matters but in relation to the defence industry market.[36]

B. Competence for Criminal Law and Justice

A turn from the EU Treaty to the Treaty on the Functioning of the European Union gives sight of some of the more expected occurrences of 'terrorism' in the text. The most straightforward of these is found in Article 83 TFEU. This Article,

[31] P Koutrakos, 'Editorial – "What to Make of a Diminished Thing?"' (2013) 38 *European Law Review* 1.

[32] For a sophisticated analysis, see R Brown, *Fighting Monsters: British–American War-Making and Law-Making* (Oxford, Hart Publishing, 2011).

[33] J Argomaniz, 'A Rhetorical Spill-over? Exploring the Link between the European Union Common Security and Defence Policy (CSDP) and the External Dimension in EU Counter-Terrorism' (2012) 17 *European Foreign Affairs Review*, Special Issue 35.

[34] The programme identifies 'security' as a thematic priority in external relations and notes that 'addressing threats, even far away from our continent, is essential to protecting Europe and its citizens'. See Council of the European Union, 'The Stockholm Programme – an open and secure Europe serving and protecting the citizens' 17024/09, Brussels, 2 December 2009.

[35] Argomaniz (n 33). See also Koutrakos (n 31). See Council Decision 2013/34/CFSP of 17 January 2013 on a European Union military mission to contribute to the training of the Malian Armed Forces (EUTM Mali), OJ 2013 L14/19, 18 January 2013. Note that this difficulty is notwithstanding the threat that instability in Mali may pose to Europe. See Europol, *EU Terrorism Situation and Trend Report 2013* (Europol, 2013) 7.

[36] See M Trybus, 'The Tailor-made EU Defence and Security Procurement Directive: Limitation, Flexibility, Descriptiveness, and Substitution' (2013) 38 *EL Rev* 4; P Koutrakos, 'Editorial – Money is the Sinews of War' (2012) 37 *EL Rev* 521.

which provides the power to adopt legislation in criminal law and criminal justice, includes terrorism as a crime against which the EU may act. The introduction of this new legal basis in the Treaty is in part a consequence of Court of Justice case law on criminal competence in the internal market – in particular in relation to environmental crimes.[37] The Treaty establishes two different legal bases for criminal law. The first legal basis in Article 83(1) TFEU allows the Parliament and the Council to adopt criminal law (or 'minimum rules concerning the definition of criminal offences and sanctions') in relation to certain specified areas. Amongst those areas, indeed first amongst them, is terrorism. This legal basis effectively replaces the framework decision with the directive as a legislative instrument. Thus, if the Framework Decision on Combating Terrorism were to be adopted today it would be a directive on combating terrorism. The second legal basis lies in Article 83(2) TFEU. It is this element of the Treaty that flows from the *Environmental Crimes* and *Ship Source Pollution* judgments of the Court of Justice.[38] This allows the use of criminal law 'and regulations' where it is necessary to 'ensure the effective implementation of a Union policy in an area which has been subject to harmonisation measures'. This idea – of criminal law as effectiveness – is problematic. It might lead the EU to support over-criminalisation and, in any event, assumes the effectiveness of criminal law. However, the use of criminal law to ensure the 'effectiveness' of EU law arises in certain counter-terrorism contexts, such as in relation to counter-terrorism financing law, and the broader idea of 'effectiveness' now appears to be a central tenet of EU criminal justice.[39] Insofar as future EU counter-terrorism action is to involve criminal justice legislation the Lisbon Treaty has made it easier for such legislation to be adopted.[40]

The institutional changes brought about by the Treaty have also given rise to hope for better compliance with the rule of law.[41] The European Parliament now has co-legislative powers in relation to most policy areas that were previously the domain of the Council. The Parliament's opinions on previous measures – such as the Framework Decision on Combating Terrorism and the Framework Decision on the European Arrest Warrant – sought a more proportionate approach to the Union's crime control objectives.[42] One might therefore hope that the measures to be adopted under the new constitutional settlement will be more respectful of the rule of law. Although it is too early to determine the full effect of the institutional changes on the legislative process early indications are that the Parliament and Council are operating in a spirit of cooperation – as the

[37] See Case C-176/03 *Commission v Council* [2005] ECR I-7879. See also the discussion by Mitsilegas in ch 7 in this book.

[38] C-176/03 *Commission v Council* [2005] ECR I-7879 ('*Environmental Crimes*'); C-440/05 *Commission v Council* [2007] ECR I-9097 ('*Ship Source Pollution*').

[39] See E Herlin-Karnell, *The Constitutional Dimension of European Criminal Law* (Oxford, Hart Publishing, 2012).

[40] See ch 7 by Mitsilegas and ch 2 by Peers in this volume.

[41] See the analysis by Murphy (n 8) ch 3 – but note too the caveats by Rijpma in this book.

[42] See the analysis in Murphy (n 8) chs 3 and 7.

agreement of several legislative measures at first reading shows.[43] In contrast with the immediate change in the European Parliament's powers, the Lisbon Treaty's full effects on the ECJ's jurisdiction will take longer to be felt. Although any new criminal justice legislation will be subject to the jurisdiction of the Court the existing limitations on that jurisdiction will remain in place for five years. These limitations on institutional accountability are, of course, more general considerations and do not apply only in relation to counter-terrorism law and policy.

C. Restrictive Measures

The adoption of restrictive measures against individuals remains perhaps the most invasive EU counter-terrorism measure. It involves the financial incapacitation of the subject of the measure with profound implications for their human rights. The operation of the EU system of restrictive measures is the subject of a large literature and a seemingly endless line of cases before the Court of Justice.[44] The leading case is that of *Kadi* – a man who was subject to such measures for over a decade as the UN Security Council held him to be an associate of the Al-Qaeda network. The *Kadi* litigation touches on all aspects of EU law, but perhaps the least impressive aspect of the judgment in *Kadi I* was with regard to the legal basis for the restrictive measures against Kadi.[45] The contested regulation was adopted on the basis of Articles 60, 301 and 308 EC. The Court's means of upholding this legal basis was an exercise in judicial alchemy. Articles 60 and 301 EC set out a legal basis for disrupting economic relations with third countries. Article 308 EC gave the power to act in furtherance of objectives of the (then) Community where no explicit power existed elsewhere in the Treaty. The combination of these powers, according to the Court of Justice, was enough to provide a basis for restrictive measures against individuals. The reasoning of the Court was unconvincing but the matter did appear, at that point, to be resolved.[46]

The apparent resolution of the legal basis problem was short-lived. The Lisbon Treaty provides an explicit legal basis for the adoption of restrictive measures. The problem is that the Treaty provides not one but two possible legal bases. Article 75 TFEU provides a specific legal basis for the EU to 'define a framework' for administrative measures against terrorism – including for the freezing of assets. Article 215 TFEU provides for the adoption of 'restrictive measures' against states or non-state entities. The Council, when adopting new legislation for restrictive measures such as those at issue in the *Kadi* litigation, has chosen to use the latter legal basis. This is dubious because it avoids democratic scrutiny (due to the lesser

[43] See ch 4 by Rijpma in this volume.

[44] For useful up-to-date information on current case law, see the European Sanctions blog: www.europeansanctions.com, last accessed 18 June 2013.

[45] Joined Cases C-402/05 P and C-415/05 P *Kadi and Al Barakaat International Foundation v Council and Commission* [2008] ECR I-6351 (*Kadi I*).

[46] See discussion in Murphy (n 8) 125–30.

role of the European Parliament under the latter provision) and is contrary to the principle of *lex specialis*.[47] However, Advocate General Bot's Opinion, and the Court of Justice's judgment, in litigation initiated by the Parliament, supports the choice of legal basis.[48] This decision may yet have broader implications for the relationship between EU internal and external security law and policy. A further point in relation to restrictive measures is the expansion of their use beyond counter-terrorism objectives.[49] The measures have their origin in sanctions against states and as such it is unsurprising that their use is not limited to counter-terrorism. However, such expansion is also an example of the normalisation of an extraordinary measure and therefore demonstrative of the potential for counter-terrorism law to have a broader impact on the legal system.

D. Europol and Terrorism

Article 88 TFEU sets out the role of Europol in counter-terrorism. It declares that Europol's missions shall be to 'support and strengthen' Member State action to prevent, amongst other threats, terrorism. Although the legal basis for Europol's work was questionable at first, the role has been put on firmer ground in recent years. The replacement of the Europol Convention with a Council decision in 2009 was a step in this direction.[50] At the time of writing a new Europol regulation was under consideration. This regulation would provide Europol with a greater role in the collection and exchange of law enforcement information and, through merging Europol with the European Police College, in the provision of training.[51]

Perhaps the most notable counter-terrorism role played by Europol to date has been in relation to the operation of the TFTP Agreements. The Agreements provide for the transfer of large volumes of data on financial transactions to US authorities for use for counter-terrorist finance purposes. On the European side it is Europol that acts as the liaison with the US authorities in the operation of the system. Europol's role has come under scrutiny insofar as it finds itself in the difficult position of playing both an enforcement and a safeguarding role under the Agreements.[52] The problems that this may cause for Europol in terms of having to resolve conflicting institutional incentives are clear. Whether they have arisen in

[47] ibid.

[48] C-130/10 *European Parliament v Council*, Opinion of AG Bot, 31 January 2012 and judgment of the Court of 19 July 2012.

[49] For a full list of current measures see: European Commission, *European Union Restrictive Measures (Sanctions) in Force*, available at: eeas.europa.eu/cfsp/sanctions/docs/measures_en.pdf, last accessed 9 July 2013.

[50] Council Decision of 6 April 2009 establishing the European Police Office (Europol) 2009/371/JHA.

[51] European Commission, 'Proposal for a regulation of the European Parliament and of the Council on the European Union Agency for Law Enforcement Cooperation and Training (Europol) and repealing Decisions 2009/371/JHA and 2005/681/JHA' COM(2013) 173 final, Brussels, 27 March 2013.

[52] S Marques da Silva, 'The TFTP Agreement: A Legal and Contextual Analysis' (Transatlantic Conference on Transparency Research, Utrecht University, 8 June 2012) copy with author.

practice or not is difficult to ascertain in light of problems of transparency in the operation of the Agreements.[53]

In broader terms Europol has struggled to prove its usefulness in counter-terrorism to Member State law enforcement agencies. It is this challenge – more so than one of legal basis – that is likely to determine its success or failure in making a contribution to European counter-terrorism action in the future.[54]

E. The Solidarity Clause

The solidarity clause in Article 222 TFEU may be an example of the direct impact of the 'war on terror' on the treaties. It was first to become part of the Constitutional Treaty and then in the aftermath of the Madrid bombing in 2004 the Member States made a declaration of solidarity. In the end the solidarity clause has proven to have greater longevity than that treaty and is now part of EU constitutional law. It provides that the Union and the Member States shall 'act jointly in a spirit of solidarity' if a Member State should suffer a terrorist attack or another 'natural or man-made disaster'. The scope of the clause is not limited to terrorism (yet another example of function creep in this field). The Union and the Member States are to 'mobilise' all available instruments including military resources. The action to be taken will depend, in part, on any request made by the Member State that has suffered from the attack but may involve prevention of a 'terrorist threat' and the protection of 'democratic institutions and the civilian population'. The clause also commits the Council to 'regularly assess the threats facing the Union in order to enable the Union and its Member States to take effective action'. In late 2012 the European Commission and the High Representative published a proposal for a Council decision on the implementation of the solidarity clause.[55] It is perhaps illustrative of the inherent limitations of the proposal that Recital 13 to the proposed decision's Preamble states that 'this decision has no defence implications'.

F. Terrorism and the Treaties

The explicit references to terrorism in the treaties each have their own story to tell. However, they are also all part of a greater narrative that has seen terrorism become a more prominent concern of EU law and policy in general. The Lisbon

[53] See Marques da Silva, ibid. See further, D Curtin, 'Official Secrets and the Negotiation of International Agreements: Is the EU Executive Unbound?' (2013) 50 *CML Rev* 423.

[54] M Den Boer, C Hillebrand, A Nolke, 'Legitimacy under Pressure: The European Web of Counter-Terrorism Networks' (2008) 46 *Journal of Common Market Studies* 101.

[55] European Commission and High Representative of the European Union for Foreign Affairs and Security Policy, 'Joint proposal for a Council decision on the arrangements for the implementation by the Union of the solidarity clause', Join (2012) 39 final, Brussels, 21 December 2012.

Treaty may make a greater operational role for EU institutions and agencies possible in this field. However, in both external and internal matters, that operationalisation of EU counter-terrorism policy remains rather under-developed. The development of the EU's capacity to take external operational action in the context of the CSDP remains at an early stage. Europol continues to struggle to develop an effective role in relation to internal or external security operations – with its actions subject to scrutiny both from those who would rather it were more effective and those who see it as a threat to human rights. However, as EU agencies shift in 'business model' towards information sharing and coordination, then the prevalence of systems of data surveillance in EU counter-terrorism may render EU agencies more important.[56] The Lisbon Treaty therefore provides the EU with scope to continue to develop its role in counter-terrorism but it is the presence or absence of political willingness that will determine whether or not that scope is used. To understand the extent of that political will it is necessary to turn to the Stockholm Programme.

III. THE STOCKHOLM PROGRAMME AND COUNTER-TERRORISM POLICY

The effect of counter-terrorism on the area of freedom, security and justice became apparent when the proposal for a European Arrest Warrant, an aim of the Tampere Programme, went from idealistic aspiration to legal reality within a year of the attacks.[57] The Hague Programme was astonishing in its preoccupation with security. It was agreed in 2004, the year of the Madrid bombings, and thus the year that Al-Qaeda made its first mark on European soil. It is therefore unsurprising that the Programme was strong on security and weak on freedom and justice.[58] Five years after the Hague Programme the EU concern with security appears to be different. It is clear that terrorism remains a key priority for the Union and its area of freedom, security and justice. It features in the Stockholm Programme both as a specific subject of attention and as a consideration in a wide range of policy fields. The Programme has since been the subject of a Plan of Action drawn up by the European Commission.[59] This Plan of Action must be taken into account when assessing the likely developments in counter-terrorism law and policy over the next five years. For the purpose of this chapter, the citations of terrorism and counter-terrorism in the Stockholm Programme may be categorised as including: first, terrorism and criminal justice; second, terrorism and internal

[56] See ch 4 by Rijpma in this book.

[57] See Murphy (n 8) ch 8.

[58] See Statewatch, 'The "Hague Programme" Annotation of final version, approved 5.11.2004' available at: www.statewatch.org/news/2004/nov/hague-annotated-final.pdf, last accessed 9 July 2013, for an annotation of the Programme by Steve Peers.

[59] European Commission to the European Parliament, the Council, the European Economic and Social Committee and the Committee of the Regions, 'Delivering an area of freedom, security and justice for Europe's citizens – Action Plan implementing the Stockholm Programme' (Communication) COM(2010) 171 final, Brussels, 20 April 2010 ('Stockholm Action Plan').

security; and third, terrorism and external relations. These are not, however, discrete categories as the line between criminal justice and internal security is somewhat artificial and that between internal and external policies is now a rather blurry one.[60] Rather, they serve as categories of convenience for the present consideration of counter-terrorism law and policy under the Stockholm Programme. Each category merits a brief consideration before the overall impact is subject to examination in the chapter's conclusion.

A. Terrorism and Criminal Justice

One of the most notable developments in EU counter-terrorism law under the Stockholm Programme is the way in which much of the policies in this area have now become part of ordinary EU criminal law and justice. There may, therefore, be much EU counter-terrorism law hidden away in the parts of the Programme and Plan that address the adoption of substantive and procedural criminal law and cooperation by criminal justice agencies. In this respect the latest Programme and Plan evidence the 'normalisation' of EU counter-terrorism law – it is not an exceptional part of EU law and policy but part of the Union's ordinary activity. Thus, the adoption of the EAW was made possible by the need to combat terrorism but it is now demonstrative of the strengths and weaknesses of EU criminal justice in general. The Action Plan promises reports on its implementation and 'appropriate follow-up'.[61] It also calls for legislation for the European Investigation Order and for common standards for evidence-gathering.[62] As these initiatives build on the existing European Evidence Warrant they too are counter-terrorism law. Indeed, the full extent to which the response to terrorism has made other EU criminal law and justice possible can merely be the subject of speculation, but the broad catalytic effect of the September 11 attacks is noteworthy.

The section of the Action Plan specifically on terrorism is notable for being light on criminal justice legislation. There is a call for a legislative proposal on 'precursors to explosives'.[63] The Plan also seeks a report on the implementation of the recent amendments to the Framework Decision on Combating Terrorism and on the operation of the Data Retention Directive.[64] It notes that the focus in criminal law will be 'primarily on mutual recognition' with harmonisation used for 'selected cases' only.[65] Therefore, despite the legal framework that the Lisbon Treaty provides, the Stockholm Programme may represent a more sober approach to harmonisation in this year after the heady enthusiasm for legislation that was prompted by the September 11 attacks. Indeed, the Programme states that crim-

[60] On the latter point see, eg ch 11 by Eckes in this book.
[61] Stockholm Action Plan, 18.
[62] ibid.
[63] Stockholm Action Plan, 40.
[64] ibid, 41.
[65] ibid, 5.

inal law should 'as a rule, be used only as a last resort'.[66] This sobriety finds some expression in the call for 'special attention, support and social recognition' for victims of terrorism but also in the need to build trust through protecting suspects' rights in criminal proceedings.[67]

Perhaps the most noteworthy aspect of the Plan in the field of criminal justice is the increasing emphasis on operational cooperation and the attempt to capacity build at EU level with Europol, Eurojust and FRONTEX all receiving attention.[68] The statement in the Action Plan that the Union should 'remove all the obstacles in the way of effective law enforcement cooperation' is indicative of the Commission's desire to drive forward EU action in this regard.[69] It seems likely that the teething problems of the EAW are, in part, responsible for the strong emphasis throughout the Programme on building mutual trust (an emphasis that is almost humorous at times – witness the proposal for a Police Erasmus Programme). The Council seeks the development of a 'genuine European law enforcement culture'.[70]

B. Terrorism and Internal Security

Although terrorism has an impact on criminal justice it also relates to the broader area of internal security. It sits alongside organised crime and 'other threats' as a target of the internal security strategy. Thus, terrorism is the subject of specific attention under the heading of 'a Europe that protects':

> The European Council considers that the threat from terrorists remains significant and is constantly evolving in response to both the international community's attempts at combating it and new opportunities that present themselves. We must not lower our guard against these heinous criminals.[71]

Although this first statement on 'terrorism' as part of 'a Europe that protects' is tabloidesque the Programme as a whole is more difficult to characterise. The Action Plan notes the 'better tools to fight terrorism' that the Lisbon Treaty provides and states that the Internal Security Strategy will be 'implemented with care and firm resolve'.[72] The Programme also makes reference to the solidarity clause as the EU commits to make 'full use of Article 222 TFEU'.[73] The four strands of the Council Action Plan are reaffirmed: prevent, protect, pursue and respond. The Stockholm Programme also includes a hat-tip to the somewhat dubious role of the EU Counter Terrorism Coordinator (although he is perhaps notably absent

[66] Stockholm Programme, para 3.3.
[67] ibid, para 2.3.4., para 2.4.
[68] ibid, para 4.2.
[69] Stockholm Action Plan, 6.
[70] Stockholm Programme, para 4.2.1.
[71] ibid, para 4.5.
[72] Stockholm Action Plan, 5.
[73] Stockholm Programme, para 1.1.

from the Commission's Action Plan).[74] The Plan calls for a methodology with 'common parameters' for the assessment of 'threats at European level' with Europol, SitCen and Eurojust all to be participants.[75]

It is remarkable how much of this aspect of the Programme focuses on prevention and counter-radicalisation. The Council Action Plan on Combating Terrorism did not result in significant action on this element of counter-terrorism policy. Nevertheless the first three items of the Council's call for action in the Stockholm Programme deal with this policy. Of course, counter-radicalisation is a key concern of the United Kingdom and it may have made a strong push for these policies in the drafting of the Programme.[76] The absence of EU action in this field to date, in comparison with an active agenda in other areas of counter-terrorism such as surveillance, may make counter-radicalisation a priority. It may simply be that the Council sees counter-radicalisation as an area where action remains possible without legislation. The Commission's Action Plan limits work in this field to 'non-legislative measures', a 'public-private dialogue' on online illegality, efforts to 'enable, reinforce and disseminate' 'ideologies that reject extremism and violence', and 'a holistic approach [to] radicalization'.[77] The Programme itself includes a rather incoherent paragraph of action that conflates 'the importance of better understanding the methods used for dissemination of terrorist propaganda' with maritime and aviation security.[78] The issue of security of goods, the 'fight against illicit use of dual use goods' and efforts to 'protect the international supply chain' are all rhetorical commitments to rather vague action in this field.[79] It is unclear why they sit alongside counter-radicalisation in counter-terrorism policy.

The action in this part of the Programme also has a strong focus on counter-terrorist finance. It is in this part of global counter-terrorism law that the EU continues to play a strong role – both as a centre for international finance and as a developer of rules.[80] The Commission will explore a European Terrorist Finance Tracking Programme to mirror the US system that has been the subject of several EU–US Agreements (and much criticism). It will also examine alternative payment methods, cooperation with financial institutions, and counter-terrorist financing and non-profit organisations.[81] The exploration of a European system of terrorist finance tracking is an example of a policy field in which European internal law comes after EU–US cooperation in the field. The same is true of the proposal for a 'common EU approach' on Passenger Name Record screening in the Action Plan. However, just as there is an increase in enforcement cooperation so too is there a call for protection for those subject to that cooperation. Thus, the

[74] ibid, para 4.5.
[75] Stockholm Action Plan, 32.
[76] Note the 2011 review of the UK Prevent Strategy: HM Government, *Prevent Strategy* (Cm 8092, 2011).
[77] Stockholm Action Plan, 40.
[78] Stockholm Programme, para 4.5.
[79] ibid.
[80] See Murphy (n 8) ch 4.
[81] Stockholm Programme, para 4.5.

Action Plan also seeks a 'new comprehensive legal framework for data protection'.[82] This is significant as data surveillance and retention remains perhaps the broadest aspect of EU counter-terrorism law and policy – the one that affects EU citizens as a whole.[83]

C. Terrorism and External Relations

The Stockholm Programme's long section on external relations, 'Europe in a Globalised World', makes clear the extent to which the area of freedom, security and justice is as much about external security as it is about internal security. This aspect of the Programme echoes the CSDP provisions of the Lisbon Treaty. It notes that even threats 'far away from our continent' can affect the security of 'Europe and its citizens'.[84] As such it is necessary to engage with third countries on a wide range of matters including terrorism. The relationship between Europol and the CSDP – to which reference is made in the Lisbon Treaty – finds expression in the Action Plan. The Plan calls for a Commission communication on Europol cooperation with external police missions.[85] The aim is to promote 'standards and good practice' and demonstrates the increasing external effect of internal European law.[86] The idea of the EU as a standard-setter in the field of security – or even more narrowly in terms of policing – runs contrary to the claim in the literature that in these areas the EU is a 'norm-taker' under the influence of the US.[87] Of course, both the EU and the US are actors on a broader global stage that seek to influence, but are also influenced by, their interactions with third countries.

Other elements of cooperation invoked are information exchange, counter-radicalisation, and the protection of 'critical infrastructures'.[88] The exchange of information with the US, in particular in relation to border security, is given emphasis.[89] European cooperation with Africa, Latin America and the Caribbean are also aspects of external relations with counter-terrorism implications.[90] The implementation of these objectives is remarkable for the extent to which it makes clear the relationship between internal and external security. Thus, the Commission Action Plan states that such policies are 'inextricably linked' and that 'continuity and consistency' in internal and external action is 'essential'.[91] The Commission gives itself the task of developing cooperation on PNR Agreements with third countries. It also

[82] Stockholm Action Plan, 29.
[83] See Murphy (n 8) ch 8.
[84] Stockholm Programme, para 7.
[85] Stockholm Action Plan, 32.
[86] Stockholm Programme, para 4.3.1.
[87] J Argomaniz, 'When the EU is the "Norm-taker": The Passenger Name Records Agreement and the EU's Internalization of US Border Security Norms' (2009) 31 *Journal of European Integration* 119.
[88] Stockholm Action Plan, 42–43.
[89] Stockholm Programme, para 2.6.
[90] ibid, para 7.5.
[91] Stockholm Action Plan, 8.

set out – and has seen implementation of – the need for a long-term agreement between the EU and US on the US Terrorist Finance Tracking Programme. These aspects of EU–US cooperation are largely articulated in early sections of the Action Plan with the result that their consideration under 'Europe in a Globalised World' consists of cross-references. Although these aspects of external relations remain enforcement-led there is also evidence here of a reaction against over-reach by existing law enforcement cooperation. Thus, there is a commitment to data protection agreements with the US and the protection of personal data in cooperation with other third countries.[92]

IV. CONCLUSION: THE CONSTITUTION OF EU COUNTER-TERRORISM TODAY

How then might we characterise the constitution of EU counter-terrorism after Lisbon and Stockholm? The above exposition of the Treaty and the Programme may confirm both the contention that we are in a post-'war on terror' world with the EU seeking to reform its counter-terrorism action in light of problems both with its efficacy and its societal impact. There is evidence that the EU is thinking again about the action it has taken since September 11. There is an emphasis on 'stocktaking' in the field of counter-terrorism – one that the Action Plan describes as a priority. A range of factors may be playing a part in prompting a reconsideration of counter-terrorism policy-making. There has been a reaction against some EU measures that were adopted on the basis of their necessity for counter-terrorism. The judgment of the European Court of Justice in *Kadi I*, the judgments of national courts in relation to the EAW and EU telecommunications surveillance, and the broader political outcry about that surveillance all represent a push-back against EU action in this field.[93] A further factor may be the new constitutional and institutional framework. The Stockholm Programme draws particular attention to new accountability through the European Parliament and national parliaments and to the broadening and deepening of judicial review – both because of the increase in the European Court of Justice's jurisdiction and the coming into effect of the Charter of Fundamental Rights. The triumvirate of values – security, justice and fundamental rights – must not be 'in isolation' but rather must go 'hand in hand'.

Does this reflect a liberalisation of EU counter-terrorism law after the security-driven action of the past decade? Not if such liberalisation would involve repealing or amending the legal measures that were adopted in pursuit of EU counter-terrorism policy. Indeed – in this respect the comment by Commissioner Malmstrom that data retention is 'here to stay'[94] is emblematic of the permanence of much EU counter-terrorism law. The current low level of legislative activity in the Action Plan

[92] See, eg Stockholm Programme, para 2.6.

[93] For a discussion see Murphy (n 8) ch 8.

[94] C Malmstrom, 'Taking on the Data Retention Directive' (European Commission Conference, Brussels, 3 December 2010). Reference: SPEECH/10/723.

may be a product of a variety of factors. It may be that the Commission (and/or the Council) believes that EU counter-terrorism law is 'done' and the aim now is to operationalise the existing law. The Commission may, alternatively, read a shift in the political climate with Member States facing greater scrutiny at national and European level in the field of counter-terrorism. The impact of the September 11, March 11 and July 7 bombings on EU action may be diminishing.[95] It may also be that after the disappointment of the Hague Programme the Commission is avoiding a difficult expectations–delivery gap by promising too much by way of legislation. A modest legislative agenda may protect against future perceptions of failure.

The Commission notes that under the Lisbon Treaty the 'new institutional framework offers the Union an unprecedented opportunity to better interlink its different counter terrorism instruments'.[96] Furthermore, the Council notes the achievement of 'maturity' in the area of freedom, security and justice should see policies 'grow in consistency'.[97] However the theme of fragmentation that runs through this book also occurs in the field of counter-terrorism law. The EU is no Leviathan. It has no sword to swing against Al-Qaeda or any other security threat. After September 11 the efforts of the EU to carve out a role in global counter-terrorism had a deleterious effect on the rule of law. The Lisbon Treaty and Stockholm Programme may offer cause for optimism for a rebalancing but that optimism has yet to be proven to be borne out in action. The pre-emptive *dispositif* of EU counter-terrorism law and policy remains a broad field in which mechanisms of restraint struggle against a power that is both difficult to characterise and to contain.

[95] Notwithstanding the time that has passed since the last Al-Qaeda bombing in Europe there remains concern as to the threat of individual acts of violence – as the murder of a British soldier in London on 22 May 2013 demonstrates.

[96] Stockholm Action Plan, 6.

[97] Stockholm Programme, para 4.1.

11

*External Relations Law: How the Outside Shapes the Inside**

CHRISTINA ECKES

I. INTRODUCTION

BY OFFERING ITS citizens an area of freedom, security and justice (AFSJ),[1] the Union barely linguistically disguises an aspiration to assume core state functions. The carefully chosen term AFSJ is not only loaded with social contract connotations but also contains a spatial notion of territorial unity that has a state flavour to it. The strengthening of the policy fields brought together under the AFSJ has been explained as a necessary complement to the internal market compensating the removal of frontiers within the EU.[2] However, AFSJ policies, arguably as all EU policies, are shaped by many pull and push forces, originating not only within the Union but also outside.

This chapter explores the extent to which the AFSJ is influenced from the outside.[3] The underlying argument is that the Union's AFSJ is not merely a product of internal compromise aiming to reconcile the – at times schizophrenic – ambitions of the Union and its Member States, who want to offer EU citizens an AFSJ governed by coherent and indiscriminately applicable policies, while ensuring the greatest possible retention of sovereign rights on the part of the Member States, but also a product of external forces. This chapter aims to demonstrate such 'outside-in' effects resulting from the Member States cooperating under international law, and the Union interacting with third parties and recognising external human rights regimes.[4] These outside-in effects will only increase with the intensification

* I would like to thank Luis Barroso for his comments on an earlier draft and Robbert-Jan Winters for his research assistance.

[1] Art 3(2) TEU.

[2] ibid.

[3] This chapter does not deal with judicial cooperation in civil matters.

[4] This chapter forms part of a broader enquiry about the implications of internationalisation for the power division within the TEU legal order: *Outside-In: Tracing the Imprint of the European Union's External Actions on its Constitutional Landscape*, funded by the Dutch Science Foundation, NWO. For a short description, see: centers.law.nyu.edu/jeanmonnet/fellows/12-13/ ChristinaEckes.html.

of litigation and, in particular, a rise in preliminary rulings in the different policy fields now falling within the AFSJ.[5] These rulings will help to ensure uniform interpretation of EU law creating an AFSJ, but they will also be the ECJ's tool to determine the rules of the inter-institutional game, the boundaries of EU law competences, and the deeper meaning of what the EU can offer in terms of freedom, security and justice. The Court will be confronted with outside-in effects, which can have constitutional consequences if, possibly only over time, they change the division of power between the institutions or the understanding of core principles. Integration is a process leading towards the establishment of *one* out of many. The process itself has consequences for the understanding of the involved parts, even before this one is created. The process of European integration has such consequences by shaping the understanding of the sovereignty of the Member States. This is a constitutional change.

Most existing literature on the external dimension of the AFSJ largely focusses on the Union's external actions, including the Union's ability to influence the outside.[6] This is an important issue, with real implications for policy-making and substantive influence of the Union beyond its borders. The intention of this chapter is to focus on the reverse question of how the outside shapes the inside. This is relevant not only in extreme cases where the outside aspires to impose rules that undermine fundamental values,[7] but also in every day policy-making, where preferences, institutional influence, and the reading of the law are changed as a result of the outside.

The chapter identifies the above-described outside-in effects on the creation and understanding of the AFSJ. Section II demonstrates that when internal policy areas become external policy the European Parliament is disadvantaged in the decision-making procedure. Even after the changes introduced by the Treaty of Lisbon this has not fully been remedied. Section III analyses how law-making under international rather than EU law has been used in the past to determine the AFSJ policies. Examples are Prüm and Schengen. Section IV turns to the substantive content of internal EU law-making in the AFSJ. It explores examples in which the internal law-making has been inspired or even influenced by (international agreements with) third countries. Section V focuses on the influence of the European Convention on Human Rights (ECHR) and the case law of the European Court of Human Rights (ECtHR) on the protection of rights in the AFSJ. The final section offers an account of how the external has influenced the AFSJ as the place of an 'imagined community'.[8]

[5] eg D Acosta Arcarazo and A Geddes, 'The Development, Application and Implications of an EU Rule of Law in the Area of Migration Policy' (2013) 51 *Journal of Common Market Studies* 179; S Peers, 'Mission Accomplished? EU Justice and Home Affairs Law after the Treaty of Lisbon' (2011) 48 *CML Rev* 661.

[6] eg M Cremona, J Monar and S Poli (eds), *The External Dimension of the European Union's Area of Freedom, Security and Justice*, College of Europe Studies 13 (Brussels, PIE Peter Lang, 2011); T Balzacq (ed), *The External Dimension of Justice and Home Affairs – Governance, Neighbours, Security*, Palgrave Studies in European Union Politics (Basingtoke, Palgrave, 2009).

[7] The case that springs to mind is of course C-402/05 P and C-415/05 P *Kadi* [2008] ECR I-6351.

[8] B Anderson, *Imagined Communities: Reflections on the Origin and Spread of Nationalism* (London, Verso, 2006).

II. UNION BORDERS: WHERE DOES THE AFSJ END?

About 50 years ago, Michel Foucault identified space as Europe's greatest anxiety.[9] He developed the concept of 'heterotopias' as a kind of 'effectively enacted utopia in which the real sites, all the other real sites that can be found within a culture, are simultaneously represented, contested and inverted' – real places that are 'placeless places' 'outside of all places', present in all cultures in the world.[10] This concept of heterotopias can inform the discussion about the AFSJ.[11] Foucault explains that heterotopias are 'capable of juxtaposing in a single real place several spaces, several sites that are in themselves incompatible', that they constitute a break with traditional time, by representing either a quasi-eternity or transitoriness, and that the access to heterotopias is restricted. These are all characteristics of the AFSJ. First, it comprises the territories and jurisdictions of the Member States, which support the Union's claim to governance while at the same time challenging it. Secondly, it, as the Union itself, alludes to eternity by being established for an unlimited period of time. Thirdly, it protects its outer boundaries and determines the criteria of access in a complex interplay with national and international law. Foucault also argues that throughout history heterotopias 'function in a very different fashion'. Thinking about the AFSJ in these terms allows considering its deeper meaning beyond the actual legal changes it imposes, as well as the potential evolvement of its function in society over time.

When discussing the external influences on the AFSJ the delimitation of space is central. From the perspective of the Member States the very creation of an AFSJ makes what was previously external (territories of other Member States) internal and defines that the territory of third countries remains external. Different forms of 'external' influences can be distinguished: direct influence from third parties, be it third countries or international organisations; the use of international law by the EU institutions resulting in an internal power change; and the use of international law by EU Member States influencing EU law. 'Influencing' is here understood as having a limiting effect on the autonomy of (some of) the internal actors, be it on their substantive choices or exercise of power within the institutional interaction.

The greatest particularity of the AFSJ is its intergovernmental legacy. This is also what makes it particularly difficult to identify 'external' influences on EU law. Is it an external influence if Member States *inter se* make agreements with the intention to later integrate them into EU law (Schengen)? Are ex-third pillar con-

[9] M Foucault, *Of Other Spaces (1967), Heterotopias.* Available at: foucault.info/documents/heteroTopia/foucault.heteroTopia.en.html (last visited 6 February 2013): 'The present epoch will perhaps be above all the epoch of space'.

[10] ibid.

[11] Even though Foucault's examples of 'heterotopias in deviation' may at first sight seem rather different in that they are specific limited spaces, such as rest homes, psychiatric hospitals, and prisons. See discussion in s VII below.

ventions international agreements? Despite the Court of Justice of the European Union's (ECJ) attempts to establish jurisdiction and a certain level of uniform interpretation throughout the European legal order,[12] the Union's pillars remained before Lisbon very different as regards decision-making,[13] the extent of jurisdiction of the ECJ,[14] and the legal effects of third pillar instruments.[15] Some of the historical heritage of the pillars has survived over time, even after the Lisbon Treaty merged all first and third pillar policies of the AFSJ under Title V of the TFEU. Indeed, even though the ordinary legislative procedure has been introduced for most policy areas,[16] special procedures requiring unanimity apply to a significant number of exceptions.[17] Furthermore, the AFSJ is the subject of numerous protocols attached to the European treaties.[18] Most importantly, these protocols contain transitional provisions and geographical limitations. Special interim rules apply to pre-Lisbon instruments; yet, time passes and on 1 December 2014, the interim rules will expire. More permanent remains the continuous shadow of the intergovernmental nature in the geographical limitations of the AFSJ, which does not correspond to the territory of the Union. The UK, Ireland and Denmark do not only continue to enjoy their pre-Lisbon opt-outs for the areas of immigration, visa and asylum (and civil law). The Lisbon Treaty extends it for the UK and Ireland to cooperation in police and criminal matters.[19] The position of the UK, Ireland and Denmark could be summarised as a default opt-out from the AFSJ with an opt-in possibility.[20] In the case of Denmark, this is limited to visa lists and formats. Also, Denmark (which signed the Schengen Agreement) is bound by the Schengen *acquis* under international law rather than

[12] Case C-105/03 *Pupino* [2005] ECR I-5285; Case C-355/04 P *Segi v Council* [2007] ECR I-1657.

[13] Even after the partial integration of third pillar policies into the TEC. Unanimity for instance remained the voting requirement in the Council even after the Treaty of Nice for family law and legal migration. The European Parliament was only consulted on these two policies and on visa lists and visa formats.

[14] References for a preliminary ruling from final courts only. See ex-Art 35 EU and ex-Art 68(1) EC.

[15] See ex-Art 34(2)(b) EU.

[16] Arts 75 (financial counter-terrorist sanctions), 77(2) (visa lists and formats), 79 (common European asylum system), 82 (approximation of criminal laws), 83 (minimum rules concerning the definition of criminal offences and sanctions for cross-border offences), 84 (crime prevention), 85 (Eurojust), 87 (police cooperation) and 88 (Europol) TFEU.

[17] Arts 77(3) (passports), 86(1) (European Public Prosecutor) 87(3) (operational police cooperation), and 89 (operation on the territory of another Member State) TFEU.

[18] Protocol 19 on the Schengen *acquis* integrated into the framework of the European Union; Protocol 21 on the position of the United Kingdom and Ireland in respect of the area of freedom, security and justice; Protocol 22 on the position of Denmark; Protocol 23 on external relations of the Member States with regard to the crossing of external borders; Protocol 36 on transitional provisions; in a more limited way: Protocol 20 on the application of certain aspects of Art 26 of the Treaty on the Functioning of the European Union to the United Kingdom and to Ireland; Protocol 24 on asylum for nationals of Member States of the European Union.

[19] The UK may until 31 May 2014 choose whether to accept the application of the Commission's infringement powers and the Court's jurisdiction for unamended third pillar instruments or to opt-out of them entirely, in which case they will cease to apply to the UK on 1 December 2014.

[20] The UK and Ireland (Protocol 21), as well as Denmark (Protocol 22), are in an opt-out default position with an opt-in possibility, with slightly different rules.

EU law.[21] This means that the ECJ does not have jurisdiction over Denmark. This geographical differentiation leads to great complexity.[22] It might also make it more difficult for EU citizens to feel that the AFSJ is their own, when it does not match the territory of the political entity establishing it or of the internal market, to which their free movement rights apply. Finally, the picture is rendered even more complex by the fact that internal and external objectives are highly interdependent[23] and the Chapter on the AFSJ does not contain explicit external Union competences, except for very specific actions.[24] Instead, competences in other areas, such as trade and Common Foreign and Security Policy (CFSP), which are not geographically limited, are also used to pursue AFSJ objectives.

III. LIMITING LAW-MAKING POWERS OF THE EUROPEAN PARLIAMENT BY TAKING IT OUTSIDE: HAS THE SWIFT SITUATION CHANGED AFTER LISBON?

Until the entry into force of the Lisbon Treaty, the European Parliament's powers to participate in external policy-making in the AFSJ were very limited. The Parliament did not have any say in the process culminating in the conclusion of international agreements in the third pillar.[25] Since Lisbon, Parliament's powers for the conclusion of international agreements have been significantly extended in all policy fields governed by the ordinary legislative procedure, including the AFSJ.[26] However, the Council remains the most powerful institution: it authorises the opening of negotiations, adopts negotiating directives, authorises the signing, and concludes international agreements. In principle (subject to exceptions), the Council acts by qualified majority. As to the involvement of the European Parliament, it is important to distinguish between the initiation and negotiation stage on the one hand and the signing and conclusion stage on the other. Parliament is not formally involved in the negotiations, apart from having the right to be informed during all stages of the procedure.[27] At conclusion stage, it can be involved in two ways: consultation or consent. The latter is required for policy fields falling under the ordinary legislative procedure.

The right to be informed, in combination with the European Parliament's powers at conclusion stage, has introduced certain political safeguards. Indeed,

[21] Art 3 of the Schengen Protocol and Art 5 of the Danish Protocol.

[22] Which also leads to litigation before the ECJ: Case C-77/05 *UK v Council* (*Frontex* decision) [2007] ECR I-11459; Case C-137/05 *UK v Council* [2007] ECR I-11593; and Case C-482/08 *UK v Council* [2010] ECR I-10413.

[23] M Cremona, 'EU External Action in the JHA Domain – A Legal Perspective' in Cremona et al, *External Dimension* 78.

[24] Art 79(3) TFEU for the conclusion of readmission agreements and Art 78(2)(g) TFEU for cooperation with third countries in the context of the EU asylum law.

[25] Ex-Art 24 and 38 EU.

[26] Art 218(6)(a) TFEU (explaining that Art 218(6)(a)(v) includes agreements that fall within the policy fields in which the ordinary legislative procedure applies).

[27] Art 218(11) TFEU.

the rationale of Article 218 TFEU requires involving the European Parliament at negotiation stage. This is also acknowledged in the Framework Agreement on relations between Parliament and the Commission.[28] The greatest strength and influence of a parliament is not consent or rejection, but deliberation in its search for a majority. If the European Parliament is fully and actively involved at an earlier stage, for instance when the negotiation mandate and directives are drawn up, it has a governing role rather than the role of the opposition. Parliament would be forced to find constructive solutions. By contrast, if the European Parliament has very little influence until the very end, it is given the role of an obstructionist: its only option is to veto the agreement if it disagrees with the final draft. The latter, however, breeds mistrust between Parliament and Commission and Council, as well as between the EU and its external negotiation partners.

The two cases in point are SWIFT and ACTA. Shortly after the Lisbon Treaty entered into force, the European Parliament showed its newly established teeth under Article 218(5) TFEU in the adoption of an agreement within the AFSJ. It voted the SWIFT Agreement down the first time (11 February 2010), only to then agree to an amended version (8 July 2010).[29] The SWIFT Agreement allows US authorities to access, subject to the approval of Europol,[30] large volumes of transaction information from the Society for Worldwide Interbank Financial Telecommunication (SWIFT) for the purpose of the Terrorist Finance Tracking Program. SWIFT is an inter-service banking company that is used in roughly 80 per cent of all international transactions.[31] This naturally raises a multitude of data protection concerns. The European Parliament was cut out of the information flow in the negotiations leading up to the conclusion of the SWIFT Agreement.[32] Crucially, the negotiations took place before the entry into force of the Lisbon Treaty and only the conclusion after. Hence, the question remains whether the involvement of the European Parliament at negotiation stage has fundamentally changed with the Lisbon Treaty. The negotiations of the Anti-Counterfeiting Trade Agreement (ACTA), which does not fall within the AFSJ but is also controversial, raises concerns in this regard.[33] The European Parliament remained excluded from the negotiations, even after Lisbon. However, in the case

[28] See Annex 3 of Decision 2010/2118 of the European Parliament of 20 October 2010 on the revision of the Framework Agreement on relations between the European Parliament and the Commission, OJ 2010 C70E/55, para 3 ('The Commission shall take due account of Parliament's comments throughout the negotiations').

[29] J Monar, 'The Rejection of the EU–US SWIFT Interim Agreement by the European Parliament: A Historic Vote and its Implications' (2010) 15 *European Foreign Affairs Review* 143.

[30] Vetting by Europol was introduced only after the EP had once voted the agreement down.

[31] G Fuster, P De Hert, and S Gutwirth, 'SWIFT and the Vulnerability of Transatlantic Data Transfers' (2008) 22 *International Review of Law, Computers and Technology* 191.

[32] C Kaunert, S Leonard and A MacKenzie, 'The Social Construction of an EU Interest in Counter-Terrorism: US Influence and Internal Struggles in the Cases of PNR and SWIFT' (2012) 21 *European Security* 474, 488.

[33] C Eckes, E Fahey and M Kanetake, 'International, European and US Perspectives on the Negotiation and Adoption of the Anti-Counterfeiting Trade Agreement (ACTA)' (2013) *Currents, International Trade Law Journal*.

of the new Passenger Name Records (PNR) Agreements the information flow to the European Parliament seems to have worked better.[34]

Executive secrecy, particularly in the area of external relations, is the rule rather than the exception. This remains a concern, including after Lisbon, for the European Parliament and for the wider public. Following the controversial adoption of the SWIFT Agreement, the General Court ruled in *Sophie in 't Veld I* on the lack of transparency in negotiating international agreements, along with the difficulties of the European Parliament and the public to access relevant information.[35] The *Sophie in 't Veld I* case is informative on the interpretation of the right of access to information. It concerned access to the opinion of the Council's Legal Service concerning a recommendation from the Commission to the Council to authorise the opening of negotiations for the SWIFT Agreement.[36] Sophie in 't Veld, a Member of the European Parliament, relied on the general Transparency Regulation for her access request, and consequently, the discussion was framed as to whether the refusal was justified under the exceptions under that Regulation.[37] The General Court ruled that

> the mere fact that a document concern[ed] an interest protected by an exception cannot justify application of that exception. Such application may, in principle, be justified only if the institution has previously assessed . . . whether access to the document would specifically and actually undermine the protected interest.[38]

Judicial review of a provision with such 'a complex and delicate nature' as the international relations exception

> must be limited to verifying whether the procedural rules and the duty to state reasons have been complied with, whether the facts have been accurately stated, and whether there has been a manifest error of assessment of the facts or a misuse of powers.[39]

The General Court's analysis led to partial annulment of the Council decision denying access to information because the Council had not established the risk of a threat to the public interest in the field of international relations concerning the undisclosed parts of the document relating to the legal basis.[40] Under this case law, *public* access to information cannot be denied simply because it concerns an international agreement, but the assessment of whether secrecy is necessary is the

[34] See S in 't Veld, 'Draft recommendation on the draft Council decision on the conclusion of the Agreement between the United States of America and the European Union on the use and transfer of Passenger Name Records (PNR) to the United States Department of Homeland Security' 2011/0382NLE. But see also the preceding media coverage: V Pop, 'Unhappy MEPs to Approve Passenger Data Deal' (2011) *EU Observer*. Available at: euobserver.com/justice/114252 (last visited 6 February 2013).

[35] See Case T-529/09 *Sophie in 't Veld v Council* (hereinafter *Sophie in 't Veld I*) [2012] ECR II-000, para 2; see also Case T-301/10 *Sophie in 't Veld v Commission* (hereinafter *Sophie in 't Veld II*), OJ 2010 C260/55, 18.

[36] *Sophie in 't Veld I*, para 2.

[37] In particular Art 4(1)(a) of Reg 1049/2001, see ibid.

[38] *Sophie in 't Veld I*, para 20. This is in line with the earlier case: Joined Cases C-514/07 P, C-528/07 P and C-532/07 P *Sweden v ASBL* [2010] ECR I-8533.

[39] *Sophie in 't Veld I*, paras 24–25.

[40] ibid, paras 59–60.

responsibility of the EU institution asked to grant access (usually the Council) and the Court will only check procedural compliance and rule out manifest error of assessment. The extent to which the European Parliament is granted access to information remains to be seen in future negotiations. After all, Parliament continues to hold veto powers in a large number of policy areas.

The involvement of Parliament is particularly important where the Council negotiates an international agreement that foresees a change of the Union *acquis* – which is perfectly possible under the hierarchy of laws within the EU. Otherwise, the executive would externally predetermine change of legislative decisions without giving the European Parliament the opportunity to influence the course of the discussion or the framing of the subject matter. Indeed, the General Court explained that the principle of transparency is applicable 'especially where a decision authorising the opening of negotiations involves an international agreement which may have an impact on an area of the European Union's legislative activity'.[41] Furthermore, the decision under the Lisbon Treaty to strengthen the role of the European Parliament in the conclusion of international agreements, where a field requires the ordinary legislative procedure internally, can be read as a reaction to the increasingly broad and detailed nature of international agreements, which govern and regulate the legal position of individuals in the same way as internal legislation.[42] The Lisbon Treaty has brought great improvement but the negotiation of international agreements, particularly those with legislative scope, remains a point of concern, including and perhaps particularly in the AFSJ.

IV. EARLY LAW-MAKING OUTSIDE THE EU FRAMEWORK AND ITS INTEGRATION

EU law offers a sophisticated legal framework in which the EU institutions and the Member States interact and make policy. It enables these actors but it also constrains them by imposing specific decision-making procedures and, albeit at times limited, judicial review by the Court. As a result groups of Member States have in the past agreed to act outside of the framework of EU law, usually due to a lack of the required support within. These international agreements have affected the development of EU law.

A. Migration Policies through the Backdoor: Schengen

In 1985 and 1990, 5 of the then 10 Member States[43] concluded an international legal framework outside of the European Treaties, the Schengen Agreement and

[41] ibid, para 89.

[42] T Tiilikainen, 'The Empowered European Parliament: Accommodation to the New Functions Provided by the Lisbon Treaty' (2011) 91 *Finnish Institute of International Affairs*, Briefing Paper.

[43] Belgium, France, Germany, Luxembourg, and the Netherlands.

the Schengen Convention implementing the earlier agreement respectively. These two instruments established for the first time the concept of free movement of persons, which initiated the abolition of border controls between participating Member States and strengthened the external border of the Union. Today free movement rights form the centrepiece of the internal market, but at the time of the inception of Schengen, the competence to regulate free movement was debateable, particularly since the Schengen Agreement also abolished the internal borders for third-country nationals.[44] A legal basis for such cooperation was introduced only with the Maastricht Treaty. Schengen was interpreted as a reaction to the slow progress within the existing institutional framework on matters of free movement.[45] It 'expressly presented as an interim arrangement pending a final regime' in the Union context.[46] Furthermore, even though Schengen was a 'parallel track',[47] it referred explicitly to the EEC legal framework[48] and stated that it 'shall apply only in so far as they are compatible with Community law'.[49] As is well-known Schengen has later been integrated into the EU legal and institutional framework[50] and Schengen cooperation has gradually been extended to include all EU Member States, except the UK and Ireland, as well as four non-EU Member States.[51] The integration required some institutional adaptations: the Schengen Secretariat was integrated into the General Secretariat of the Council[52] and the EU concluded an agreement with Iceland and Norway to allow for their enhanced observer status. The UK and Ireland obtained opt-outs, but 'may at any time request to take part in some or all of the provisions of the Schengen *acquis*'.[53] Indeed from 2000/2002 onwards, they have taken part in some aspects of Schengen, such as the Schengen Information System (SIS). At the same time, the UK was not allowed to participate in the new Visa Information System[54] or Frontex,[55] because these legal instruments

[44] J Schutte, 'Schengen: Its Meaning for the Free Movement of Persons in Europe' (1991) 28 *CML Rev* 564.

[45] G Papagianni, *Institutional and Policy Dynamics of EU Migration Law*, Immigration and Asylum Law and Policy in Europe 10 (Leiden, Martinus Nijhoff Publishers, 2006) 13. See also: Commission, 'The abolition of border controls of persons at intra-Community borders' (Communication) COM(88) 640 final, 7 December 1988.

[46] C Timmermans, 'Free Movement of Persons and the Division of Powers between the Community and its Member States: Why do it the Intergovernmental Way?' in H Schermers et al (eds), *Free Movement of Persons in Europe: Legal Problems and Experiences* (Leiden, Martinus Nijhoff Publishers, 1993) 362.

[47] Papagianni, *Institutional and Policy Dynamics*, 13.

[48] Preamble, Arts 1, 3, 6, 11, 17, 20, 21, 22, 24, and 26.

[49] Art 134 Schengen Convention.

[50] In 1997, the Protocol on the Schengen *acquis* integrated the Schengen *acquis* (which consists of the 1985 Agreement, the 1990 Convention, Accession Protocols, Decisions of the Executive Committee, and Declarations of the Central Group) into the Union *acquis* (eur-lex.europa.eu/LexUriServ/LexUriServ.do?uri=OJ:L:2000:239:0001:0473:EN:PDF).

[51] Iceland, Liechtenstein, Norway, and Switzerland. Iceland and Norway had already concluded the 1957 Nordic Passport Control Agreement with Denmark, Finland, and Sweden.

[52] Council Decision 1999/307/EC of 1 May 1999 laying down the detailed arrangements for the integration of the Schengen Secretariat into the General Secretariat of the Council, OJ 1999 L119/49.

[53] Art 4 Schengen Protocol.

[54] Case C-482/08 *UK v Council*, cited above (n 22).

[55] Case C-77/05 *UK v Council* (*Frontex* decision), cited above (n 22).

were found to build on the existing Schengen *acquis* in which the UK is not participating. Acceding Member States do not automatically join Schengen.

Schengen has become EU law and has further developed as part of EU law[56] but it remains an interesting example of how international cooperation can lead to differentiated integration within the EU and impact on the creation and substantive content of EU law. Schengen and justice and home affairs cooperation under the former third pillar largely overlapped[57] and the free movement introduced by Schengen is used as one of the fundamental justifications for the necessity of cooperation and coordination between police and judicial authorities to compensate for the open borders. Moreover, the SIS forms a core element of current cooperation.

B. The Prüm Convention

The Prüm Convention[58] is another example of Member States' use of international law to create institutionalised cooperation with an eye on later integrating it into what is now the AFSJ. In 2005, seven Member States[59] agreed to

> further development of European cooperation, to play a pioneering role in establishing the highest possible standard of cooperation especially by means of exchange of information, particularly in combating terrorism, cross-border crime and illegal migration, while leaving participation in such cooperation open to all other Member States of the European Union.[60]

This was after the adoption of the Maastricht, Amsterdam and Nice Treaties, which brought the policy areas covered by Prüm squarely within the EU framework. Schengen had been integrated into EU law by then and the former third pillar policies of asylum, migration, and judicial cooperation in civil matters had been moved to the first pillar, with the effect that the Commission had the right of initiative and that the European Parliament was consulted. In certain areas the latter even had the prospect of becoming a co-legislator.[61] It is hence a fair assessment that Prüm was 'not a mere technical attempt to accelerate the flow of information among signatories. It is, fundamentally, a significant countervailing political force

[56] See, eg the Schengen Borders Code (Reg 562/2006).

[57] S Peers, *EU Justice and Home Affairs Law* (Oxford, Oxford University Press, 2011) 37.

[58] Convention between the Kingdom of Belgium, the Federal Republic of Germany, the Kingdom of Spain, the French Republic, the Grand Duchy of Luxembourg, the Kingdom of the Netherlands and the Republic of Austria on the stepping up of cross-border cooperation particularly in combating terrorism, cross-border crime and illegal migration, Prüm (Germany), 27 May 2005, Council Secretariat, 10900/05, (Brussels, 7 July 2005).

[59] Austria, Belgium, France, Germany, Luxembourg, the Netherlands, and Spain.

[60] ibid, Preamble, Recital 3. Article 1(4) also expresses the intention to have the provisions of the Convention brought into the EU legal framework. Article 51(1) confirms that the Convention is open to all other EU Member States.

[61] Ex-Art 67 EC; see also: S Peers, 'EU Justice and Home Affairs Law (Non-Civil)' in P Craig and G de Búrca (eds), *The Evolution of EU Law*, 2nd edn (Oxford, Oxford University Press, 2011) 274–75.

against the European Union's AFSJ'.[62] However, the conclusion that Prüm 'creates a hierarchy within the EU . . . some Member States can decide to create a new structure that will apply to all . . . this produces a multiple level game within the EU that will vitiate its credibility'[63] overstates it. The geographical differentiation in the AFSJ more broadly seems to be at least as problematic in terms of credibility and community building.[64] In any event, by agreeing Prüm, the states successfully avoided the procedural constraints of EU law, both the decision-making procedures within the institutions and the conditions of enhanced cooperation.[65] The European Parliament was virtually excluded. On substance, the participating Member States made a great effort to ensure compatibility with EU law.[66] Similar to Schengen's references to the EEC, Prüm explicitly refers to secondary EU legislation, third pillar measures and Schengen.[67] At the same time, Prüm establishes a database, restricted to the Prüm signatories, that competes with the existing EU law principle of availability, pursuant to which the authorities of any Member State should have the same right of access to information held by any other authority in the Union including the authorities within the state where the data are held.[68] Institutionally, Prüm relied to some extent on the EU institutions. For instance, the contracting parties are required to submit joint progress reports to the Council and the Commission.[69] At the same time, the Commission cannot initiate infringement proceedings and the Court is in principle excluded from adjudicating any disputes under Prüm. As is well known, Prüm did not remain a parallel agreement but was partially included into the EU law framework. In the process, the Commission and the European Parliament remained side-lined,[70] while the Council took the driving seat under the then third pillar.[71]

[62] T Balzacq, D Bigo, S Carrera, and E Guild, 'The Treaty of Prüm and EC Treaty: Two Competing Models for EU Internal Security' in T Balzacq and S Carrera (eds), *Security versus Freedom? A Challenge for Europe's Future* (Aldershot, Ashgate, 2006) 115–16.

[63] ibid, 116.

[64] See below.

[65] Ex-Art 11 EC and ex-Arts 43–45 EU. T Balzacq, 'The Treaty of Prüm and the Principle of Loyalty (Art 10 TEC)' (2006) Briefing Paper, European Parliament, Directorate-General Internal Policies, Brussels.

[66] Art 47 Prüm Convention requires compliance with EU law and ensures that future EU law 'arrangements' take precedence over the Convention.

[67] Secondary EU legislation: Arts 20(1), 23(1), and 40; Third Pillar measures: Art 16, and the 1990 Schengen Convention: Arts 21(2), 27(2), and 30.

[68] This principle had at the time of the conclusion of Prüm already been endorsed by the European Council (European Council of 4–5 November 2004) and promoted by the Commission, 'Proposal for a Council framework decision on the exchange of information under the principle of availability' COM(2005) 490 final, Brussels, 12 October 2005.

[69] Art 1(5) Prüm Convention.

[70] The European Data Protection Supervisor argued that the Community institutions should have been involved from the start ('Opinion of the European Data Protection Supervisor on the proposal for a Council Framework Decision on the exchange of information under the principle of availability' COM(2005) 490 final, OJ 2006 C116/8, para 48).

[71] Council Decision 2008/615/JHA of 23 June 2008 on the stepping up of cross-border cooperation, particularly in combating terrorism and cross-border crime, OJ 2008 L210/1. See also: Council Decision 2008/616/JHA of 23 June 2008 on the implementation of Decision 2008/615/JHA on the stepping up of cross-border cooperation, particularly in combating terrorism and cross-border crime, OJ 2008 L210/12; Council Decision 2008/617/JHA of 23 June 2008 on the improvement of cooperation between the special intervention units of the Member States of the European Union in crisis situations, OJ 2008 L210/73.

Schengen and Prüm may be seen as exceptional, yet they should not be seen as of historical value only. Indeed, by adopting a number of international law instruments to mitigate the Eurocrisis[72] the Member States have recently demonstrated that they remain ready to cooperate outside the EU framework on subject matters that at least partially fall under Union competence, possibly affecting areas of exclusive competence. This, at the very least, raises questions of whether such cooperation complies with the spirit of EU law.[73]

V. EXTERNAL PRESSURES ON EU LAW-MAKING: SUBSTANTIVE AND INSTITUTIONAL ISSUES

Substantive EU law is also subject to direct external influences. Not only do Member States conclude international agreements *inter se* to enhance cooperation further than would be possible at that point in time under EU law but the Union also concludes international agreements with third countries. In the latter case, the Union is in principle in the same position as other international actors: its interests are shaped in interaction and it has to accommodate the interests of the other parties to reach an agreement. However, besides these substantive influences interaction with the outside also has institutional consequences. In a legal construction as complex as the Union, in which many different players cooperate, each of whom enjoy separate international legal personality, interaction with the outside is particularly prone to cause internal struggles for power and visibility.

A. PNR: Substance Determined from the Outside?

The general assumption in the AFSJ continues to be that external action is closely related and follows internal action, 'as if the existence of an internal *acquis* was a pre-condition for the exercise of external powers'.[74] This is confirmed by the limited explicit external competences of the Union in the AFSJ and the close interknitting of external and internal objectives. However, examples to the contrary exist, for instance the Passenger Name Record (PNR) Agreements signed with the US.[75]

[72] Treaty on Stability, Coordination and Governance in the Economic and Monetary Union (Fiscal Compact), signed on 2 March 2012. Available at: european-council.europa.eu/media/639235/st00tscg26_en12.pdf (last visited 31 January 2013); Treaty Establishing the European Stability Mechanism, signed on 2 February 2012. Available at: www.esm.europa.eu/pdf/esm_treaty_en.pdf (last visited 31 January 2013).

[73] In the AFSJ, Art 73 TFEU leaves room for future cooperation between Member States outside the Union framework on issues of security.

[74] S Poli, 'The Institutional Setting and the Legal Toolkit' in Cremona et al, *External Dimension*, 49.

[75] (1) The first one was signed in 2004: Agreement between the European Community and the United States of America on the processing and transfer of PNR data by air carriers to the United States Department of Homeland Security, OJ 2004 L183/84; Council Decision 2004/496/EC of 17 May 2004, OJ 2004 L183/83 and Commission Decision 2004/535/EC of 14 May 2004, OJ 2004 L235/11; (2) after its annulment an interim agreement was signed in 2006: Agreement between the European Union and

The Union and the US have concluded four PNR Agreements, which have set consecutive legal frameworks for the transfer of PNR data by carriers operating passenger flights between the territory of the Union and the US to the US Department of Homeland Security (DHS) and the subsequent use of that data to prevent, detect, investigate and prosecute terrorist offences, related crimes, and other serious cross-border crimes. Several MEPs, including Dutch MEP Sophie in 't Veld who initially acted as the rapporteur for the European Parliament, the European Data Protection Supervisor (EDPS) and Article 29 Working Party on Data Protection, consisting of representatives from the national data protection authorities, expressed concerns over data protection safeguards.[76] However on 19 April 2012, the European Parliament approved the fourth PNR Agreement, even if it is identical to the previous one, which the Parliament had annulled by the ECJ.[77] MEP Sophie in 't Veld explained in 2010 that 'the provision of PNR data is part of the conditions the United States have imposed in exchange for a derogation from the visa regime'.[78] A rejection of the Agreement by Parliament 'would cause problems for air carriers and would negate whatever purposes the system might be used for'.[79]

External pressures work in several ways. In the EU, cooperation with the US as such is seen as a strategy to contain terrorism.[80] This cooperation has then in turn an influence on *how* the EU interest is constructed.[81] Political science scholars have argued that 'in line with social constructivist literature, it is important to conceptualize interests as being mutually constituted through interactions amongst political actors'.[82] They use the PNR Agreement as an example where the

the United States of America on the processing and transfer of PNR data by air carriers to the United States Department of Homeland Security, OJ 2006 L298/29; Council Decision 2006/729/CFSP/JHA of 16 October 2006, OJ 2006 L298/27; Letter to the Council Presidency and the Commission from the Department of Homeland Security (DHS) of the United States of America, OJ 2006 C259/1 and Reply by the Council Presidency and the Commission to the letter from the USA's Department of Homeland Security, OJ 2006 C259/4; (3) in 2007 a new permanent agreement was signed: Agreement between the United States of America and the European Union on the processing and transfer of Passenger Name Records to the United States Department of Homeland Security, OJ 2007 L204/18; Council Decision 2007/551/CFSP/JHA of 23 July 2007, OJ 2007 L204/16; European Parliament resolution of 12 July 2007 on the PNR Agreement with the United States of America, OJ 2008 C175E/564; (4) and finally in 2011: Agreement between the United States of America and the European Union on the use and transfer of Passenger Name Records to the United States Department of Homeland Security, OJ 2012 L215/5.

[76] S in 't Veld, Report, cited above (n 34).

[77] Joined Cases C-317/04 and C-318/04 *EP v Council and Commission* [2006] ECR I-4721.

[78] EDRi-gram 8.5, of 10 March 2010, PNR Agreements with US and Australia on the European Parliament's Agenda. Available at: www.edri.org/edrigram/number8.5/pnr-eu-us-australia-postponed-ep (last visited 6 February 2013).

[79] ibid.

[80] European Council, Anti-Terrorism Roadmap, SN 4019/01, Brussels, 2001; Council of the European Union, EU Plan of Action on Combating Terrorism, 10586/04, Brussels, 2004, 13; Council of the European Union, The European Union Counter-Terrorism Strategy, 14469/4/05, Brussels, 2005, 7.

[81] This is widely accepted for continuous Member State interaction within the EU framework.

[82] C Kaunert, S Leonard and A MacKenzie, 'The Social Construction of an EU Interest in Counter-Terrorism: US Influence and Internal Struggles in the Cases of PNR and SWIFT' (2012) 21 *European Security* 474. See also: C Kaunert, 'Conclusion: Assessing the External Dimension of EU Counter-Terrorism – Ten Years on' (2012) 21 *European Security* 578, 582.

US has exercised 'significant influence on the shaping of the EU interest'.[83] The internal legislation on the transfer of passengers' information is clearly inspired by the EU's external actions, that is cooperation with third countries.[84] The Commission presented a proposal for a framework decision setting up an internal 'EU PNR scheme' only after the conclusion of the first PNR Agreement with the US.[85] The PNR Directive, which could extend passenger-tracking systems to all flights to and from countries outside the EU, is still in the making,[86] but it is fair to say that it benefits from the already concluded PNR Agreements with the US and Australia,[87] not only because of the already established structures and practices, but also in terms of acceptance. This is not to argue that the Union is a monolithic block that passively follows the US lead. The different internal players, that is the EU institutions and the Member States, have different stakes. It has, for instance, been shown that the Commission was ready to take advantage of external pressures in order to advance European integration in the particular area of counter-terrorism.[88]

B. Pressure on the Pillar Structure

International cooperation has never taken into account the pre-Lisbon Union pillar structure. In the past, the distinction between the first and the third pillar has indeed constituted a split across the landscape of AFSJ policies. Arguably, the Lisbon Treaty bridged this split to a large extent. However, to appreciate the influence of the external it is worth recalling the uneasy cross-pillar approach of the Union when concluding international agreements. Two illustrative examples[89] are the UN Convention against Transnational Organised Crime (Palermo Convention)[90] and

[83] ibid.

[84] See also: J Argomaniz, 'When the EU is the "Norm-Taker": The Passenger Name Records Agreement and the EU's Internationalization of US Border Security Norms' (2009) 31 *Journal of European Integration* 119.

[85] Discussion on the introduction of the 'EU PNR scheme' started after the European Council of 25–26 March 2004 invited the Commission to bring forward a proposal on an EU common approach on the use of PNR data for law enforcement purposes. See, 'Proposal for a Council framework decision on the use of Passenger Name Record (PNR) for law enforcement purposes' COM(2007), 654 final, 6 November 2007.

[86] See the resubmitted proposal: Brussels, 2 February 2011, COM(2011), 32 final 2011/0023 (COD).

[87] PNR Agreement with Australia: 10093/11, of 13 September 2011, Agreement between the European Union and Australia on the processing and transfer of Passenger Name Record (PNR) data by air carriers to the Australian Customs and Border Protection Service.

[88] C Kaunert and S Leonard, 'EU Counter-Terrorism and the European Neighbourhood Policy: An Appraisal of the Southern Dimension' (2011) 23 *Terrorism and Political Violence* 286; C Kaunert, *European Internal Security: Towards Supranational Governance in the Area of Freedom, Security and Justice?* (Manchester, Manchester University Press, 2010).

[89] See also: Cremona, 'EU External Action', above (n 23) 85.

[90] United Nations Convention against Transnational Organized Crime, adopted by General Assembly resolution 55/25 of 15 November 2000. It entered into force on 29 September 2003. Available at: www.unodc.org/unodc/treaties/CTOC/index.html (last visited 30 January 2013).

the PNR Agreements.[91] As to the first, two of the Protocols to the Palermo Convention, on smuggling of migrants and on trafficking of persons respectively, were concluded by the then Community based on its competences under different parts of the first pillar, that is development cooperation[92] and migration policy.[93] Because of procedural differences of the two policy areas the Community concluded each of the Protocols in two separate decisions 'in so far as the provisions of this Protocol fall within the scope of' either of the two policy areas.[94] To add to the confusion, a third Protocol, on illicit manufacturing and trafficking of firearms, required a separate conclusion since this issue fell at least partially under the Member States' competence for security.[95] Hence, in addition to the Community's conclusion of certain aspects of this third Protocol,[96] the Council agreed a common strategy on those aspects that fell under what was then the third pillar.[97] The need to adopt six EU instruments to conclude three protocols to an international convention in two different Council formations and the uncertain scope of these instruments 'in so far as the provisions fall' within a particular policy field demonstrate the mismatch between taking uniform external action and fragmented internal policy-making powers. Necessarily, this is not only an obstacle to uniform external action, it also pressures the Union to unify its internal approach.

In the case of the PNR Agreements, adoption was not only made more complex by the pillar structure, but resulted in a successful legal challenge of the first PNR Agreement.[98] The first PNR Agreement was originally concluded on the basis of Article 95 EC – largely because this was the legal basis of the earlier adopted Data Protection Directive, which determined the legal requirements for data exchange between EU carriers and US authorities. However, the Court struck down the Council decision concluding the Agreement.[99] It considered the PNR Agreement

[91] EU–US PNR Agreement, see above (n 75).

[92] Ex-Arts 177 et seq EC (now Arts 208 et seq TFEU).

[93] Part III Title IV EC (ex-Arts 61 et seq EC).

[94] See, eg Council Decision 2006/616/EC of 24 July 2006 on the conclusion, on behalf of the European Community, of the Protocol against the smuggling of migrants by land, sea and air, supplementing the United Nations Convention against Transnational Organised Crime concerning the provisions of the Protocol, *in so far as the provisions of this Protocol fall within the scope of Articles 179 and 181a TEC* and Council Decision 2006/617/EC of 24 July 2006 on the conclusion, on behalf of the European Community, of the Protocol against the smuggling of migrants by land, sea and air, supplementing the United Nations Convention against Transnational Organised Crime concerning the provisions of the Protocol, *in so far as the provisions of the Protocol fall within the scope of Part III, Title IV of the TEC*; available at: eur-lex.europa.eu/JOHtml.do?textfield2=262&year=2006&Submit=Rechercher&serie=L (last visited 6 February 2013).

[95] Ex-Art 296 EC (now Art 346 TFEU).

[96] Council Decision 2001/748/EC of 16 October 2001 concerning the signing on behalf of the European Community of the United Nations Protocol on the illicit manufacturing of and trafficking in firearms, their parts, components and ammunition, annexed to the Convention against Transnational Organised Crime.

[97] Common Position 2000/130/JHA of 31 January 2000 on the proposed Protocol against the illicit manufacturing of and trafficking in firearms, their parts and components and ammunition, supplementing the United Nations Convention against Transnational Organised Crime, based on ex-Art 34(2)(a) EU.

[98] Joined Cases C-317/04 and C-318/04 *EP v Council and Commission* [2006] ECR I-4721.

[99] Council Decision 2004/496/EC of 17 May 2004, OJ 2004 L183/83.

to fall outside the scope of the Data Protection Directive and consequently also outside the scope of Article 95 EC, because the agreement concerned 'processing operations concerning public security and the activities of the State in areas of criminal law'.[100] The Union had to conclude a new agreement under what was then the third pillar.[101]

As is well-known, the particular difficulties of drawing lines between first and third pillar competences have disappeared with the Lisbon Treaty. Similarly, much of the decision-making in the AFSJ has become subject to the ordinary legislative procedure.[102] Nonetheless, the dividing line between the AFSJ and CFSP remains in place and the Union will still have to bridge this split to accommodate external demands. The joint legal basis of the new PNR Agreement is Article 218(6) TFEU in combination with Articles 82(1)(d) and 87(2)(a) TFEU, governing police and judicial cooperation. The latter two provisions are also the legal basis for the proposed PNR Directive. The PNR Agreement is not based on Article 16 TFEU on data protection.[103] While on the one hand police and judicial cooperation, that is data exchange rather than protection, is the objective of the PNR Agreement, one could argue on the other hand that the Agreement's purpose is to determine the conditions under which this exchange takes place and hence to protect the personal data of passengers on European air carriers. If an international agreement on the basis of Article 16 TFEU was to be concluded, this would also open the door for an argument in favour of using the complementary CFSP competence for data protection under Article 39 TEU.

VI. INTERNATIONAL HUMAN RIGHTS CONTROL OF EU MIGRATION AND SECURITY POLICIES

Another form of direct external pressure is exercised by international organisations and human rights regimes. The ECtHR's case law has the particular potential of becoming influential in the AFSJ.[104] Not only because these are areas of law in which civil liberties are submitted to far reaching restrictions but also because the ECJ has not yet built up a large body of case law in this particular field.[105] The

[100] Joined Cases C-317/04 and C-318/04 *EP v Council and Commission*, para 56.

[101] Based on ex-Arts 24 and 38 TEU. See above (n 75) for the second EU–US PNR Agreement.

[102] Arts 77 et seq TFEU.

[103] Art 16 is only included in the Recitals. See criticism by: S in 't Veld, Report, above (n 34) para 8.

[104] In 2010, 2011 and 2012, 90 judgments of the ECJ and AG Opinions refer to the ECHR. In the three previous years (2007–09), 68 judgments and Opinions made a reference to the Convention. The largest share of references to the Convention in these years was made in cases concerning the AFSJ: 9 Court decisions and 13 AG Opinions (list with the author). While the references to the ECHR have increased, the specific value given to the Convention and the ECtHR's case law would have to be analysed in more detail. The increase in total numbers contains no further information on in how many cases the Court could have used the ECHR and did not do so.

[105] Until the entry into force of the Lisbon Treaty, the ECJ only had limited jurisdiction on third pillar matters and until 1 December 2014 the transitional provisions continue to limit the Court's jurisdiction over pre-Lisbon instruments.

recent *MSS* ruling of the ECtHR[106] demonstrated the influence of external control. In *MSS*, the ECtHR struck a blow to European asylum policy by finding Belgium to be in violation of Article 3 ECHR for sending an asylum seeker back to Greece where their rights under the Convention were blatantly infringed.[107] External pressure was necessary to fully expose the weakness of a system built on the idea of mutual trust that assumes all Member States are safe third countries.[108] The main objective of the Dublin II Regulation is to determine which Member State is responsible for examining an asylum application lodged by a third-country national on Union territory. In principle, each application is reviewed by the Member State through which the asylum seeker first entered the EU. It aims to prevent 'asylum shopping' and multiplication of administrative procedures. However, this assumes that all Member States, at the very least, offer asylum in compliance with the requirements of the ECHR.[109] The ECtHR's ruling in *MSS* exposed that there are no effective internal EU checks of minimum standards and that Member States – at least under EU law – are largely able to free themselves from unpopular 'problems' such as asylum seekers without ensuring the national, European and international standards of human rights protection.[110]

The ECtHR's *MSS* ruling triggered immediate reactions by the EU institutions. The European Parliament asked the Commission whether it would take action against Greece and similar cases.[111] However against Greece in particular, the Commission had already launched an infringement procedure for the deficient conditions of its national asylum system two years earlier (and hence before the *MSS* ruling).[112] In December 2011, the Commission took the ECtHR's ruling in *MSS* as the main argument that reform of the Dublin II system was urgently necessary.[113] Equally in December 2011, the ECJ addressed, in a case joining preliminary questions from Ireland and Wales, whether Member States are obliged not to transfer asylum seekers if such transfer would violate human rights (*NS*).[114] It discussed

[106] *MSS v Belgium and Greece* (30696/09) (2011) 53 EHRR 2. Numerous cases that raise similar allegations are pending before the court.

[107] Greece was equally found in violation of the Convention.

[108] Council Regulation 343/2003/EC of 18 February 2003, OJ 2003 L50/1 (Dublin II Regulation), Recital 2.

[109] As well as the 1951 Convention relating to the Status of Refugees (Refugee Convention).

[110] 75% of the nearly 30,000 irregular EU external border crossings between October and December 2011 occurred at the Turkish border with eastern Greece, southern Bulgaria or Cyprus (Eastern Mediterranean route): Commission to the European Parliament and the Council, 'Biannual report on the functioning of the Schengen area – 1 November 2011 – 30 April 2012' (Communication) COM(2012) 230 final, Brussels, 16 May 2012, 3.

[111] European Parliament, 'Judgment by the European Court of Human Rights in the Case of MSS v Belgium and Greece' Parliamentary Questions of 10 February 2011, E-001222/2011.

[112] Commission to the European Parliament, the Council, the European Economic and Social Committee and the Committee of the Regions on Enhanced Intra-EU Solidarity in the Field of Asylum, 'An EU agenda for better responsibility-sharing and more mutual trust' (Communication) COM(2011) 835 final, Brussels, 2 December 2011, 11.

[113] ibid, 7.

[114] Joined Cases C-411/10 and C-493/10 *NS v Secretary of State for the Home Department* and *ME and Others v Refugee Applications Commissioner* [2011] nyr.

the *MSS* case[115] and adhered to the ECtHR's ruling by declaring it an obligation of the transferring Member State to examine the asylum application itself in cases such as *MSS*. In light of the wording of the Dublin II Regulation, this is quite a stretch.[116] Hence, even though the problems undermining EU asylum law were known to the EU institutions before the *MSS* ruling the latter emphasised the urgency of the need to take reform action, served as an authoritative argument in the discussion, and influenced the ECJ's reading of EU law in departure from the general spirit of mutual trust.

Furthermore, the envisaged accession to the ECHR will finally submit the Union to an external human rights control mechanism.[117] It will give EU citizens the same protection vis-à-vis acts of the Union as they presently enjoy from their Member States. Rulings of the ECtHR will become directly binding on the ECJ. As a consequence, the ECJ will no longer be able to hold the ECtHR's decisions at arm's length – even though this is mainly rhetorical before accession.[118] Further with the prior involvement mechanism, applicable in cases where the EU is a co-respondent, the two courts will enter into a direct institutionalised discourse that will give both courts more influence over the other's approach.

VII. HOW THE OUTSIDE SHAPES THE INSIDE'S IMAGINATION

Besides the external influences on substantive law and institutional balance in the AFSJ the outside also influences the inside at a deeper level. The Union's understanding of the 'self' – its identity – stands in a reflexive relationship with the outside. Identity can be defined as 'those attributes that make you unique as an individual and different from others' or 'the way you see or define yourself'.[119] It expresses the self as distinguished from 'others'. Individuals' identities are multifaceted: they are part of many different distinguishable 'norm-generating communities'[120] with which they share elements of their identity, such as gender, nationality, age,[121] but also increasingly being 'European'. National identity forms one layer of individual identity and concerns the identity shaping characteristics of a population. The details of how national identity is shaped and to what unit it applies are contentious;[122] yet at the core of identity is *distinction over time*. National

[115] ibid, para 88 et seq.

[116] See in particular Art 3(2) and Recital 2 of the Dublin II Regulation, cited above (n 108).

[117] See, for details on the implications of accession, C Eckes, 'EU Accession to the ECHR: Between Autonomy and Adaptation' (2013) 76 *MLR* 254.

[118] ibid. See also: Art 52(3) Charter of Fundamental Rights.

[119] E Olson, 'Personal Identity' (2002) in E Zalta et al (eds), *The Stanford Encyclopedia of Philosophy*. Available at: plato.stanford.edu/archives/fall2002/entries/identity-personal/ (last visited 6 February 2013).

[120] P Berman, 'Global Legal Pluralism' (2007) 80 *Southern California Law Review* 1155, 1170.

[121] See in more detail: A Smith, *National Identity* (London, Penguin Books, 1991) 15.

[122] D Miller, *Citizenship and National Identity* (Cambridge Polity Press, 2000); D Miller, *On Nationality* (Oxford, Oxford University Press, 1995); Smith, *National Identity*; W Bloom, *Personal Identity, National Identity and International Relations* (New York, Cambridge University Press, 1993);

identity emerges by contrast to the 'not national' or 'foreign'.[123] 'What we habitually forget [in this context] is that, like any other collectivity, the national polity is an "imagined community,"[124] not an inevitable one'.[125] In this regard, it is much like the European Union, even if the latter is less deeply rooted in the consciousness of EU citizens and differs depending on nationality.[126] Indeed, the Union's success in establishing itself as an imagined community remains contentious,[127] and any construction through law and the media can be accused of remaining an elite identity.[128]

Two dimensions of European identity should be distinguished: a Habermasian,[129] civic identity and a cultural identity.[130] The former refers to citizens' attachment to the political and the institutional system of the European Union, and ultimately with the project of European political integration. The AFSJ is characterised by a greater ambition than other policy fields to contribute to civic identity. With its allusion to territorial unity, it 'reach[es] deep into issues of frontier control, asylum and immigration, and policing long imagined to be at the very core of sovereign territorial control',[131] decides who forms part of the community and who does not, and ultimately creates an 'inside area' that implies that everything else is 'outside'. The latter refers to a cultural and normative commonality that makes fellow Europeans feel more alike and closer to each other than to non-Europeans.

Indeed as any form of identity, the sense of being European is closely linked to what is not European. This is true not only for the cultural but also for civic identity. At the community and ultimately identity forming level, the external is relevant not only because of who is in and who is out, but also who one is by distinction or even opposition.[132] Only outside of Europe, being European is a distinguishing characteristic. On the one hand, introducing a 'European area' and linking it intimately with largely unrelated value-loaded policies that constitute the core of state sovereignty requires a focus on the *inside*. It makes the area the

P Boerner (ed), *Concepts of National Identity: An Interdisciplinary Dialogue – Interdisziplinäre Betrachtungen zur Frage der nationalen Identität* (Baden-Baden, Nomos Verlagsgesellschaft, 1986).

[123] Smith, *National Identity*, 8.

[124] See Anderson, *Imagined Communities*, cited above (n 8). Anderson argues that the development of the printed press provided the foundation for the development of national consciousness by creating a common, standardised language. This form of communication essentially allowed previously disconnected people to connect on an imaginative level and see themselves as part of a larger community.

[125] J Boli, 'Sovereignty from a World Polity Perspective' in S Krasner (ed), *Problematic Sovereignty – Contested Rules and Political Possibilities* (New York, Columbia University Press, 2001) 54.

[126] Eurobarometer 71 – Future of Europe, see map at 35. Available at: ec.europa.eu/public_opinion/archives/eb/eb71/eb713_future_europe.pdf (last visited 3 March 2013).

[127] U Haltern, 'On Finality' in A von Bogdandy and J Bast (eds), *Principles of European Constitutional Law* (Oxford, Hart Publishing, 2006).

[128] Paul Brass, *Ethnicity and Nationalism: Theory and Comparison* (Aldershot, Gregg Rivals, 1991).

[129] Habermas speaks of 'constitutional patriotism', eg J Habermas, 'Citizenship and National Identity: Some Reflections of the Future of Europe' (1992) 12 *Praxis International* 1.

[130] M Bruter, 'Winning Hearts and Minds for Europe – The Impact of News and Symbols on Civic and Cultural European Identity' (2003) *Comparative Political Studies* 1148.

[131] T Heller and A Sofaer, 'Sovereignty – The Practitioners' Perspective' in S Krasner (ed), *Problematic Sovereignty*, 36.

[132] The reference to European identity in the Preamble of the EU Treaty refers explicitly to the external.

place of EU citizens, their own.[133] The Union does so by referring to the area as a pre-existing place.[134] It asserts this spatial dimension in a self-reflective way: linked by common values the community of EU citizens share a common area that is embodying these common values and that combines this normative dimension with a physical one: the actual territory governed by EU law. This is where the above-mentioned concept of heterotopia becomes explanatory: the area is a real place representing other real places, for example the territory of the Member States, as well as imagined places such as a legal space in which the Union guarantees its citizens to be free, safe and fairly treated. On the other hand, any inside necessarily requires delimitation from what is *outside*, from what it is not. Having common values implies that there are also other values that are not constitutive for the community of EU citizens and their area. In the political and legal context, openness towards the outside, that is international law and international relations, is traditionally seen as a particular virtue that distinguishes the EU from third countries, such as the US.[135] In this way, the outside plays an ambivalent role in influencing EU values and interests but also in defining the commonality of EU citizens by distinction.

VIII. CONCLUSION

Outside-in effects differ from case-to-case and in different policy areas.[136] This chapter identified and discussed different ways in which the AFSJ is influenced from the outside. In the AFSJ, the situation is particularly complex because it covers issues that lie at the core of sovereignty and immediately affect the rights of individuals, because the former split between the first and the third pillar, the continuous prominence of Member States, and the geographical limits stand in the way of uniformity and coherence, and because it remains a relatively young and fast-developing field of Union action.

The Union's relationship and interaction with third countries and international organisations under international law is not only a matter of external relations. It does not only concern the Union's role in the world, but also directly affects what happens within the Union legal order. This includes the policy directions that the Union takes in relation to its citizens and the relationship between the EU institutions and the Member States. At least in practice, Member States submit to Union rule. National courts apply Union law and consider compliance

[133] H Lindahl, 'Finding Place for Freedom, Security and Justice: The European Union's Claim to Territorial Unity' (2004) 1 *Webpapers on Constitutionalism and Governance beyond the State* 8.

[134] ibid, 9.

[135] The Union's external 'self' is influenced by a sense of opposition to the US, see: C Eckes, 'EU Climate Change Policy: How Much Governance is Just?' in F Amtenbrink and D Kochenov (eds), *European Union's Shaping of the International Legal Order* (Cambridge, Cambridge Uniuversity Press, 2013).

[136] See, eg for environmental policy: C Eckes, 'Environmental Policy "Outside-In": How the EU's Engagement with International Environmental Law Curtails National Autonomy' (2012) 13 *German Law Journal* 1151.

with Union authority as part of the national rule of law. The extreme of withdrawal or judicial rebellion based on a *Solange* reasoning notwithstanding,[137] the legal situation of citizens of the Member States under national law is also determined by European law.[138] This makes it crucially important to consider who determines EU law, not only in the case of the extreme but also in the day-to-day experience of determining policy priorities.

More often than not, the internal effects are co-determined by internal actors. They are not imposed on the Union but rather enhanced or used by internal actors to push a particular development of EU law. This is the case where groups of Member States have pushed further developments through channels of international law, as we saw in the cases of Schengen and Prüm. This is also the case where the Commission proposes internal legislation mirroring external commitments, as in the case of the PNR Agreements. By contrast, the change in the institutional balance when legislative action is determined by international agreements, as it still occurs after Lisbon – albeit no longer at conclusion but only at negotiation stage – appears to be a general and nearly unavoidable consequence of international law-making that finds parallels at Member State level. Similarly, where individuals initiate proceedings before the ECtHR, this is not as such a strategy of one of the internal players of the EU. Yet, rulings of the ECtHR not only draw attention to human rights violations resulting from Member States implementing EU law, but also shape the understanding of rights and specific policy-making within the Union. Finally, the understanding of the AFSJ as part of European identity creation is affected by the outside. This influence is intensified by the fact that the Union possesses only nascent 'imagined identity'.

[137] BVerfGE 37, 271, of 29 May 1974 (*Solange I*); BVerfGE 73, 339, of Decision of 22 Oct 1986, 2 BvR 197/83 (*Solange II*).

[138] On Union citizenship more generally, see S Coutts, 'Citizenship of the European Union' in this volume.

Index